UNDERSTANDING CYBER WARFARE AND ITS IMPLICATIONS FOR INDIAN ARMED FORCES

UNDERSTANDING CYBER WARFARE AND ITS IMPLICATIONS FOR INDIAN ARMED FORCES

by

Col R K Tyagi

(Established 1870)

United Service Institution of India

New Delhi

Vij Books India Pvt Ltd

New Delhi (India)

Published by

Vij Books India Pvt Ltd
(Publishers, Distributors & Importers)
2/19, Ansari Road
Delhi – 110 002
Phones: 91-11-43596460, 91-11-47340674
Fax: 91-11-47340674
e-mail: vijbooks@rediffmail.com

Paperback Edition 2015

The views expressed in this book are those of the author in his personal capacity. These do not have any official endorsement.

Contents

Appendices

Foreword

Information and Communication Technology (ICT) with its all pervasive nature has ushered in the Information Age with direct impact on the manner we communicate and conduct our daily business. It has created a virtual world with no boundaries where the rules of engagement are being constantly defined by the world community with very little interference from the government. This virtual world called "cyber space" has not only opened new avenues for interaction, development and exchange of views but as a natural corollary, it also has negative manifestations and is becoming more hostile providing an option for conducting warfare. Worldwide, people, and in some cases the governments, are engaged in the exploitation of cyber space for illegal activities like espionage, theft of technology, financial frauds and so on. They have, accordingly, developed means and methods to carry out such activities by way of viruses, root kits, malware and so on.

These are the initial steps in the evolution of cyber warfare. This fast evolving means of conducting warfare with its ability to disrupt networks, systems and their functionality; its suitability for the conduct of asymmetric warfare; its offence dominant characteristic and the ability to launch attacks at the speed of light; its unique ability of power projection and all pervasive application in civilian and military domains; together with the near impossibility of attribution coupled with low cost, has made cyber warfare the new dimension of warfare.

The recent stuxnet attack on the Iranian nuclear facility has not only demonstrated the most critical ability of cyber warfare entering the physical space but has also legitimized cyber attack as a Nation State activity. This has lead to both the weaponisation of cyber space and the consequent threat to the Critical Information Infrastructure (CII). Accordingly, development of Cyber Security capabilities in all its three dimensions vis Computer Network Attack, Computer Network Defence and Computer Network Exploitation, has become a national imperative. It is believed that more than 140 nations across the world are engaged in developing technologies and capabilities for offensive cyber warfare.

A viable cyber warfare capability would entail having a National Doctrine for Cyber Warfare and the associated cyber security policies. The objectives of the doctrine should be to develop credible cyber deterrence and devise means of eliminating threats and not just defining defensive measures. Thus, it would clearly define responsibilities and accountability for the security of ICT systems and components; codify normative behavior in cyber space and more importantly, the response that a particular cyber incidence would get. Other major challenges for capability building are the awareness of the people and armed forces towards cyber security; building a reservoir of cyber warriors and leaders with requisite skill sets; a dedicated organization, development of cyber security standards to include security of the supply chain; development of language skills, R&D in cryptography, codes and build up of cyber weapons. Equally important is the knowledge of the capabilities of the likely adversaries in the field of cyber warfare.

Notwithstanding our strength in the field of ICT, such capabilities, skill sets and the much needed synergy amongst all concerned in the nation, would take a long time -assuming that we have and can display necessary political will and resolve. We must make haste and concentrate more on *'implementation'* of our policies and doctrine with full involvement of our people. In this context, this book written by Colonel R K Tyagi would be of immense value in creating awareness of this topical subject amongst professional military people, general public and scientific community and providing a base for building the much needed capabilities in *Cyber Warfare*.

Davinder Kumar

Lieutenant General (Retd)

Preface

Ever since Cyber warfare came to be recognized as the fifth domain of warfare, military planners and theorists, the world over have begun to ponder over this aspect of warfare. Militaries draw up their doctrines, policies and drills based on past experiences. However, in the field of cyber warfare there is no past experience. The much talked about cyber attacks on Estonia, allegedly by Russia for which attribution could not be conclusively established, were only attacks on informational sites of the government and no critical infrastructure or military sites were attacked. The enormity and the after effects of the attacks had far reaching echo.

The book is divided into two parts. Part 1 deals with cyber warfare in general. Chapter 1 describes the unique characteristics of cyber space leading up to it being called as the fifth domain of warfare. Chapter 2 discusses the recent cyber attack on Estonia and the Stuxnet attack on Iranian Nuclear facilities. Chapter 3 examines how the established Principles of War can be applied in cyberspace. Chapter 4 discusses the cyber strategy of US and China, primarily because US is undoubtedly the leader in this field and China is a fast emerging super power and has relevance in Indian context. Chapters 5 and 6 deal with offensive and defensive aspects of cyber warfare. Chapter 7 deals with cyber deterrence and considering the unique nature of cyber weapons, both offensive and defensive and the need of secrecy, the chapter discusses how cyber deterrence can be practiced. Chapter 8 deals with the new challenge facing the militaries the world over- leadership in cyber domain. It attempts to identify the desirable attributes of the cyber commander.

Part 2 is devoted to the Indian context. Chapter 9 discusses in detail the impact of ICT on the life of an ordinary indian citizen and slowly it has become an integral part of our lives. Chapter 10 looks at the cyber challenges facing the country. Chapter 11 discusses the implications for the Indian Armed Forces and the last Chapter summarizes the recommendations.

Acknowledgements

It was on bright February morning that, Maj Gen YK Gera (Retd), Consultant and Head of Research of Centre for Strategic Studies and Simulation (CS 3), announced that all researchers would be required to produce a book on their respective research topics. It was not amusing to say the least as one was nearing the end of the study leave and as was the norm had prepared the Monograph of 45 pages. Writing a book was a totally different ball game.

Without reference to a vast range of material available at the USI Library it would have not been possible to write this book. There is a mass of footnotes in the text which were required to keep the work updated and current. Some of the works cited in the References and Bibliography have been extensively cited in the text to highlight a point or reinforce an argument.

Compatriot Research Fellows at USI were more than forthcoming with their valuable advise whenever sought and we often had brainstorming sessions wherein on a large number of issues were leant clarity. My sincere thanks are due to Gururaj, Harish, Sandeep and Vivek for their valuable time and advise.

Maj Gen Gera has been both, the guiding and driving force in motivating us to write this book. His inputs on the chapter on Principles of War were very valuable. He was always available for any advise and help sought was always forthcoming. He has been the true mentor for all of us. My sincere thanks to him for all the support.

Lt Gen PK Singh, PVSM, AVSM (Retd), Director, USI, deserve special appreciation for spearheading the idea that Research Scholars of USI should produce the book instead of Monograph. He deserve our sincere thanks for creating the atmosphere and resources required to carry out the research work. He was always approachable for any advise and help. My sincere thanks to him.

My sincere thanks to the USI library staff for all their help during the course of writing this book. My special thanks are due to the office staff of CS 3, Aparna, Dharambir and Tiwari for all their help extended during my stay at USI and while writing this book.

My most special and profound thanks are due to Brig Abhimanyu Ghosh (Retd), Director, National Security Council Secretariat, who painstakingly carried out the peer review of the book and offered many useful suggestions which I have to a large extent incorporated in the text.

Lastly, I thank my wife Shikha and daughters, Esha and Richa, who bore my absence at odd hours while I was working overtime to complete this book.

20 May 2013 - RK Tyagi

Acronyms

Back Door – Also, Trapdoor. An intentional breach in the security of a computer system left in place by designers or maintainers. A hidden software or hardware mechanism used to circumvent security controls. A breach created intentionally for the purpose of collecting, altering or destroying data."

Breach – The successful defeat of security, which could result in system penetration or Violation of a system's controls that exposes information assets or system components.

C4I – Stands for Command, Control, Communications, Computers, and Intelligence.

CERT – Computer Emergency Response Team --This term was chosen for the first team, founded in December 1988 at the Carnegie Mellon University Software Engineering Institute (Pittsburgh, PA) by ARPA. Although the team was officially called CERT/CC, now CERT Coordination Center many users simply think of this team as "the" CERT.

Cyber Boundary – The cyber/ kinetic boundary is the decision point when a commander must decide whether and how to move from a purely cyber war to one involving conventional forces, or kinetic weapons. Crossing the boundary is an escalatory step that may lead to the war spiraling out of control.

Cyber Power – Is the ability to use cyber space to create advantages and influence events in all the operational environments and across the instruments of power.

Cyber Space – Is a global domain within the info environment whose distinctive and unique character is framed by use of electronics and the electromagnetic spectrum to create, store, modify, exchange, and exploit info via interdependent and interconnected networks using information communication technologies.

Cyber Strategy – Is the development and employment of strategic capabilities to operate in cyber space, integrated and coordinated with the other operational domains, to achieve or support the achievement of objectives across the elements of national power in support of national security strategy.

Cyber War -- Actions taken to achieve information superiority over an adversary – to deny, exploit, corrupt or destroy an enemy's information while protecting your own.

Daemon -- Pronounced *demon* or *damon,* a process that runs in the background and performs a specified operation at predefined times or in response to certain events. Sometimes referred to as *System Agents* and *services.* Typical daemon processes include print spoolers, e-mail handlers, and other programs that perform administrative tasks for the operating system. The term comes from Greek mythology, where daemons were guardian spirits.

Data Driven Attack – An attack form that is encoded in data that appears harmless and executed by a user or a process, often behind a firewall.

DBA – Dominant battlefield awareness. Applies to own-system advantage in terms of sensor, reconnaissance and intelligence data in a particular "battle space."

Derf – The act of exploiting a terminal unwittingly left logged on.

Digital Signature -- A digital guarantee that a file has not been altered, as if it were carried in an "electronically-sealed" envelope. The "signature" is an encrypted digest (one-way hash function) of the text message, executable or other file.

E-mail Bombs – Code that when executed sends many messages to the same address(s) for the purpose of using up disk space and/or overloading the E-mail or web server.

EMP/T Bomb – Electromagnetic pulse transformer, which disables or destroys an electronic network. Similar to a HERF Gun but many times more powerful.

Ethernet Sniffing -- This is listening with software to the Ethernet interface for packets that interest the user. When the software sees a packet that fits certain criteria, it logs it to a file. The most common criteria for an interesting packet is one that contains words like login or password.

Firewall – A form of web security that stands between a private network and the Internet to prevent unwanted traffic from passing either way. Some firewalls have proxy functions built in. Often the distinction between a firewall and a proxy is blurry. True firewalls generally support packet-filtering, proprietary application filtering, and some proxy functions.

Flooding Programs -- Code which when executed will bombard the selected system with requests in an effort to slow down or shut down the system.

Hacker – A person who breaks into systems for which they have no authorization. They penetrate information systems; to browse, steal, or modify data; deny access or service to others; or cause damage or harm in some other way.

Hacking Run – An extended hack session that goes beyond normal working times, especially if more than 12 hours long.

HERF Gun -- High Energy Radio Frequency gun. They shoot a high power radio signal at an electronic target and knock it out of commission.

Honeypot – A decoy server set up either inside or outside a firewall to lure and trick an intruder. It is designed to make hackers/crackers think they are on a valid production system. It is used to catch and stop an intruder or detect and track intruder techniques and test system vulnerability.

IP Sniffing – Stealing network addresses by reading the packets. Harmful data is then sent stamped with internal trusted addresses.

IP Spoofing – An attack whereby an active, established, session is intercepted and co-opted by the attacker.

Keystroke Monitoring – A device or software that records every key struck by a user and every character of the response that the user gets.

Leapfrog Attack – An attack in which the hacker gains access to a site or server from a third party site. Use of user ID and password information obtained illicitly from one host to compromise another host. The act of TELNETing through one or more hosts in order to preclude a trace (a standard cracker procedure).

Network Worm -- A program or command file that uses a computer network as a means for adversely affecting a system's integrity, reliability or availability. A network worm may attack from one system to another by establishing a network connection. It is usually a self-contained program that does not need to attach itself to a host file to infiltrate network after network.

One-Time Password – In network security, a password issued only once as a result of a challenge-response authentication process. Cannot be "stolen" or reused for unauthorized access.

Packet sniffing – A technique in which a software program is planted at remote junctions in a computer network. The program monitors information packets as they are sent through networks and reveals user names and passwords to the hacker, who is then able to break into the system.

Rootkit – A hacker security tool that captures passwords and message traffic to and from a computer. A collection of tools that allows a hacker to provide a backdoor into a system, collect information on other systems on the network, mask the fact that the system is compromised, and much more. Rootkit is a classic example of Trojan horse software.

SET – Short for Secure Electronic Transaction, a new standard that enables secure credit card transactions on the Internet. SET has been endorsed by virtually all the major players in the electronic commerce arena.

Sneaker – A person hired to break into a system to test its security.

Sniffer – A program and/or device that monitors data traveling over a network. Sniffers can be used both for legitimate network management functions and for stealing information off a network. Unauthorized sniffers can be extremely dangerous to a network's security because they are virtually impossible to detect and can be inserted almost anywhere. This makes them a favourite weapon of hackers.

Stealth Viruses – Viruses that attempt to hide from detection programs by hiding their presence in boot records or files. When such viruses are run, they install a resident extension. This resident extension intercepts various disk accesses, determines if its own code is part of the disk access, and removes the code before giving the data to the calling program. The result is that the virus can be in several places on the disk. Normal reads of the disk will not reveal it.

Trapdoor – A secret way of gaining access to a program or online service.

Vulnerability – This term refers to any weakness in any system (either hardware or software) that allows intruders to gain unauthorized access or deny service.

Zombie – A computer that has been implanted with a daemon that puts it under the control of a malicious hacker or organization without the knowledge of the computer owner. Zombies are used by malicious hackers to launch DoS attacks. The hacker sends commands to the zombie through an open port. On command, the zombie computer sends an enormous amount of packets of useless information to a targeted Web site in order to clog the site's routers and keep legitimate users from gaining access to the site. The traffic sent to the Web site is confusing and therefore the computer receiving the data spends time and resources trying to understand the influx of data that has been transmitted by the zombies.

CHAPTER 1

CYBERSPACE - THE FIFTH DOMAIN OF WARFARE

Introduction

The principle strategic objective of warfare for centuries has been the physical occupation of territory. The warfare extended into the four natural domains of land, sea, air and space which led nations to possess armed forces and weapon systems of these domains to achieve battlefield supremacy over their adversaries. War is typically defined as the use of force, or violence, by a nation-state to compel another to fulfil its will. Military conflict is a way for nation-states to achieve their political objectives when other means, such as diplomacy, are not working or are less expedient than violence. The use of force, however, may be less obvious in a new battle space made up of bits and bytes, where the borders between countries blur, the weapons are much more difficult to detect, and the soldiers can easily be disguised as civilians. It is difficult to envision cyber warfare because history lacks experience in cyber conflict. There is no past to learn from, much less envision how a national-level cyber conflict would be fought.

Evolution of Information warfare has led to 'Revolution in Military Affairs '. The paradigms of warfare have transformed in last two to three decades which forced the nations to shift into the fifth domain of warfare – the cyber domain. The impetus came when cyberspace was classified by the US government as strategically important to national security.[1] Cyber-attacks against Estonia in 2007 and Georgia in 2008 effectively moved the warfare in the cyber domain. These attacks spurred the militaries to understand their own capabilities and their adversaries' capabilities.

Cyber-attacks on military infrastructure, government and

1 The National Military Strategy of the USA – www.defencelink.mil/news/Mar2005/d20050318nms.pdf

communication systems and financial institutions pose a rapidly growing but little understood threat to national security in particular and international security in general. This could become a decisive weapon of choice in future conflicts between states. Simply speaking cyber warfare is knowledge warfare. Cyber-attacks in recent political conflicts have evoked little appreciation of how to assess cyber-attacks. Potentially we are now, in relation to the issue of cyber warfare, at the same stage of intellectual development as we were in the 1950s in relation to nuclear warfare. [2]

Future state-to-state conflicts as well as conflicts involving non state actors such as Al-Qaida and other terrorist org would increasingly be characterized by reliance on asymmetric warfare techniques, particularly cyber warfare. "History teaches us that in asymmetric warfare the most heavily armed do not always win" says Ignacio Ramonet.[3] Hostile states could easily hide behind rapidly advancing technology to launch attacks undetected. Unlike conventional and nuclear arms, there are no agreed international controls on the use of cyber weapons. The unfettered access to cyber weapon systems (i.e. computers and internet access) and armies (i.e. botnets that can captured or rented), coupled with the capacity for such attacks to strike at a nation's strategic vulnerabilities presents a uniquely dangerous threat. Failure by any nation to proactively address this threat risks something like a digital Pearl Harbour or a 9-11.

Israel gets hit by over 1000 cyber-attacks per minute. This was stated by Issac Ben-Israel, senior security advisor to Prime Minister Binyamin Netanyahu, which he divides into hierarchy of threats. He said that cyber security is about "securing different life systems regulated by computers. In Israel we realised this 10 years ago". In order to ensure the country is well protected, said Ben-Israel, a list of 19 major infrastructures was drawn up in 2002. On the list were things like power production, water supply, banking and other services of central importance. "We faced a legal problem- how do you force the private sector infrastructure to protect themselves

2 Military Balance 2010 published by International Institute for Strategic Studies, London.

3 Ignacio Ramonet, "Unjust means" November 1, 2001- www.mondediplo.com/2001/11/01unjustified.

against cyber-attacks? So we changed the laws," Ben-Israel said. "People accepted this law because of the experience of Scud missiles in 1991. The threat was real and people felt it was real" he said. He pointed out to Israel as a model for effective collaboration between industry, defence and academia on how to attack the legal, political and societal issues raised by cyber-attacks- but noted "there is still a lot to do". One of the things that Israel did was to create a Cyber Warfare Administration to combat cyber terrorism.[4]

Our nation's digital national security infrastructure is routinely penetrated some of which have crossed the critical line: they have compromised critical systems as was evident during the Chinese attack now famously called 'shadow in the cloud'. It is imperative for us to adopt a new approach. We need to understand cyber warfare in all its dimensions. There is also the need to pro-actively address the problem of operational and planning aspects of cyber-attacks i.e. how a terrorist group or a nation state could plan, org, launch and conduct a real, large scale attack. There is a need to have a comprehensive debate and discussion on cyber warfare in order to evolve a new strategic approach.

Sun Tzu said, "Attaining one hundred victories in one hundred battles is not the pinnacle of excellence. Subjugating the enemy's army without fighting is the true pinnacle of excellence." It aptly fits in the scenario of information age. Complex computer networks control important functionalities of a nation. Internationally, no acceptable definition exists however we can broadly say that cyber war is a war of the information where in the attacker seeks to gain control over the key information and knowledge. US DoD defines cyber warfare as" An armed conflict conducted in whole or part by cyber means. Military operations conducted to deny an opposing force the effective use of cyberspace systems and weapons in a conflict. It includes cyber-attack, cyber defence, and cyber enabling actions".[5] It is therefore a part of a larger military campaign, and attacks are likely to have both real world and cyber components.

---

4 Arutz Sheva- www.IsraelNationalmews.com accessed 14 Feb 2011.

5 http://www.pcmag.com/encyclopedia_term/0,1237,t=DOD+cyberspace+glossary&i=62535,00.asp

According to a recent UN Security Council Resolution, "Cyber warfare is the use of computers or digital means by a government or with explicit knowledge of or approval of that government against another state, or private property within another state including: intentional access, interception of data or damage to digital and digitally controlled infrastructure. And production and distribution of devices which can be used to subvert domestic activity." [6]

A successful cyber war depends upon two things: means and vulnerability. The 'means' are the people, tools, and cyber weapons available to the attacker. The vulnerability is the extent to which the enemy economy and military use the Internet and networks in general. One does not know who has what cyber war capabilities exactly. But a growing number of states have organized cyber war units and ever more skilled Internet experts for combat in this domain.

Cyber warfare is a component among many capabilities related to the cyberspace offensive and defensive operations that are a subset of Information War. Future state to state conflicts will be characterized by asymmetric techniques where in cyber warfare would be used to disable the adversary's critical infrastructure (communication, power etc.), financial institutions and government systems. Increased dependence by nations on computer technology to harness its benefits has made them vulnerable for exploitation by the adversary. The attack on Estonia is an example of cyber vulnerabilities.

Cyberspace

Cyberspace, the fifth domain of warfare after land, sea, air, and space, is all of the computer networks in the world and everything they connect and control via cable, fiber-optics or wireless. It is not just the Internet – the open network of networks.[7] From any

6 UN Security Council, Resolution 1113 (2011), 5 March 2011.

7 The Internet is an open network of end points, devices, and computer networks that communicate with each other using the TCP or IP communications protocol. It is built in an open, decentralized manner, and from any end point in it is possible to communicate with any other end point.

network on the Internet, one should be able to communicate with any computer connected to any of the Internet's networks. Thus, cyberspace includes the Internet plus lots of other networks of computers, including those that are not supposed to be accessible from the Internet. Some of those private networks look just like the Internet, but they are, theoretically at least, separate. Other parts of cyberspace are transactional networks that do things like sending data about money flows, stock market trades, and credit card transactions. In addition, there are the networks which are Supervisory Control and Data Acquisition (SCADA) systems that just allow machines to speak to other machines: control panels talking to pumps, elevators, generators, etc. Thus, cyberspace is composed of the now two billion computers existing, plus servers, routers, switches, fiber-optic cables, and wireless communications that allow critical infrastructures to work.

What is cyberspace? There are more than ten definitions by various experts but the one by Daniel T. Kuehl is most comprehensive. In the Chapter "From Cyberspace to Cyberpower: Defining the problem" Kuehl defines "cyberspace as a global domain within the information environment whose distinction and unique character is framed by the use of electronics and the electromagnetic spectrum to create, store, modify, exchange, and exploit information via interdependent and interconnected networks using information- communication technologies".[8] Kuehl further explains that these interdependent and interconnected information networks and systems reside simultaneously in both physical and virtual space and within and outside geographic boundaries. Their users range from entire nation-states and their component organizational elements and communities down to lone individuals and amorphous transnational groups who may not profess allegiance to any traditional organization or national entity. They rely on three distinct yet interrelated dimensions that in the aggregate comprise the global information environment: the physical platforms, systems and infrastructures that provide global connectivity to link information systems, networks, and

8 The work is included in the compilation "Cyber Power and National Security" edited by Franklin D. Kramer, Stuart H. Starr and Larry K. Wentz and published by Vij Books India Pvt Ltd, New Delhi.

human users; the massive amounts of information content that can be digitally and electronically sent anywhere, anytime, to almost anyone, a condition that has been enormously affected and augmented by the convergence of numerous informational technologies; and the human cognition that results from greatly increased access to content and can dramatically impact human behaviour and decision-making.

Warfare of the 21st Century involving opponents possessing even a modicum of modern technology is not possible without access to cyberspace. New operational concepts such as 'Network Centric Warfare' in an 'informationalized battlespace' would be impossible without cyber-based systems and capabilities. The ability to reprogram the targeting data within a weapon on its way to the target, then rely on real-time updates from a GPS satellite to precisely strike that target, is possible only through the use of cyberspace. Cyberspace exists across the other domains of land, sea, air, and space and connects these physical domains with the cognitive processes that use the data that is stored, modified, or exchanged. However, it is the use of electronic technologies to create and 'enter' cyberspace, and use the energies and properties of the electromagnetic spectrum (EMS) that sets cyberspace apart from the other domains, and what makes cyberspace unique.[9]

One characteristic of cyberspace is that it cannot exist without being able to exploit the naturally existing EMS. Without the EMS, not only would millions of information and communications technologies (ICT) be unable to communicate with each other, but the ICTs themselves would be unable to function. Integrated circuits and other microelectronic devices depend on electrons to function.

A second characteristic is that cyberspace requires man-made objects to exist, which again makes cyber-space unique when compared to the land, sea, air, and space domain. Cyberspace would not exist were it not for the ability of human beings to innovate and manufacture technologies capable of exploiting the various properties of the EMS.

9 Kuehl, "From Cyberspace to Cyber power: Defining the Problem", ibid

A third characteristic is that cyberspace can be constantly replicated. There can be as many cyberspaces as one can possibly generate. But there is one portion of the air, sea, or land domain that is important: the portion that is contested. With cyberspace, however, there can be many in existence at any one time – some contested, some not. In addition, for the most part, nothing is final in cyberspace. And due to relatively inexpensive and readily available hardware, IT systems and networks, if damaged, can be quickly repaired and reconstituted.

A fourth characteristic is that the cost of entry into cyberspace is relatively cheap. The resources and expertise required to enter, exist in, and exploit cyberspace are modest compared to those required for exploiting the land, sea, air, and space domains. Generating strategic effects in cyberspace does not require a budget of billions, large numbers of manpower and weapons. With modest financial outlays, a small group of motivated individuals and access to networked computers can provide entry into cyberspace. The character of cyberspace, however, is such that the numbers of actors are able to operate in the domain and potentially generate strategic effect is exponential when compared to the other domains.

A further characteristic is that, for the time being, the offense rather than the defence is dominant in cyberspace, for a number of reasons. First, defences of IT systems and networks rely on vulnerable protocols and open architectures, and the prevailing defence philosophy emphasizes threat detection, not elimination of the vulnerabilities. Second, attacks in cyberspace occur at great speed, putting defences under great pressure, as an attacker has to be successful only once, whereas the defender has to be successful all the time. Third, range is no longer an issue in cyberspace since attacks can occur from anywhere in the world. Fourth, the attribution of attacks is particularly difficult, which is complicating possible responses. And fifth, modern society's overwhelming reliance on cyberspace is providing any attacker a target-rich environment, resulting in great strain on the defender to successfully defend the domain.

Many consider cyberspace as the newest and most important

addition to the global commons, which comprise four domains: maritime, air, space, and now cyber. Maritime and air are the international oceans and skies that do not fall under the jurisdiction of any nation. Outer space begins at a point above the earth where objects remain in orbit. And cyberspace is the EMS that enables digital processing and communications. The maritime domain has been used by humans for millennia, air for a century, and space for six decades. Cyberspace as the newest and most important of the global commons has been widely available for less than thirty years, yet more than a quarter of the world's population now uses it every day, and that number continues to expand. Thus, cyberspace has become the center of gravity for the globalized world, and for nations the center of gravity not only for military operations but for all aspects of national activity, to include economic, financial, diplomatic, and other transactions.

Cyberspace can also be seen as the 'terrain' of technology mediated communication. Reduced to basics, cyberspace is the proverbial ether within and through which electromagnetic radiation is propagated in connection with the operation and control of mechanical and electronic transmission systems. Moreover, it is a medium in which information can be created and acted on anytime, anywhere, and by essentially anyone.

Cyberspace is qualitatively different from the sea, air, and space domains, yet it both overlaps and continuously operates within all of them. More importantly, it is the only domain in which all instruments of national power – diplomatic, informational, military, and economic – can be concurrently exercised through the manipulation of data and gateways. Just like the other commons, it is one in which continued uninhibited access can never be taken for granted as a natural and assured right. Were unimpeded access to the EMS denied through hostile actions, satellite aided munitions would become useless, command and control mechanisms would be disrupted, and the ensuing effects could be paralyzing. Accordingly, cyberspace has become an emerging theater of operations that undoubtedly will be contested in future conflicts. Successful exploitation of this domain through network warfare operations can allow an opponent to dominate or hold at risk any or all of the global commons. Yet uniquely among the other three, cyberspace is a domain in which the classic constraints of distance, space, time, and investment are reduced, sometimes dramatically, both for us and for potential enemies.

Cyber Power

Stuart H Starr describes cyber power as the "ability to use cyberspace to create advantages and influence events in other operational environments and across the instruments of power."[10] Its strategic purpose revolves around the ability in peace and war to manipulate perceptions of the strategic environment to one's advantage while at the same time degrading the ability of an adversary to comprehend that same environment. Transforming the effects of cyber power into policy objectives is the art of strategy, defined as "managing context for continuing advantage according to policy." Basically, cyber power is the capability to control IT systems and networks in and through cyberspace. "Cyber power is the use, threatened use, or effect by the knowledge of its potential use, of disruptive cyber-attack capabilities by a state."[11] Power depends on context, and cyber power depends on the resources that characterize the domain of cyberspace. And across the other elements and instruments of power, cyber power creates synergies between those elements and connects them in ways that improve all of them.

Cyber power is shaped by multiple factors. While cyberspace just exists as an environment, cyber power is always a measure of the ability to use that environment. Technology is one factor, because the ability to 'enter' cyberspace is what makes its use possible. That technology is constantly changing, and some users – countries, societies, non-state actors, etc. – may be able to leap over old technologies to deploy and use new ones to dramatic advantage. Organizational factors also play a role, because organizations reflect human purposes and objectives, and their perspectives on the creation and use of cyber power are shaped by their organizational mission, be it military, economic or political. But the element most closely tied to cyber power is information. Cyberspace and cyber

10 Ibid 2.

11 Ibid.

power are dimensions of the informational instrument of power, and there are myriad ways that cyber power links to, supports, and enables the exercise of the other instruments of power. Thus, information is the bedrock of cyber power.

Cyber power relies on hardware and software. Hardware is the mechanical, magnetic, electronic, and electrical devices comprising a computer system, such as the central processing unit, disk drives, key-board, or screen. Cables, satellites, routers, computer chips, and the like are also considered hardware. Software consists of the programs used to direct computer operations and uses. Malware is malicious software that interferes with normal computer and Internet-based application functions and is a key weapon in cyber warfare.

Cyber power has three main characteristics: it is ubiquitous, it is complementary, and it can be stealthy. Land, sea, air, and space power are able to generate strategic effect on each of the other domains. But nothing generates strategic effect in all domains so absolutely and simultaneously as cyber power, because cyber power is ubiquitous.

Unlike land, sea, and airpower, but in some respects like space power, cyber power is a complementary instrument, particularly when used autonomously. It is indirect because the coercive ability of cyber power is still limited. While cyber- attacks can be damaging and disruptive, neither the attacks suffered by Estonia in 2007 and by Georgia in 2008, nor the Stuxnet attack on Iranian nuclear facilities in 2010/11, have been really coercive. This may well change in the future. But for this to happen, coercion must first be proven. Shutting down a power grid via cyber power, for example, would most likely have catastrophic consequences. But rather than coercing its victim to concede to an attacker's demands, it may only invite an even more catastrophic response. Thus, until cyber power will prove its coercive capability, it can be said to be a complementary instrument.

The last characteristic, that cyber power can be stealthy, makes it attractive to many users. They can use this ability to wield it surreptitiously on a global scale without it being attributable to the perpetrator. Databases can be raided for classified or proprietary information without the owners being any wiser after terabits of data have been stolen. Malicious software can be planted in adversary IT systems and networks without knowledge until these weapons are activated and cause their intended damage. Such stealthy use of cyber power, aided by the inherent difficulties of attributing the identity and motivation of most attackers, makes it an attractive instrument for governments and other actors.

Cyber power can be used to produce preferred outcomes within cyberspace, or it can use cyber instruments to produce preferred outcomes in other domains outside cyberspace. The key elements of cyber power are the science of the electromagnetic spectrum, the technology of electronics, and integrated manmade infrastructure. The key aspect of cyber power is its capability to manipulate or access a target's cyber infrastructure via exploitation and attack. Means of cyber power come via cyber warfare. Cyber warfare is the use of cyber power to either inflict or threaten punishment against an adversary, or to achieve political objectives through force without the opponent's acquiescence. As states begin to focus their energies on developing doctrine and weapons for conducting cyber warfare operations, it is essential that we move beyond the realization that cyberspace is an important new battleground for conducting warfare operations and recognize the need to come to an understanding of what rules regulate this new battleground. Decision making in time requiring defensive measures or military crisis is guided by doctrine and rules of engagement, but in the case of cyber-attacks and cyber warfare they do not currently exist.

Cyber power is exerting itself as a key lever in the development and execution of national policy. Its capabilities challenge the strategist to integrate those capabilities with other elements and instruments of power. And this requires the crafting of a cyber-strategy, which is "the development and employment of capabilities to operate in cyberspace, integrated and coordinated with the other operational realms, to achieve or support the achievement of objectives across the elements of national power."[12]

Cyberspace is now attracting the attention of the military strategists. If cyberspace is the new domain then its dominance will become the key in the outcome of cyber war. This implies achieving superiority in the cyber domain. This brings us to an interesting question. If cyberspace includes networks and systems which are interconnected globally, then how does one dominate or achieve superiority? The key aspect therefore is of controlling cyberspace by attaining operational superiority both, by offensive and proactive efforts. Few countries, US primarily closely followed by Israel, China and to some extent UK are engaged in seriously developing the skills and resources required in achieving superiority in cyber domain while most of the other countries are simply watching what they are doing.

Cyber strategy builds on a systematic and structured combination of "ends" (goals and objectives), "means" (resources and capabilities), and "ways" (how the means are used to accomplish the ends), tempered with due analysis and considerations of the risks and costs. To develop a national strategy for cyberspace, therefore, is to simultaneously create cyber resources and procedures that can contribute to the achievement of specific national security objectives. The most important part of cyber strategy concerns the ends for which cyber capabilities might be used. These ends are part of the larger military, political, economic, diplomatic, and national security objectives being sought. Cyber power is created to support the attainment of larger objectives: strategic goals across the elements of national power as a means of satisfying the vital national needs and interests of the National Security Strategy. The key contribution of a national strategy for cyberspace will be to explicitly and clearly demonstrate how it makes possible the attainment of all the other strategies, most especially the National Security Strategy.[13]

12 Daniel T Kuehl, in "From Cyberspace to Cyber power: Defining the Problem".

13 Ibid.

Indian Cyberspace Today

India fared poorly in cyber defence in the recently released report published by Brussels based Security and Defence Agenda (SDA)-a think tank. India needs to invest, quickly and substantially in improving the cyber defence of its vital infrastructure installations. One cannot sit back and wait allowing things to happen.

India needs to adopt a different approach in framing policies towards defending against cyber-attack than it has against other forms of attack. First, it is difficult to identify the attacker particularly when some nations sponsor private attackers. Second, it may be difficult to follow through with threats of counter attacks one does not know how damage the attacks could do. Thirdly, by the time the attacker is located the damage has already been done. One of the major problems with cyber warfare policy would be the lack of definition of what constitutes an act of cyber war. The distinction between a simple cyber-attack and cyber war really does not exist.

The discovery of the worm, Stuxnet in 2009 has been a watershed in the perception of threats in cyberspace. It has made the nations sit up and take cognisance of the threat that cyber-attacks could cripple its critical national infrastructure. The aim of Stuxnet was to cripple the Programmable Logic Controller controlling the speed of centrifuges in nuclear plants of Iran and it strongly suggests it was a work of not a way side hacker but that of state intelligence agency. It has acted as a starting point in cyber arms race.

India's adversaries know fully well that it cannot be defeated in conventional political, economic and military manner. Consequently, they now seek to attack India through warfare by other means (WBOM). While the first form i.e. the kinetic attack which includes suicide attacks have not yielded desired results it is the second form of WBOM which is non- kinetic and is important here as cyber warfare falls in this category. In fact cyber warfare is most attractive means of non –kinetic warfare which have enthused our adversaries.

On 07 March 2012, US weapons manufacturer Northrop

Grumman released a report "Occupying the Information High Ground: Chinese Capabilities for Computer Network operations and Cyber Espionage," wherein it warns of Beijing's integration of network operations into broader military and intelligence context and of the threat this represents to US economic and strategic interests. The report states that more than 50 Chinese universities are conducting research on information security, funded by five national grant programs as part of a broad national policy.

The Security and Defence Agenda (SDA) Report which is based on interviews with global experts finds that 57 percent respondents feel cyber arms race is underway. Other findings are:-

(a) 36 percent believe cyber security is more important than missile defence.

(b) 43 percent feel damage or disruption to CNI as the greatest threat.

(c) 45 percent feel that cyber security is as important as border security.

As states begin to focus their energies on developing doctrine and weapons for conducting cyber warfare operations, it is essential that we move beyond the realization that cyberspace is an important new battleground for conducting warfare operations and recognize the need to come to an understanding of what rules regulate this new battleground. Decision making in time requiring defensive measures or military crisis is guided by doctrine and rules of engagement, but in the case of cyber-attacks and cyber warfare they do not currently exist.

Cyber power is now a fundamental fact of global life. In political, economic, and military affairs, information technology provides and support critical elements of operational activities. It is imperative that India incorporates cyber power into its strategic calculations.

CHAPTER 2

RECENT CYBER ATTACKS

ESTONIA

Brief History[1]

Estonia is a former colony of the erstwhile Soviet Union. It is mainly a low lying country that is bordered by Russia, Latvia and Baltic Sea. Estonians are one of the longest-settled European people and have lived along the Baltic Sea for over 5,000 years. The Estonians were an independent nation until the 13th century A.D. The country was then subsequently conquered by Denmark, Germany, Poland, Sweden, and finally Russia, whose defeat of Sweden in 1721 resulted in the Uusikaupunki Peace Treaty, granting Russia rule over what became modern Estonia.

In 1346, the Danes who possessed northern Estonia, sold the land to Teutonic Knights of Germany, who already possessed southern Estonia and Latvia. They reduced the Estonians to serfdom. In 1526, the Swedes took over. Estonia entered a period of peace and prosperity under Swedish rule. Although the lot of the Estonian peasantry did not improve much, cities, boosted by trade, grew and prospered, helping the economy speedily recover from the ravages of war. Under Swedish rule, Estonia was united for the first time in history under a single ruler. This period is often referred to as 'the good old Swedish time'. After 1721 Russia succeeded Sweden as the ruling power, the Estonians were subject to double bondage- the Balts and the czarist officials. The late 19th century was also a period of rampant industrialization, marked by the rise of large factories and an extensive railway network that linked Estonia with Russia. Socialism and discontent accompanied those grim workplaces, with demonstrations and strikes led by newly formed worker parties. Events in Estonia mimicked those in Russia,

1 Estonia – http://en.wikipedia.org/wiki/Estonia

and in January 1905 as armed insurrection flared across the border, Estonia's workers joined the fray. Tension mounted until autumn that year, when 20, 000 workers went on strike. Tsarist troops brutally responded by killing and wounding 200.

Tsar Nicholas II's response incited the Estonian rebels, who continued to destroy the property of the old guard. Subsequently, thousands of soldiers arrived from Russia, quelling the rebellions and then executed 600 Estonians and sent hundreds off to Siberia. Trade unions and progressive newspapers and organizations were closed down, and political leaders fled the country.

More radical plans to bring Estonia to heel - such as sending thousands of Russian peasants to colonize the country - were never realized. Instead, Russia's bumbling tsar had another priority: WWI. Estonia paid a high price for Russia's involvement - 100, 000 men were drafted, 10, 000 of whom were killed in action. Many Estonians went off to fight under the notion that if they helped defeat Germany, Russia would grant them nationhood. Russia, of course, had no intention of doing so. But by 1917 the matter was no longer simple for the Tsar's to decide. In St Petersburg Nicholas II was forced to abdicate, and the Bolsheviks seized power. As chaos swept across Russia, Estonia seized the initiative and on 24 February 1918, effectively declared its independence. Estonia had a brief spell of freedom (1918-1920) but shortly after World War II started it was again occupied by Russian troops and was incorporated as the 16th Republic of USSR in 1940. Deportations and WW II devastated the country. Tens of thousands were conscripted and sent not to fight but to work (and usually die) in labor camps in northern Russia. Thousands of women and children were also sent to gulags.

When Russia fled the German advance, Estonia welcomed the Nazis as liberators. Fifty-five thousand Estonians joined home-defence units and Wehrmacht Ost battalions. The Nazis, however, would not grant statehood to Estonia and viewed it merely as occupied territory of the Soviet Union. Hope was crushed when the Germans began executing communist collaborators. Seventy-five thousand people were shot (5000 of who were ethnic Estonians). Thousands fled to Finland, while those who remained faced conscription into the German army (nearly 40, 000 were conscripted). In early 1944 the Soviet army bombed major cities of Estonia and exacted revenge upon 'Estonian traitors'.

The Nazis retreated in September 1944. Fearing the advance of the Red Army, many Estonians also fled and around 70, 000 reached the West. By the end of the war one in 10 Estonians lived abroad. All in all, Estonia lost over 280, 000 people in addition to those who emigrated, 30, 000 were killed in action; others were executed, sent to gulags or exterminated in concentration camps.

After the war Estonia was immediately annexed by the Soviet Union. This began the grim epoch of repression, with many thousands tortured or sent to prison camps and 19, 000 Estonians executed. Farmers were brutally forced into collectivization, and thousands of immigrants flooded the country from different regions of the Soviet Union. Between 1939 and 1989 the percentage of native Estonians fell from 97 percent to 62 percent.

As a result of the repression, beginning in 1944, Estonians formed a large guerrilla movement. Calling themselves the 'Forest Brothers', 14, 000 Estonians armed themselves and went into hiding, operating in small groups throughout the country. Unfortunately, the guerrillas had little success against the Soviet army, and by 1956 the movement had been effectively destroyed.

The dissident movement in Estonia gained momentum, and on the 50th anniversary of the Stalin-Hitler pact, a major rally took place in Tallinn. Over the next few months, more and more protests were held, with Estonians demanding the restoration of statehood. In the late 1980s, looser controls on freedom of expression under Soviet leader Mikhail Gorbachev reignited the Estonians' call for self-determination. By 1988, hundreds of thousands of people were gathering across Estonia to sing previously banned national songs in what became known as the "Singing Revolution."The song festival was one of Estonia's most powerful vehicles for protest. The biggest protest took place in 1988 when 250, 000 Estonians gathered on Tallinn's Song Festival grounds. This brought much international attention to the Baltic plight.

An Independent Nation

In November 1989 the Estonian Supreme Soviet declared the events of 1940 an act of military aggression and therefore illegal. Disobeying Moscow, Estonia held free elections in 1990. In November 1988, Estonia's Supreme Soviet passed a declaration of sovereignty; in 1990, the name of the Republic of Estonia was restored, and during the August 1991 coup in the USSR, Estonia declared full independence. Unlike the experiences of Latvia and Lithuania, Estonia's revolution ended without blood spilled.

US, UK, France, Italy and the majority of other western democracies considered illegal the annexation of Estonia by the USSR. They retained diplomatic relations with the representatives of the independent Republic of Estonia and never recognized Estonia as a legal constituent of Soviet Union. The first country to diplomatically recognize Estonia's reclaimed independence was Iceland. Soviet Union recognized Estonia on 06 Sep 91. UN membership was accorded on 17 Sep 91. Estonia adopted free market economy which led to foreign investments and improved economy. Estonia, slowly but surely, drifted away from Russia and looked more and more towards the West. It became the member of European Union and NATO in 2004. In Mar 2007, Estonia allowed internet voting for Parliamentary elections, becoming the first country to do so.

In early 2007, the Government of Estonia decided to relocate a World War II Soviet era War Memorial from the city of Tallinn to a military cemetery outside the city. This enraged the Russian Government and many Russian citizens who saw it as a slight. It is generally accepted that this was the catalyst for the cyber-attacks that followed soon after. These cyber-attacks served as a wakeup call about the potential damage that could be inflicted on a highly wired country.

Did the attacks achieve the objective set by the attackers? Was Estonia as a nation really got damaged from these attacks? In order to answer these questions it would be relevant to look at Estonia through traditional levers of power- political/diplomatic, informational, military and economy (P/DIME).

Politics/Diplomatic

Estonia follows the framework of a parliamentary representative democratic republic in which he Prime Minister is the head of the Government in a multi-party system. The Parliament of Estonia is elected by the people for a four year term and has 101 members. It elects and appoints several high officials of the state, including the President. The executive branch or the Government of Estonia is headed by the Prime Minister who is nominated by the President and approved by the Parliament. The Prime Minister has the right to appoint his ministers.[2]

Estonia has pursued the development of the e-state and e-government. Internet voting is used in elections in Estonia, the first such voting took place in 2005 local elections and parliamentary elections in 2007 in which 30,275 people voted over the Internet.

After attaining independence, Estonia has pursued a foreign policy of close cooperation with its Western European partners with the most prominent being its joining NATO and European Union in 2004. As Estonia aligned more and more towards the West its relations with Russia went on a steady decline. It now sought to deal with Russia as a full partner and not as a former colony. Russia still attempted to exert control over Estonia on the pretext of expressing concern for over hundred thousand ethnic Russians living there.

Post-independence Estonia sought to forge closer ties with the Nordic countries particularly Finland and Sweden. In fact Estonians consider themselves as Nordic rather than Baltic. It sought to improve its diplomatic relations with members of European Union and also countries such as Bosnia, Kosovo and Serbia which it saw as future NATO and European Union members. This realigned also led to a shift in economic interdependence and trade from Russia ((92 percent in 1992) to the Nordic countries (Finland and Sweden)

Estonia deliberately leaned towards European Union as it sees that as a source of diplomatic strength and protection. Through 2004 till 2007 Estonia slowly tried to distance itself from Russia and

2 Background Note: Estonia – http:/www.state.gov/r/pa/ei/bgn/5377.htm

sought to deal with Russia on equal footing. It saw EU and the West as the tool to do this.

Information[3]

Estonia is one of the most wired countries in the world. It is one of the few countries in the world which allowed voting for national elections over the internet. This exhibits its confidence and trust, as a nation, on its Information Systems. 57 percent of the population had internet connections in 2007 which has now gone up to 75.1 percent in 2010 (ITU). 93 percent of people aged sixteen to twenty four use the net in 2007, 86.3 percent aged twenty five to thirty four and 77.8 percent aged thirty five to forty four used the net.

Estonia has achieved relatively high ICT levels given its income, based on remarkable growth in ICT access and uptake between 2002 and 2007. Indeed, since the launch of the Estonian Information Policy in 1998, 14 the country has made great strides in ICT development. The public sector led the way and offered some of the most advanced eGovernment services, and implementing very successful ICT policy initiatives, such as the Tiger Leap Programme, aimed at the internetization of schools. The results proved how strong policies can be drivers of ICT-led development.

The Baltic States have made significant improvements in their evolution towards becoming information societies. Estonia, Latvia and Lithuania all increased their ranks (by five, three and eight places respectively). Lithuania and Estonia are among the top ten countries worldwide that have increased their index values most between 2002 and 2007. This is due to improvements in both access and usage indicators. For example, Estonia and Lithuania have one of the highest mobile subscription penetration rates globally (148 per cent up from 65 per cent and 145 per cent up from 47 per cent in 2002, respectively). Latvia has considerably improved household access to computers and Internet (49 and 51 per cent respectively, up from 15 and 8.5 per cent in 2002).

Estonia thus was fully embracing and exploiting the benefits

3 Statistics Estonia –http://www.stat.ee

of information technology both in the government sector as well as private sector. All government agencies were equipped with information technology needed to discharge their functions. While rapid employment of information technology enabled Estonia to harness information power, it at the same time increased its vulnerability to cyber-attacks. The main cyber warfare facility in 2007 was CERT which was founded in 2006. Estonian information security procedures were not capable of preventing cyber-attacks but once started they were able to respond effectively.

Military

Estonian Defence Forces comprise Army, Navy, Air Force and paramilitary National Guard Organization *Kaitseliit*. The military service is compulsory for men between 18 to 28 years. At moment the main strategic goals are to be able to defend the country's interests and development of the armed forces which would be ready to interoperate with other armed forces of NATO and EU and also contribute to NATO and UN missions. Estonia in 2006-07 was driven by its desire to be a contributing power to NATO and EU. Estonia identified Ukraine, Georgia, and Moldova as security priorities. 2006 was a strong year which resulted in increased defence spending by 33 percent in 2007 over 2006(Baltic Security and Defence Review 2007).

Estonia also sought to upgrade its fighting capabilities and procured night vision equipment and advanced light weaponry. Estonia contributed its troops to NATO missions in Afghanistan and Iraq (Baltic Security and Defence Review 2007).

Estonian actions indicate that it was trying to distance itself from security reliance on Russia. It pursued a military policy that looked towards West. This reduced its dependence on Russia and gave it the chance shake off reliance on Russian security institutions and norms that were reminiscent of the cold war era. Estonia was thus becoming a catalyst for change in Eastern Europe.

Economic[4]

Estonia was rapidly becoming an economic powerhouse in 2006 in the Baltic region. The GDP grew by 7.9 percent in2007 alone. Most significant sectors are IT, Transportation, Energy, Tourism and Banking. In 2006 Estonia adapted 3G mobile communications networks granting unprecedented mobile access for Estonian users (ITU).

The country was nearly energy independent by meeting over 90 percent of its electricity needs with locally mined shale oil. It imported petroleum products from Western Europe and Russia (natural gas). Estonia broke free from the shackles of the communist era and privatized farming thus making it more efficient. Railway dominates the cargo sector carrying 70 percent of the goods. Road transport accounts for carrying 90 percent of the passenger traffic.

Cyber Attacks: 2007[5]

On April 26-27, 2007, in downtown Tallinn, Estonia, government workers took down and moved a Soviet era monument commemorating World War II called the Bronze Soldier, despite the protests of some 500 ethnic Russians Estonians. They considered this monument as a symbol of honour to the Red Army who fought against German Nazis. However the Estonians viewed it as a symbol of foreign occupation and used to protest every year for its removal from Tallinn. This incident sparked anger all across Russia which in turn led to cyber-attacks on Estonia.

Same night by about 10 PM local time digital intruders began probing Estonian Internet networks, looking for weak points and marshaling resources for an all-out attack. Bursts of data were sent to important nodes and servers to determine their maximum capacity- that the attackers would exceed with floods of data, crashing servers and clogging connections. By 1 am on 28 April Estonia finally realized it was under cyber-attack.

4 Economy of Estonia - http://en.wikipedia.org/wiki/Economy_of_Estonia

5 Hackers take Down the Most Wired Country in Europe by Joshua Davis in Wired Magazine : Issue 15.09

The cyber-attacks launched were very coordinated and well planned. The attacks were carried out in two phases. The first phase was carried out by what is called hacktivists. Relatively primitive and simple attack tools were used against Estonia by ordinary people who were instructed to attack Estonia on Russian web sites and those on which the attack tools were posted. These attack tools were directed against mainly government web sites and some leading parties in Estonia. Main targets of attacks were:-

(a) Estonian Presidency and Parliament

(b) Government Ministries

(c) Political Parties

(d) Prominent news organizations

(f) Banks

(g) Communication infrastructure

The second phase of attack used more sophisticated tools mainly botnets. Rough estimate indicate that attacks came from 75 or more jurisdictions using 1 million or more computers without people who owned these computers knowing anything about it. The attacks were so intensified that Estonia had to block foreign access to sites under siege.

Analysis of Attacks

The attacks were steady though not uniform during the period of attack. The attacks lasted for about three weeks and the number of attacks recorded is given in Table 2 below:-

Table 2. Number of Attacks

Attacks	Date
21	2007-05-03
17	2007-05-04
31	2007-05-08
58	2007-05-09
1	2007-05-11

Most of the attacks lasted form 1 min to 1 hour while some were recorded for more than 10 hours that caused enormous damage to the target systems. Table 3 below shows the duration of attacks.

Table 3. Duration of Attacks

Attack	Time
17	less than 1 minute
78	1 min -1 hour
16	1 hour - 5 hours
8	5 hours to 9 hours
7	10 hours or more

Bandwidth used for attacks is given below in Table 4.

Table 4. Bandwidth used for Attacks

Atacks	Bandwidth measured
42	Less than 10 Mbps
52	10 Mbps - 30 Mbps
22	30 Mbps - 70 Mbps
12	70 Mbps - 95 Mbps

The attacks carried out against Estonia were of DoS and DDoS type ranges from simple PING flood to more sophisticated botnets. According to the Asymmetric Threats Contingency Alliance (ATCA), Russia hired illegal botnets for short time to amplify the attack by involving millions of computers in the assault on Estonia.

Data from Arbor Network Active Threat Level Analysis System (ATLAS), which claims to be able to monitor 80 percent of the internet traffic, reveals that 128 unique DoS attacks targeted IP addresses within Estonia over three weeks of conflict and most of which were ICMP PING flood that targets whole system instead of a particular port or service within the server [10]. Analysis of the ATLAS data also revealed that there were more than one botnets involved in the assault, making it difficult to track down the perpetrators. On the basis of the data collected from ATLAS, out of 128 unique DoS attacks, 115 were ICMP flood, 4 were TCP SYNC flood, and 9 were generic traffic flood.

Attacks on Estonia were quite heavy and most likely DDoS attacks were used in which attacker compromises large number of computers to launch heavy attacks. The attacker sends commands to a master computer that in turn forwards the instructions to daemon's installed on Zombies to launch heavy coordinated attacks against the target.

Response by Estonia

Estonian Internet Security professionals though could not prevent the attacks from happening in the first place they were however, not unable to defend their system. The response was coordinated by CERT, Estonia. He response was systematic, well-coordinated with willing cooperation among various government agencies. Here being a small country helped shape quick and effective response.

During the first wave of attacks, network security specialists attempted to erect barriers and firewalls to protect primary targets. As the attacks increased in intensity, these began to crumble. Estonia acted politically to get the international community to intervene and also asked allies in EU and NATO for help. Estonian Defence Minister Jaak Aaviksoo mulled invoking NATO Article 5, which states that an assault on one allied country obligates the alliance to attack the aggressor? Never before had an entire nation been targeted on almost every digital front almost at once, and never before had a government itself fought back.

Hillar Aarelaid, head of Estonian CERT called upon contacts in Finland, Germany, Slovenia and other countries to assemble a team of hackers and computer experts to defend the country. Aarelaid and his team, after the first wave of attacks had gradually managed to block access to many of the hackers targets and restored a degree of stability within the networks.

On May 8 at exactly 11 pm, as Aarelaid and his team watched, Estonia was slammed with a traffic surge almost 200 fold increase. Globally, nearly 1 million computers were sending traffic to various Estonian sites thereby squeezing the bandwidth of the entire country.

Aarelaid and his team chased the sources upstream and found a botnet comprising hijacked computers in US. As they identified the IP addresses, rapid fire emails were sent to network providers to block the IP. The aim was to block traffic before it enters Estonia's major international connections. By dawn they had deflected the attacks. By May 10 the attacks slowly decreased as Aarelaid managed to take the botnets offline by having the ISPs block the IO addresses.

During the defence of Estonia's Internet system, many computers used in the attack were traced back to computers in Russian government offices. What could not be determined was whether these computers were simply Zombies hijacked by bots or were actively used by government personnel.

Lessons

Had the state of Estonia not been the most wired country in the world, these attacks would have quietly faded away from public memory. Ever since it broke away from the former Soviet union, Estonia steadily embraced the Western model of development. Estonia was the first country to conduct elections on line and performed 90 percent of their banking online. For a nation that spawned the global telecommunications phenomenon as Skype, the 2007 attacks were a watershed moment. Estonia's experience and subsequent actions continue to offer lessons for security managers of more advanced threats today.

Professional Networks are Critical. The informal relationship among technology professionals through old fashioned social networking was the key to government- private sector response to the crisis of 2007. Estonia is a small nation and the technical people not only knew each other fairly well but also abroad and this helped. Estonia's two-person CERT recruited help, both of national and foreign experts. This resulted in quick and effective response. US and Sweden in particular aided the response by halting internet traffic before Estonia. The government also turned to local, private specialists who could help. What is the lesson – Use meaningful project collaboration to connect with colleagues in various agencies and in private sector.

Go Beyond Partnership. Cyber-attack will be directed not only against government sites but also that of private infrastructure. It was therefore realized that cooperation had to extend beyond information sharing and needed to be institutionalized, voluntary associations were insufficient to create the kinds of relationships necessary to coordinate an effective cyber response. While large organisations had the resources to maintain their systems, small and medium ones were vulnerable. All needed incentives and prodding to share the details of breaches.

Coordinated Response with Foreign Powers. Estonia has today developed its cyber security strategy around engagement with foreign partners' networks and intelligence agencies. It played a leading role in setting up the NATO Cooperative Cyber Defence Centre of Excellence in Tallinn, which stages attack scenarios and encourages members to share best practices.

Be Ahead of the Threat. Without official processes in place in 2007, Estonia's response team tried to defeat each traffic wave separately. As the attacks continued and origins of traffic were traced to diverse set of servers around the world, the team had to block all traffic from abroad. The liberty to shut off all foreign traffic India does not have as it impact the economy adversely. The lesson therefore is that India's public and private networks cannot be unprepared.

STUXNET WORM[6]

General

In 2010 Iran announced that computer of the control systems at one of its nuclear processing facilities have been infected by a worm

6 W32.Stuxnet Dossier by Symantec Security Response

called Stuxnet. It was known that such a worm was possible but the attack on the nuclear installation made it an important threshold in cyber-attacks for two reasons. First, this incident proved that indeed a worm could be implanted in high security system to inflict physical damage. Second, given the complex nature of the worm, the understanding of Seimens Control Systems and nuclear installations and the resources required developing it and finally to implant it on computers not connected to internet suggests a state sponsored attack.

Stuxnet is a Windows-specific computer worm first discovered in July 2010 by VirusBlokAda, a security firm based in Belarus. It is the first discovered worm that spies on and reprograms industrial systems, and the first to include a programmable logic controller (PLC) rootkit. It was specifically written to attack Supervisory Control and Data Acquisition (SCADA) systems used to control and monitor industrial processes. Stuxnet includes the capability to reprogram the PLCs and hide its changes.

A Deadly Worm

Stuxnet is the most significant example of a cyber-war attack against another nation state's critical infrastructure since the Russian gas pipeline explosion in June 1982. In 1982 US learned from a Russian scientist that Soviets were stealing data on US technology, so CIA deliberately hatched a plot to insert a Trojan horse in gas pipeline regulator software that it knew would be stolen by the Russians. The Russians stole the software and used it Siberian natural gas pipeline. The Trojan horse corrupted the gas pipeline regulation resulting in a massive explosion that was captured by orbiting satellites. The incident was later declassified and well documented in the now famously known Farewell Dossier.

Stuxnet is a large, complex piece of malware with many different components and functionalities. Stuxnet is a threat that was primarily written to target an industrial control system or set of similar systems. Industrial control systems are used in gas pipelines and power plants. Its final goal is to reprogram industrial control systems (ICS) by modifying code on programmable logic controllers to make them work in a manner the attacker intended and to hide those changes from the operator of the equipment. In order to achieve this goal the creators amassed a vast array of components to increase their chances of success. This includes zero-day exploits, a Windows rootkit, the first ever PLC rootkit, antivirus evasion techniques, complex process injection and hooking code, network infection routines, peer-to-peer updates, and a command and control interface.

Stuxnet is a watershed event in Cyber Warfare because of the level of sophistication in the design of the worm indicates that significant resources and expertise was required to design and release the worm. The most significant indicators of a state-sponsored cyber threat are the exploitation of multiple Odays (vulnerabilities not previously known or disclosed by the software vendor) to execute the attack, two different target platforms — Windows and Siemens — needed to execute the attack, and the specific domain knowledge of the target system that was required for the worm. Whoever created Stuxnet developed four previously unknown zero-day attacks and a peer-to-peer communications system, compromised digital certificates belonging to Realtek Semiconductor and JMicron Technology, and displayed extensive knowledge of industrial systems. This is not something that a run-of-the-mill hacker can pull off. Many security researchers think that it would take the resources of a nation state to accomplish.

While there are many groups versed in Windows libraries, C/C++, and reverse engineering, there is a much more limited set of people with the domain knowledge of Siemens industrial control system, and a much, much smaller subset that has knowledge of both. There are so many different types of execution needs that it was clear this was a work by a team of people with varied backgrounds, from the rootkit side to the database side to writing exploits. The malware, which weighed in a nearly half a megabyte -- an astounding size, was written in multiple languages, including C, C++ and other object-oriented languages. Hence it would take fairly large amount of resources to plan, assemble the team, design the exploits, have access to O days, test, get intelligence on the target plant, put people in place with access, then run the operation. Possibly this would require a 1 to 2 year program with huge financial outlay. This puts it almost exclusively in the realm of nation states, or extremely well-funded transnational terrorist groups.

In order to follow the above argument let us examine a possible attack scenario as given in the *Stuxnet Dossier* by *Symantec.*

> *Industrial control systems (ICS) are operated by a specialized assembly like code on programmable logic controllers (PLCs). The PLCs are often programmed from Windows computers not connected to the Internet or even the internal network. In addition, the industrial control systems themselves are also unlikely to be connected to the Internet.*
>
> *First, the attackers needed to conduct reconnaissance. As each PLC is configured in a unique manner, the attackers would first need the ICS's schematics. These design documents may have been stolen by an insider or even retrieved by an early version of Stuxnet or other malicious binary. Once attackers had the design documents and potential knowledge of the computing environment in the facility, they would develop the latest version of Stuxnet. Each feature of Stuxnet was implemented for a specific reason and for the final goal of potentially sabotaging the ICS.*
>
> *Attackers would need to setup a mirrored environment that would include the necessary ICS hardware, such as PLCs, modules, and peripherals in order to test their code. The full cycle may have taken six months and five to ten core developers not counting numerous other individuals, such as quality assurance and management.*
>
> *In addition their malicious binaries contained driver files that needed to be digitally signed to avoid suspicion. The attackers compromised two digital certificates to achieve this task. The attackers would have needed to obtain the digital certificates from someone who may have physically entered the premises of the two companies and stole them, as the two companies are*

in close physical proximity.

To infect their target, Stuxnet would need to be introduced into the target environment. This may have occurred by infecting a willing or unknowing third party, such as a contractor who perhaps had access to the facility, or an insider. The original infection may have been introduced by removable drive.

Once Stuxnet had infected a computer within the organization it began to spread in search of Field PGs, which are typical Windows computers but used to program PLCs. Since most of these computers are non-networked, Stuxnet would first try to spread to other computers on the LAN through a zero-day vulnerability, a two year old vulnerability, infecting Step 7 projects, and through removable drives. Propagation through a LAN likely served as the first step and propagation through removable drives as a means to cover the last and final hop to a Field PG that is never connected to an untrusted network.

While attackers could control Stuxnet with a command and control server, as mentioned previously the key computer was unlikely to have outbound Internet access. Thus, all the functionality required to sabotage a system was embedded directly in the Stuxnet executable. Updates to this executable would be propagated throughout the facility through a peer-to-peer method established by Stuxnet.

When Stuxnet finally found a suitable computer, one that ran Step 7, it would then modify the code on the PLC. These modifications likely sabotaged the system, which was likely considered a high value target due to the large resources invested in the creation of Stuxnet.

Victims attempting to verify the issue would not see any rogue PLC code as Stuxnet hides its modifications.

*While their choice of using self-replication methods may have been necessary to ensure they'd find a suitable Field PG, they also caused noticeable collatera*l damage by infecting machines outside the target organization. The attackers may have considered the collateral damage a necessity in order to effectively reach the intended target. Also, the attackers likely completed their initial attack by the time they were discovered.

Unleashing of the Stuxnet worm was a watershed in the security world. Some observers consider it to be the most sophisticated malware ever publicly disclosed. Stuxnet contains malware aimed at the programmable logic controllers (PLCs), designed to destroy SCADA networks: those that run factories, the electric power grid, refineries, pipelines, utilities, and nuclear power plants. Most industrial systems are run on computers which use Microsoft's Windows operating system. Hackers constantly probe software for what are known as "zero days" vulnerabilities; weak points in the code never foreseen by the original programmers. On a sophisticated and ubiquitous piece of software such as Windows XP, which counts around 35 million lines of code, discovering even one single "zero day" vulnerability is extremely uncommon. The makers of Stuxnet found, and utilized, four of them. No one in cyber security had ever seen anything like it. It targeted a specific component; the frequency converters made by the German equipment manufacturer Siemens that regulate the speed of the many thousands of spinning centrifuges used in the Iranian uranium enrichment process. The worm then took control of the speed at which the centrifuges spun, making them turn so fast in a quick burst that they would be damaged but not totally destroyed. At the same time, the worm masked that change in speed from being discovered at the control panel – with a rootkit piece of code that intercepts security queries and sends back false 'safe' messages, indicating that the worm is innocuous.

Infection Statistics

As of September 29, 2010, the data has shown that there are approximately 100,000 infected hosts. The following graph shows the number of unique infected *hosts* by country:-

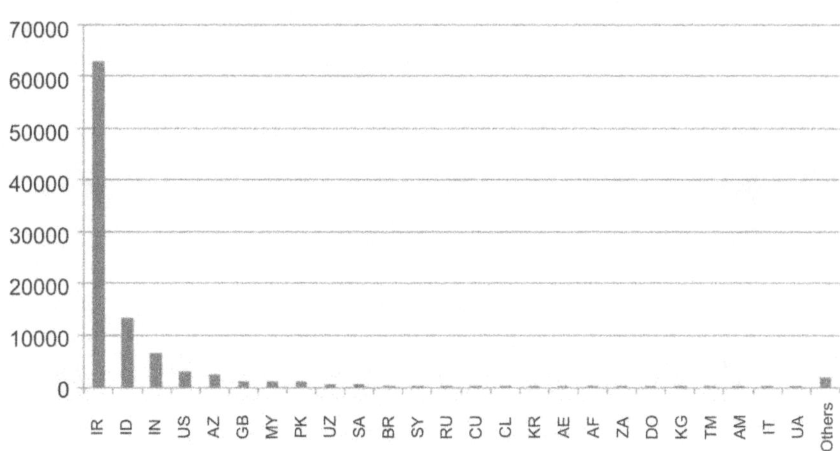

Symantec observed over 40,000 unique external IP addresses, from over 155 countries. Looking at the percentage of infected hosts by country, they found that approximately 60 percent of infected hosts were in Iran:-

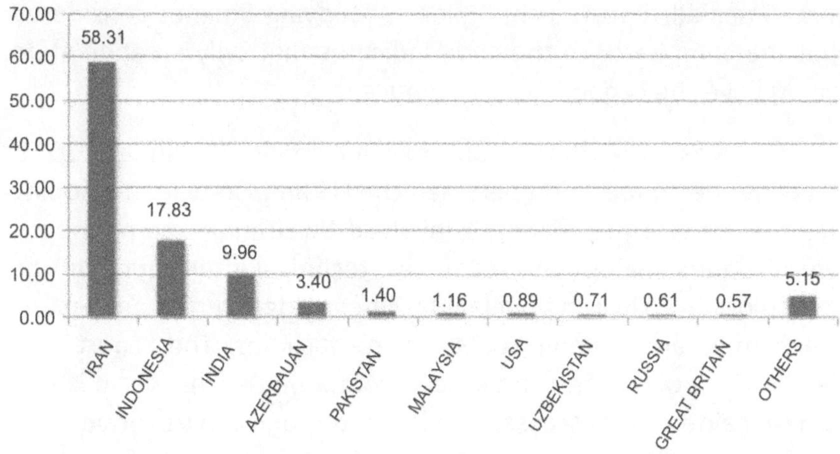

Stuxnet aims to identify those hosts which have the Siemens Step 7 software installed. The following chart shows the percentage of infected hosts by country with the Siemens software installed.

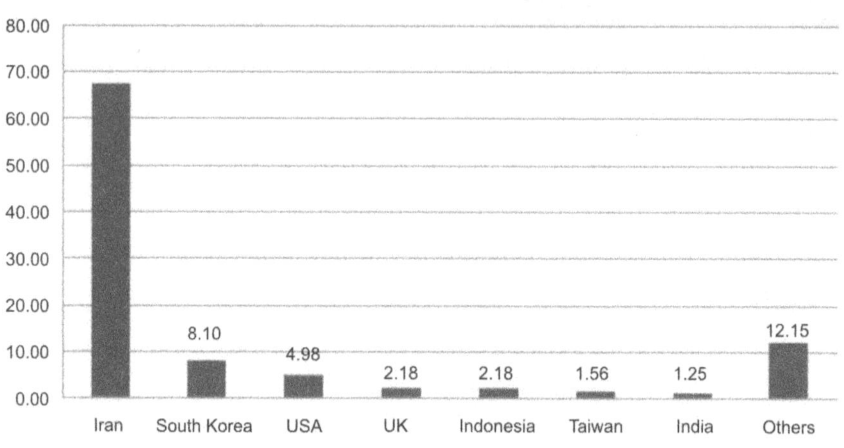

Origin and Target[7]

Symantec estimates that the group developing Stuxnet would have been well-funded, consisting of five to ten people, and would have taken six months to prepare. *The Guardian*, the BBC and *The New York Times* all reported that experts studying Stuxnet considered that the complexity of the code indicates that only a nation state would have the capabilities to produce it.

The *New York Times* published an article 25 January 2011, detailing the cooperation between the US and Israel in developing the Stuxnet worm. Creating it involved three major components, which require major state resources: technical intelligence on the technology used in Iran's nuclear facilities; programming and testing capabilities; and human access to the facilities. The report only details some of the first and second components. The worm is said to have gained initial access to a system through a 'blue rubber-clad swivel-style USB drive.' In a rare moment of openness from Iran, its president confirmed on 29 November 2010 that the centrifuges had been damaged by Stuxnet. And the Busher nuclear power plant that was scheduled to go operational on 21 August 2010 did not. If Stuxnet managed to severely damage the steam turbine in the Busher plant, repairing or replacing it may cost a significant amount

7 Stuxnet - http://en.wikipedia.org/wiki/stuxnet

of money – up to several million dollars. Presently, it looks like more than 5,084 out of 8,856 centrifuges have been taken offline at the Natanz facility, with unknown damage in Fordow and other centrifuge plants. All this translates to multi-million dollar damage.[8]

According to David Sanger from the New York Times, an Israeli military official had estimated that an air strike against the Iranian nuclear program would cause a delay of two or three years. So it looks like Stuxnet achieved pretty much what air strikes would have achieved, only at much less cost, without known fatalities, and without a full-blown war in the Middle East. It seems to have been successful in temporarily disabling the epicenter of Iranian nuclear research. A sophisticated half-megabyte of computer code apparently accomplished what a half-decade of UN Security Council resolutions could not. The cost of development of Stuxnet has been estimated to be around $10 million. The cost of air strikes would have been multiple, only counting material, not fatalities and injuries. Assuming that only one fighter jet would have been lost in a military campaign against Iran is certainly naïve; there would have been several. And there would have been many dead and many injured, significant destruction by Iranian missiles fired in retaliation and a huge amount of collateral damage just by the oil price jumping. All this did not happen with Stuxnet. Thus, in military terms, it was a bargain. If the alternative is conventional military strikes with explosives or maybe even weapons of mass destruction, cyber strikes might be the better deal, not only for the attacker, but especially for the attacked.[9]

Israel, perhaps through Unit 8200, has been speculated to be the country behind Stuxnet in many media reports and by experts such as Richard Falkenrath, former Senior Director for Policy and Plans within the United States Department of Homeland Security. When questioned whether Israel was behind the virus in the fall of 2010, it was reported that some Israeli officials broke into "wide smiles", fueling speculation that the government of Israel was involved with its genesis. Some have also referred to several clues in the code such

8 DCAF HORIZON 2015 WORKING PAPER No. 7 "On Cyber Warfare" by Fred Schreier.

9 Ibid.

as a concealed reference to the word "MYRTUS", believed to refer to the Myrtle tree, or Hadassah in Hebrew. Hadassah was the birth name of the former Jewish queen of Persia, Queen Esther. However, it may be that the "MYRTUS" reference is simply a misinterpreted reference to SCADA components known as *RTUs* (Remote Terminal Units) and that this reference is actually "My RTUs"–a management feature of SCADA. Also, the number 19790509 appears once in the code and might refer to the date "1979 May 09", the day Habib Elghanian, a Persian Jew, was executed in Tehran. These data are not conclusive, since, as written by Symantec, "Attackers would have the natural desire to implicate another party." According to the New York Times, a former member of the United States intelligence community speculated that the attack may have been the work of Unit 8200. Yossi Melman, who covers intelligence for the Israeli daily newspaper Haaretz and is at work on a book about Israeli intelligence, also suspected that Israel was involved. He noted that Meir Dagan, head of the national intelligence agency Mossad, had his term extended in 2009 because he was said to be involved in important projects. Additionally, in the past year Israeli estimates of when Iran will have a nuclear weapon had been extended to 2014. "They seem to know something, that they have more time than originally thought", he added.

Additionally, in 2009, a year before Stuxnet was discovered, Scott Borg of the United States Cyber-Consequences Unit (US-CCU) had suggested that Israel might prefer to mount a cyber-attack rather than a military strike on Iran's nuclear facilities. There has also been speculation on the involvement of NATO, the United States and other Western nations. It has been reported that the United States, under one of its most secret programs, initiated by the Bush administration and accelerated by the Obama administration, has sought to destroy Iran's nuclear program by novel methods such as undermining Iranian computer systems. However, solid evidence pointing to Western (and specifically American) involvement has been scarce.

Though Israel has not publicly commented on the Stuxnet attack, it has since confirmed that cyberwarfare is now among the pillars of its defence doctrine, with a military intelligence unit set up to pursue both defensive and offensive options.

Symantec has reported that the majority of infected systems were in Iran (about 60 percent), which has led to speculation that it may have been deliberately targeting "high-value infrastructure" in Iran including either the Bushehr Nuclear Power Plant or the Natanz nuclear facility. On 29 November 2010, Iranian president Mahmoud Ahmadinejad admitted for the first time that a computer virus had caused problems with the controller handling the centrifuges at its Natanz facilities. According to Reuters he told reporters at a news conference in Tehran, "They succeeded in creating problems for a limited number of our centrifuges with the software they had installed in electronic parts".

What was Needed to Carry Out the Attack[10]

Stuxnet presents a good case study on the type of capabilities a defence must be prepared to counter. Speculation about what was needed to develop and carry out the attack includes the following:-

(a) The developers were able to gain access to the industrial controller's schematics and design documents.

(b) They would have needed to obtain the associated Siemens industrial controllers, as well as technical and design considerations.

(c) Perhaps they also acquired centrifuges similar to those in the Iranian facility.

(d) They obtained knowledge of the computing environment in the facility.

(e) It is likely that they set up a mirrored environment that would include the necessary industrial controllers and other hardware, such as the programmable logic controllers, to test the worm.

(f) They would have needed to obtain at least two compromised

10 A Cyber worm that Knows no Boundaries by Isaac R Porche III, Jerry M Sollinger, Shawn Mckay- RAND Corporation 2011

digital certificates.

(g) They needed knowledge of unknown or unpublished (i.e. zero day) exploits in Microsoft software.

(h) Finally, they developed a means to implant the worm on computers or portable flash drives that might eventually be connected to the programmable logic controllers.

Implications of the Success of Stuxnet

It is important to understand the implications of the success of Stuxnet in order to be able to offer credible defence against such attacks. These are listed below:-

(a) First is that it is now for sure that a worm capable of inflicting severe physical damage can be developed.

(b) Second the complex nature of the worm suggests it was a state sponsored effort.

(c) Third is that control systems not only that of nuclear plants but that of other critical infrastructure such as power, banking, airlines, railways water supply systems etc can be targeted.

(d) All the above systems involve both private and government entities. Trying to coordinate defensive activities across government agencies is a challenging task and if we add private sector then the coordination becomes even more complex and difficult.

Defending Against Stuxnet

The most significant implication of Stuxnet is that it demonstrated there are serious actors, state or non-state, waging offensive cyber warfare against critical infrastructures of non-friendly countries. It also signaled to the hacker and private sector community that they have much to learn from the state-sponsored groups who demonstrated they play on a different level while revealing some of their tactics and techniques. The upshot is Stuxnet is a real demonstration of actual cyber warfare that can and likely will be waged against any country's critical infrastructure. State sponsorship of Stuxnet type worm makes it difficult to defend against it. A state may devote substantial manpower to cyber warfare, but defending against a state sponsored threat will require a well-coordinated response with best capabilities available in government and industry. Also in the case of Stuxnet, no one has credibly claimed responsibility, so the cyber deterrence effect if prophesied cannot be practiced.

Some of the conventional methods to thwart off threats as posed by Stuxnet may be examined for their effectiveness.

(a) **Isolate Command and Control Networks from Public Networks.** Many critical infrastructures share command, control, and telemetry over the Internet or other shared public network. Though convenient and cost-efficient, it leads to serious risks.

(b) **Passwords and Access Control.** Employing passwords and access control is mandatory. People handling computer systems, particularly those associated with critical infrastructure need to be very religious in in using the passwords the right way. Many of the problems whether in SCADA networks or others start with a lack of access control and poor passwords. In the case of Stuxnet, even good passwords and access control could not have stopped it. The reason is a computer account with proper credentials is infected. Once infected, the authorized user account is able to access the Siemens ICS so even rigorous passwords and access control features would not have stopped Stuxnet.

(c) **Patching and Compliance.** Implementing a rigorous patching regime for security compliance is now a routine among practicing security professionals. Most security professionals have been trained their security program revolves around timely patching and compliance to regulations or guidelines for secure configuration control. Let's assume that victim computers in the Stuxnet attacks were fully patched. Would it have stopped the attack? No. Oday exploits were used in the attack, which means the vulnerability wasn't known, let alone a patch available to be applied.

(d) **Anti-virus Update.** As these attacks were unknown at the time of attack, a fully updated anti-virus product would not have detected them. Stuxnet was able to re-infect "cleaned" systems because it actually injected its code in every single Step 7 program on the PC so that when *any* Step 7 program was open or run, the computer got re-infected. This also shows traditional anti-virus will not be able to effectively restore infected systems to a clean state.

(e) **Intrusion Detection/Prevention Systems**. The same applies for intrusion detection and intrusion prevention systems as for anti-virus products. None of these would have stopped the attack, because these products are primarily signature driven and there were no exploit signatures available to detect Stuxnet at the time of its release.

Duqu

On 01 Sep 2011, researchers at Laboratory of Cryptography and System Security of the Budapest University discovered a worm very similar to Stuxnet and named it Duqu (also called as son of Stuxnet) because it creates files with file-name prefix-DQ. It shares a great deal of code with Stuxnet; however the payload is completely different. Instead of a payload designed to sabotage an industrial control system, the payload has been replaced with general remote access capabilities. The creators of Duqu had access to the source code of Stuxnet and the attackers intended to use this capability to gather intelligence from a private entity to aid future attacks on a third party. The installer is concealed in a word file and when the file is opened, the malicious code executes itself and installs the main binaries. Duqu infections were reported from eight countries, including France, Netherlands, Switzerland, India and Ukraine.[11]

"Duqu's purpose is to gather intelligence data and assets from

11 The Christian Science Monitor 03 Nov 2011

entities, such as industrial control systems manufacturers, in order to more easily conduct a future attack against another third party. The attackers are looking for information such as design documents that could help them mount future attack on an industrial control facility." Symantec says.

Duqu was designed to last for only 36 days and then remove itself from the system it infected which limits its detection. Although Duqu might not represent a major threat in itself, it does reflect a trend in the use of malware towards gathering massive amounts of information for use in future attacks. In the grand design of next major cyber incident, Duqu appears to be a scout.

Lessons

Some of the important lessons which can be derived are listed below:-

(a) A nation should be prepared to handle, if possible prevent Stuxnet like threat from non-friendly countries.

(b) Treat your critical infrastructure as vulnerable and determine steps to be taken for its protection.

(c) Stuxnet like worm is most likely to target critical infrastructure- government, private or military, which would adversely affect everyone makes it abundantly clear that defence against such a worm is everybody's problem.

(d) The defence mechanism would require a coordinated and structured response from government, private sectors and military. This implies setting up an apex body which can coordinate and direct all agencies involved.

(e) Stuxnet like worm, once implanted can lie dormant for a specified period, howsoever long it may be, until it encounters the precise combination of events it is designed to exploit. It would then execute its programme and cause the damage. This leads us to two important conclusions:-

(i) Regular checks of critical infrastructure with the specific aim of detecting such worms.

(ii) In the event of attack though initial damage would be done, plugging the gap would prevent repetition of the worm.

(f) Duqu has been designed for espionage activities. The possibility of his worm finding its way into critical infrastructure systems or military systems is very real.

(g) It is vitally important that personnel manning computer systems are trained to be security conscious to the core as by and large this is the weakest link in the chain particularly so for networks which are isolated from internet.

Conclusion

Stuxnet represents the first of many milestones in malicious code history – it is the first to exploit four zero-day vulnerabilities, compromise two digital certificates, and inject code into industrial control systems and hide the code from the operator. Whether Stuxnet will usher in a new generation of malicious code attacks towards real-world infrastructure—overshadowing the vast majority of current attacks affecting more virtual or individual assets—or if it is a once- in-a-decade occurrence remains to be seen.

Stuxnet may represent the opening of a new chapter in the use of cyberspace to achieve the strategic effect of neutralizing a potent international threat, suggesting that cyber-attacks can be seen as another long-range strike weapon – faster than missiles or aircraft, not as destructive, but cheaper and possibly covert. This sophisticated SCADA attack, now seen as a 'game changer,' demonstrated the potential of future cyber-attacks and cyber warfare. It is also an excellent example demonstrating that political and strategic effect can be achieved without the need for armed conflict.

Stuxnet has shown that the strategic utility of cyber weapons is their ability to disrupt, deny, and deceive an adversary's strategic intentions. While it certainly damaged the Iranian program and confused its technicians, the attack's overall effect seems to have been less impressive. Iran has replaced all of its damaged centrifuges and has resumed enriching uranium. This is significant, as it suggests that cyber-weapons are not the 'silver bullet' replacement for more-traditional military instruments that they have been purported to be. It has not coerced the Iranian regime into abandoning that program. Stuxnet also shows that effective cyber-attacks require large, complex operations, and entail a massive intelligence burden. It now seems that the Iranian nuclear facilities are under a renewed attack with a worm called 'Stars,' and more recently with a Trojan called 'Duqu.'

There are clear limitations and disadvantages of such attacks, however. This, not least brought about by the porous borders of cyberspace, which, as exemplified in the case of Stuxnet, led to the infection of thousands of additional computers both in Iran and beyond. As of yet, there exists no ascertained ability to estimate or forecast the scope of unintended consequences and collateral damage of cyber-attacks. For attacks that disable networks, there could be unpredictable damage not only to the target, but also to non-combatants, neutrals, allies, or even the attacker, depending on the interconnections of the target network or the systems attacked. This makes the political risk of collateral damage and unintended second and third order consequences unpredictable, and carries with it the risk of escalating a conflict.

If Stuxnet was indeed created by a state and if the target was uranium-enrichment plants of Iran, then it was as much a weapon of war as a cruise missile. Most experts agree that a kinetic attack using cruise missiles, smart bombs or a nuclear warhead against another country's means of producing weapons is an act of war. Using carefully engineered software to accomplish the same thing would fall under the same definition. Still, without a declaration of war, the Stuxnet attack could be viewed as cyber sabotage.

Stuxnet is of such great complexity—requiring significant resources to develop—that few attackers will be capable of producing a similar threat, to such an extent that we would not expect masses of threats of similar in sophistication to suddenly appear. However, Stuxnet has highlighted direct-attack attempts on critical infrastructure are possible. The real-world implications of Stuxnet are beyond any threat we have seen in the past.

CHAPTER 3

PRINCIPLES OF WAR AND CYBER WARFARE

Introduction

Modern military doctrine draws from a deep well of experience, knowledge and philosophy that spans centuries enduring many political, economic, and scientific revolutions. The oldest and most profound treatise is Sun Tzu's "Art of War". Traces of almost all the strategic patterns and principles developed over centuries can be found in this book. Much of our current understanding of military concepts such as grand strategy, center of gravity, decisive point, and commander's intent can be traced to this book.

The principles of war have evolved as a formal lesson for militaries so that they can train and equip themselves for victory in the battlefield. There are no runners up in war and this thought has fired military theorists such as Clausewitz, Jomini and Fuller to document their thoughts, based on their experience and those preceding them, in a logical and rational manner for future militaries. It was only in the 20th century, when World War 1 led to the final formulation of modern principles of war. In 1916, British Gen John Fredrick Charles Fuller published a military journal "The Principles of War" and his article was the first detailed explanation of the eight modern principles of war. Based on the work of Fuller, after First World War, the Principles of War were formally introduced in its training by the British Army.[1] Over the years, as the world went through industrial revolution and the new domains of air and space entered the realm of warfare, some more principles have emerged. Now with the cyberspace becoming the fifth domain of warfare are these principles of war relevant or we need new ideas and principles. In order to examine that it would be prudent to examine the evolution of principles of war.

---

1 http://en.wikipedia.org/wiki/Principles_of_War

Evolution of Principles of War

According to Chinese tradition, "Art of War" was written by Sun Tzu in the 4th century B.C., and is one of China's Seven Military Classics. Some scholars argue that gaps in logic and anachronisms in the text point to multiple authors and they contend that "Art of War" is a compilation of different texts that were brought together over time. Nonetheless, the book has an internal consistency which implies it is the product of one school of military thought. "Art of War" was translated for the West by a Jesuit missionary to Peking, Father JJM Amiot, whose interpretation of "The Art of War" was published in Paris in 1772, towards the close of period during which the Chinese writings had caught the fancy of French intellectuals. It received favourable reviews and was again published in 1782, and may have had an influence on the battlefield victories of Napoleon, who was an avid reader and most probably familiar with its contents.[2]

At just about the same time Sun Tzu was writing, the ancient Greeks were formulating their own military philosophy. At the Battle of Marathon in 490 B.C., the Athenians under the battlefield command of Miltiades routed the Persian armies. Although he was not thinking specifically in terms of the nine modern principles of war, Miltiades' tactics showed a grasp of the principles of mass and economy of force.

Art of War has survived for 2,500 years because its advice is not only compelling, but concise, easy to understand, and flexible. Sun Tzu does not give military leaders a concrete plan of action, but a series of recommendations that can be adapted to new circumstances. Sun Tzu's concepts have been successfully applied to disciplines other than warfare, including sports, social relationships, and business.

The first 'principles of war' as enunciated by Sun Tzu are five 'factors': moral influence, weather, terrain, command, and doctrine. Other principles which emerge from reading his "Art of War" are deception, speed, know your enemy, and that to win without fighting is the acme of skill. The most striking aspect of Sun Tzu's

2 Sun Tzu's "Art of War" translated by Samuel B Griffith, Oxford University Press, 1963.

preaching is about what constitutes ideal war which is winning without bloodshed. By playing on the psychological weaknesses of the opponent, by maneuvering him into precarious positions, by inducing feelings of frustration and confusion, a strategist can get the other side to break down mentally before surrendering physically. The state that wins wars with few lives lost and resources squandered will thrive for a long time. Most wars, certainly, are not waged rationally, but those campaigns in history that have followed this principle stand out (Napoleon at Ulm, TE Lawrence in the desert campaign of World War 1).

Sun Tzu was one of the earliest theorists to identify what armies must do to be successful in the conduct of warfare. He included "how to" chapters on basic ideas dealing with maneuver, ground formations, and planning attacks. Sun Tzu's definitions of these basic ideas are similar to some of the definitions taught today. For example, Sun Tzu wrote that upon maneuvering forces, one should place his enemy in a position of disadvantage through flexible application of combat power. Although Sun Tzu did not specifically state that maneuver was an enduring principle of war, his teachings highlighted the importance of the concept. Though Sun Tzu did not explicitly provide a list of principles, but his writings certainly laid an intellectual foundation from which such principles were subsequently drawn. His concepts of deception, freedom of action, adaptability, and flexibility can be directly related to modern principles of war. Theorists, such as Major General Carl von Clausewitz and Swiss-French-Russian general and military theoretician Baron Antoine Henri Jomini, in the 18th and 19th century used theorists, such as Sun Tzu, as the basis for their research on the conduct of war.

Interestingly, the 19th century military thought was dominated by two men, one German and the other Swiss - Clausewitz and Jomini. Again, both drew much of their experience during the Napoleonic Wars and both sought to explain why it was that war waged in Napoleonic terms differed from the formalism that had marked 18th century military theory. Jomini, inspired by Napoleon's victories in northern Italy joined Helvetian legion. His interest in the conduct of war led him to write a study of Fredrick the Great which was published in 1803. In 1805 Napoleon, who had noted his writings with approval, appointed Jomini as a colonel on Ney's staff and thus saw action at the battles of Austerlitz (1805), Jena-Auerstadt (1806), and Eylau (1807) and thereafter Spain.[3]

In the later campaigns of Napoleon Bonaparte, military strategists further explored the principles of war. Jomini, after studying Napoleon's methods and strategies, said "There exist a small number of fundamental principles of war the application of which has been in almost all time crowned with success." According to Jomini, Napoleon proved that an Army usually succeeds when it operates against its enemy's lines of communication, masses its force against a fraction of the enemy's, attacks the enemy's weakest point in force, and attacks the enemy speedily at the right place and time. These ideas became the foundation for some of the later principles that we study today. The Napoleonic era saw the science of land warfare taken to new heights, both ideologically and technologically. Antoine Henri Jomini was the first to express the idea that a small number of principles should guide the commander's efforts on the battlefield. Although he never explicitly identified the general principles to which he referred, Jomini articulated two basic concepts which have been taken as principles. Jomini's thoughts on freedom of maneuver to bring masses of one's own troops against fractions of the enemy's and his thoughts on the ability of a military power to strike in the most decisive direction can both be linked to modern day principles of war.

Jomini summarized the Principles of War using four maxims. The first was to project the mass of an army by strategic movements, successively, upon both the decisive points of a theater of war and upon the communications of the enemy as much as possible without compromising one's own capabilities. The second maxim was to maneuver to engage fractions of the hostile army with the bulk of one's forces. The third maxim was to maneuver the mass of forces upon the decisive point or upon that portion of the hostile line that it is of the first importance to overthrow. The fourth maxim was to ensure that the massing of forces should not only be thrown

3 Introduction by Charles Messenger to "Art of War" by Jomini

upon the decisive point, but should also engage at the proper time and with the requisite energy.[4] These maxims developed into the basic principles of mass, objectives, offensive, maneuver, surprise and security.

Unlike Jomini or General Fuller, none of the early theorists explicitly outlined their Principles of War; however, these early theorists did explore critical concepts and fundamentals that would involve into the documented Principles of War in use by militaries today. Early theorists provided the basic foundation for theorists of the future to use in developing the principles of war.

Still later, World War I led to the final formulation of modern principles of war. Because of the inefficiency, waste, and inconclusiveness that characterized that war, military theorists concluded they needed a new approach to war. By approaching it in a scientific way, as a "military science," they began to develop the modern principles. In 1916, British Gen John Frederick Charles (J.F.C.) Fuller published a military journal article entitled "The Principles of War, With Reference to the Campaigns of 1914–1915." His article was the first detailed explanation of eight modern principles of war.

While Jomini saw war as a science, Clausewitz, Jomini's contemporary, viewed war at the strategic level as an art. Clausewitz began to study warfare after the Prussian loss at the battle of Jena-Auerstedt in 1806 against Napoleon. From his reflection and research, Clausewitz first published his findings in 1812 under the title "Principles of War".[5] The principles that Clausewitz identified in his 1812 publication were his first attempt to develop a training aide for rebuilding the Prussian army. Clausewitz listed his principles as offense, defence, governing the use of troops and terrain. "Principles of War" was the precursor to Clausewitz's "On War" that outlined not only the basics of how to fight at the tactical level, but also how to consider the conduct of war at the strategic level.

---

4 Jomini, The Art of War.

5 Carl Von Clausewitz, The Principles of War.

WW I produced a demand for principles which could help prevent a repetition of the disastrous waste of life and resources in that conflict. Beaufre[6] suggested that the one principle of war, based on the writings of Foch, was to reach the decisive point thanks to freedom of action gained by sound economy of force, warning against an over commitment to one course of action until the decisive moment arrives. Gen Fuller in his book, "The Foundations of the Science of War", wrote the original nine Principles of War that became the bedrock for contemporary joint operations.[7] Fuller wrote of three groups of principles: mental principles—direction, concentration, and distribution; moral principles—determination, surprise, and endurance; and physical principles—mobility, offensive action, and security. These prefigure the modern British army 'components of fighting power'—conceptual, moral, and physical Based on his formative experiences during World War I, Fuller attempted to identify what went wrong.

Nations continue to develop the Principles of War according to the external and internal conditions confronting them. While the nine basic principles have remained relevant other principles have been formulated due to changed environment resulting from external, internal conditions or combination of both.

The Nine Principles of War, which we study today, are crucial to successful military planning and actions. These Principles of War as enunciated by US Army are:-

1. Objective
2. Offensive
3. Mass
4. Economy of force
5. Maneuver
6. Unity of command

---

6 Beaufre, Andre, Introduction to Strategy (London, 1965).

7 Fuller, John F. C., Foundations of the Science of War (London, 1925)

7. Security

8. Surprise

9. Simplicity

The Joint Doctrine of the Indian Armed Force, published by Headquarters, Integrated Defence Staff, Ministry of Defence, June 2007, gives out the following Principles of War for the Indian armed forces:-

(a) Selection and Maintenance of Aim.

(b) Maintenance of Morale.

(c) Offensive Action.

(d) Surprise.

(e) Concentration of Force.

(f) Economy of Effort.

(g) Security.

(h) Flexibility.

(i) Cooperation.

(j) Simplicity

(k) Administration.

(l) Intelligence.

The principles of War have withstood the test of many battles over a long period of time primarily because they represent a confluence of many ideas refined over centuries. They are sufficiently broad based to be applied to various operations of war. They are the foundation from which the militaries conduct their operations, and hence it is important we analyze their relevance to cyber war.

Application of Principles of War in Cyber War

The Principles of War enunciated above were primarily developed for land warfare with strategic objective of physical occupation of territory. If we were to apply the principles of war in cyber domain we need to draw an analogy of terrain and weapons in the cyber domain. Computer systems can be considered as the tool for offensive as well as defensive actions. We can therefore say that Software loaded on the computer systems is the terrain on which cyber warfare is waged. Viruses and packets can be considered as the weapons of cyber war. This represents a new, revolutionary approach to warfare as geographical boundaries are no longer relevant, attacks will be launched at a speed which would be more than speed of light, where blood may not be shed, where militaries may be just left sitting in full battle readiness with their weapon systems primed waiting for the enemy and still war will be lost or won. This implies that some changes in military doctrines would be required and for that we need to examine how we can apply the conventional principles of war in cyber war.

We have seen from foregoing discussion that there are generally two predominant traditions for principles of war—the western view of Clausewitz and the eastern view of Sun Tzu. Clausewitz's western Newtonian world conceptualizes war using mass, objective, and maneuver among other principles in a state-on-state kinetic war for a political objective. However, Sun Tzu's eastern world conceptualizes war focusing on the criticality of intelligence, deception to defeat the mind of the enemy, and knowing that relationships between things matter most in the strategy of war.

When developing principles of war for cyberspace, we should look to Clausewitz for guidance when kinetic force-on-force effects seem to be required, but also look to Sun Tzu for guidance because intelligence, deception, and the relationship between things in cyberspace requires a different way of thinking; where force-on-force is often less effective toward achieving our objective than appropriate non-kinetic methods. Sun Tzu's principles of intelligence, deception, and disposition are important guides for non-kinetic cyberspace operations. Interestingly, the interconnection and integration of networks occur as the mind of the commander—including things such as intelligence fusion centers and cyber support. The best way to attack this mind is by using deception and gathering intelligence in cyberspace.

Selection and Maintenance of Aim

The objective of war is the destruction of the enemy's armed forces and will to fight. Selection of the aim starts at the political and strategic levels. The purpose of Selection and Maintenance of Aim is to direct every military operation toward a clearly defined, decisive, and achievable goal. With cyber operations, computer network operations need to be integrated into the stated objective. Leveraging the ability of the cyber domain, offensive cyber operations can enable strategic, operational, and tactical effects through functional missions such as strategic attack, counter air, counter land, counter sea and space control.

In the information age revolution in military affairs (RMA), with its promise of the capability to render the enemy strategically paralysed in a relatively short period of time, the focus is less on the enemy's armed forces and more on his leadership, command and control (C2) structures and communication infrastructure.

Depending on the objective of the Commander, a cyber-effort may either involve either attack or defence. For example, an objective may be to disrupt an enemy's command and control through a cyber-attack directed against a power grid. Through computer network attack, a joint force commander can disable a power grid without using kinetic weapons. As a result, the joint force commander does not need to take into consideration the need to rebuild the power infrastructure during post-conflict operations. By including cyber capabilities in such a direct role, equal to a conventional bombing campaign against the same target, a joint force commander can significantly reduce the amount of time required to bring about stability and meet the national strategic objectives.

Offensive Action

The purpose of an offensive action is to seize, retain and exploit the initiative. Conventionally this principle may indicate that initiative involves seizing terrain, a more contemporary understanding significantly broadens the definition. Just as airpower seizes, retains and exploits the initiative in the air domain, cyber can seize, retain, and exploit the initiative in the cyber domain. A recent example of a cyber-offensive was the computer network attacks launched against Estonia by supposedly non-state actors in Russia described earlier. Its crippling effect on the economy and the people in general was quite substantial as Estonia was one of the most wired countries of Europe. Nations will only move towards increasing digitization in future as benefits of technology attract its citizens and herein lies the essence of cyber war. The offensive in cyber war may include a network, electronic warfare or a physical attack to seize the domain for exploitation and follow-on operations. The attack will disrupt not only the government, military and private networks but most importantly it will immediately disrupt the normal routine of the common citizen of the country unlike in conventional war where these effects are felt much later and in much lesser degree.

Cyber-attacks, however, are recognized by states as a means for countering an opponent that is superior in conventional and traditional military power. Any informational infrastructure or that which relies thereon can be bugged, hacked, infected, tapped and penetrated. Thus, a multifaceted cyber-attack employing various techniques could be highly disruptive to the targeted enemy. The basic notion of and that which most attacks are designed to do go beyond mere annoyance, agitation and irritation to inflict sustained uncertainty, confusion, chaos, and to provoke a feeling bordering on fear. Some attacks also seek to disable or prevent an action.

The 2008 incursion into Georgia by Russian military forces, cyber-offensive was launched against the Georgian military and government. Russian forces conducted a full-spectrum offensive to deny the use of radio waves as well as to prevent the use of the Internet within the country of Georgia. As a result, the Russian cyber offensive blinded the Georgian military and reduced drastically their command and control capacity.

No commander can inflict damaging consequences on an enemy if his forces remain in the defensive mode. Only through offensive action can a commander compel an enemy to comply with a commander's intentions. An attack, with exclusively cyber-forces, can retain an offensive nature that potentially convinces an enemy to face a more desirable situation than any alternative. Clausewitz says "If the enemy is to be coerced you must put him in a situation that is even more unpleasant than the sacrifice you call on him to make." However, the essence of cyber offensive can best be expressed in the words of Sun Tzu "Hence to fight and conquer in all your battles is not supreme excellence; supreme excellence consists in breaking the enemy's resistance without fighting."

Sun Tzu's principles of war are based on the concept that all warfare is based on deception, that the general must attack the mind of the enemy, and kinetic weapons are only to be used when there is no alternative. These concepts are very relevant for cyberspace, where an opponent can win without kinetic fighting.

Surprise

The aim of surprise is to strike at a time, place, or in a manner for which the enemy is unprepared. Surprise in conventional operations is achieved by speed, effective intelligence, deception, and application of unexpected combat power, security, use of unfavourable terrain, operational security, variation in tactics and methods of operations, information superiority and asymmetry. In the cyber domain it would imply having freedom of maneuver to be able to conduct a surprise cyber-operation where and when it is least expected. This is synonymous to what Sun Tzu said" take advantage of the enemy's lack of readiness, make your way by unexpected routes, and attack unguarded spots."

Surprise in cyber war can be achieved by launching a computer network attack in which friendly cyber-elements destroy a country's command and control capability through a quick strike. Cyber-attacks on Estonia and Georgia clearly demonstrate this fact as both the nations had not expected the attacks of such severity and dimension.

Concentration of Force

Concentration implies the massing the effects of all combat capabilities and other means at the desired place and time to produce decisive results. As in kinetic warfare cyber-firepower can be concentrated at the right place and the right time for decisive results. The attack on Estonian essential services, such as banking leading to its collapse, exemplifies the application of this principle in cyber space. Commanders can mass electronic warfare resources at the right location to blind an enemy or to force him to move. Also cyber-attack can be launched to deny the enemy its satellite or communications infrastructure.

The cyber war waging capabilities of nations is still limited in scope and application other than US which is ahead of all other countries. The commanders would therefore have to employ their finite resources of cyber capabilities judiciously by prioritizing them and deciding where and when to mass forces and intended effects to complete a given mission.

Economy of Force

The purpose of economy of force is to allocate minimum essential combat power to achieve desired effects. It requires astute strategic planning and judgment by political and military leaders, and places a premium on the need for flexibility of thought and action.

Cyber warfare is inherently an application of this kinetic principle of war. Since cyber-warfare is the epitome of asymmetric warfare, economy of force is inherent.

A cyber-effort can save the finite human, material financial resources in accomplishing a mission in place of traditional firepower; it is obvious that this principle of war applies to the cyber domain. It would make more sense to employing cyber-resources to dwarf the enemy than the conventional resources which are scarce and difficult to replace as reserves would be finite.

Security

The aim of security is to never allow the enemy to acquire an unexpected advantage. Security results from the measures taken to protect itself from surprise, interference, sabotage, intelligence, surveillance and reconnaissance threat.

One of the biggest challenges we face today is that of cyber security – protecting computer networks. The notion of a cyber-attack that shuts down power/communications will entail serious consequences. It is therefore important that Commander must weigh the mission impact of a computer network attack on his forces and constantly determine what can be isolated with the least negative effect.

Different and layered measures need to be built in to provide security to cyber based systems. Encryption of the data will only provide basic security. Blocking of websites may be useful as a very short term measure but may have a negative impact it continued indefinitely as it may hinder own operations which may be critical to mission's success.

Loading software to fix a non-mission critical vulnerability during an operation might have negative impact. If unavoidable it should be thoroughly checked for any malware. It is here Indian Armed Forces are most vulnerable as most of the equipment and weapon systems are ex-import and some are under Annual Maintenance Contract with the OEM.

Another computer network defence capability is self-imposed degradation. If an enemy is exploiting friendly cyber-capabilities for their own operations, friendly forces can degrade or isolate the capability the enemy is using. However, it will effect own operations also. Global Positioning System (GPS) satellite constellation is an example of this capability. Therefore, the commander would have to consider first the impact on own or friendly forces operating outside the area of operations.

Security is both critical and valid in a cyber-context. It is necessary to coordinate all cyber-security capabilities in order to eliminate potential vulnerabilities that may exist. This will ensure that a nation's cyber-capacity is secure and available when needed for combat operations.

Lastly, cyber-security personnel will need to remain vigilant and updated at all times. They will need to continuously check for vulnerabilities in own systems and update security measures.

Flexibility

Flexibility is modification of the principles of mobility or maneuver. Its aim is to place the enemy in a position of disadvantage through the flexible application of combat power. It indicates the ability to react quickly to changing situations, in order to rapidly shift points of efforts to react to unforeseen opportunities or contingencies. It calls for flexibility of mind, rapid decision-making and a clear understanding of the commander's intent. It requires ability to rapidly and efficiently deploy forces to the correct time and place.

Cyber-assets are characterized by speed, reach, flexibility and the technical ability of personnel manning those assets. While similar cyber-advantages may generally be available to both warring nations, it is the type and degree of disadvantages that will vary in most cases.

Cooperation

Cooperation may produce coordination by giving a single commander the required authority which unifies action. Implicitly it implies that a single commander directs and coordinates the actions of all the forces towards a common mission.

By definition, Cooperation is currently out of alignment with respect to the conduct and management of cyber forces operating in the cyber-domain. This is primarily due to non-availability of any publication on command and control of cyber operations. While command and control functions for the other four domains of warfare are well documented, rules for cyberspace are still being evolved.

Command and control of each war fighting capability is critical. The nature, reach, speed and aftermath of cyber-attack justify that command and control of cyber related activities must be assigned to a single organization to avoid severely disjointed efforts on behalf of joint forces and to decisively establish unity of command within the operational environment.

Simplicity

The purpose of simplicity is to prepare clear, uncomplicated plans and concise orders to ensure thorough understanding throughout the chain of command. A good simple plan with concise clear words minimises the chances of confusion.

Clausewitz has pointed out "Everything in war is simple, but the simplest thing is difficult." War presents a complex scenario where uncertainty looms large. Clausewitz calls it "fog of war." The commander should be able to "see" through "fog" in order to take advantage of any opportunity that might occur. This can be achieved by developing and adhering to a simple plan, the commander can reduce the fog and see the complex battlefield more clearly.

Cyber-operations are going to more complex and challenging to any commander as cyber-domain trespasses into the other four domains(all domains are interdependent) and will have a bearing on the progress of operations in these domains. Hence, it is imperative that cyber-operations plans be kept simple and should be integrated seamlessly in the overall operational plan to ensure success in the mission.

Administration

Successful conduct of military operations requires effective and efficient logistics and administrative support. Sustaining own forces in the thick and thin of war is the key to achieve success.

Just as it is important to keep the lines of communications open for logistics and administrative support in kinetic war, in cyber-domain sustaining the connectivity would be the key. If an optical fiber cable is cut all connectivity would be lost. Therefore alternate paths need to be provided to ensure cyber-operations are sustainable in adversity.

Intelligence

Even small forces can achieve significant victory by using intelligence based on detailed reconnaissance and accurate information. Concentration of force and surprise rely upon the quality of intelligence that is available. In cyber-war information and intelligence on the enemy's critical infrastructure such as banking, communication and power grids, transportation and public works infrastructure and even social structure, institutions and political actors should be collected, analysed, disseminated and exploited when required.

Recently discovered virus, Duqu, is an example of gathering intelligence on enemy's critical infrastructure through cyber means. Crippling the enemy's critical infrastructure at the right time with speed, precision and surprise is likely to have serious impact on its capability and capacity to wage the war and will ultimately weaken his resolve or the will to fight.

As sun Tzu said" If you know the enemy and know yourself, you need not fear the result of a hundred battles. If you know yourself but not the enemy, for every victory gained you will also suffer a defeat. If you know neither the enemy nor yourself, you will succumb in every battle." He further points out" Thus, what enables the wise sovereign and the good general to strike and conquer, and achieve things beyond the reach of ordinary men, is foreknowledge."

Information collection and evaluation was so important to Sun Tzu that the entire final chapter of Art of War is devoted to espionage. Spies are called the "sovereign's most precious faculty" and espionage a "divine manipulation of the threads." The cost of spying, when compared to combat operations, is said to be so low that it is the "height of inhumanity" to ignore it; such a commander is "no leader of men, no present help to his sovereign, no master of victory."

It is the above logic that is making the nations acquire cyber-warfare capability. However, intelligence would still be a major contributing factor to mission's success.

Kenneth Geers in his paper "Sun Tzu and Cyber War"[8] argues that cyber-warfare practitioners should also use Art of War as an essential guide to military strategy. However, cyberspace possesses many characteristics that are unlike anything Sun Tzu could have imagined in ancient China. There are at least ten distinctive aspects of the cyber battlefield.

(a) The Internet is an artificial environment that can be shaped in part according to national security requirements.

(b) The rapid proliferation of Internet technologies, including hacker tools and tactics, makes it impossible for any organization to be familiar with all of them.

(c) The physical proximity of adversaries loses much of its relevance as Cyber-attacks are launched without regard to terrestrial geography.

(d) Frequent software updates and network reconfiguration change Internet geography unpredictably and without warning.

(e) In a reversal of our historical understanding of warfare, the asymmetric nature of cyber-attacks strongly favours the attacker.

(f) Cyber-attacks are more flexible than any weapon the world has seen: they can be used for propaganda, espionage, and the destruction of critical infrastructure.

(g) Cyber-attacks can be conducted with such a high degree of anonymity that defence strategies such as deterrence and retaliation are not credible.

(h) It is possible that a lengthy and costly cyber war could take place without anyone but the direct participants knowing about it.

8 http://www.ccdcoe.org/articles/2011/Geers_SunTzuandCyberWar.pdf

(j) The intangible nature of cyberspace can make the calculation of victory, defeat, and battle damage a highly subjective undertaking.

(k) There are few moral inhibitions to cyber warfare because it relates primarily to the use and exploitation of information in the form of computer code and data packets; so far, there is little perceived human suffering.

Some Additional Principles

Cyber domain has definitely some very distinctive features as we have seen above and therefore it quite logical to presume that that there may be some more principles peculiar to the cyber domain. As experience and knowledge is presently lacking in the field of cyber warfare, we can only propose tentatively some additional principles which may get refined with time.

(a) **Cyber-warfare must have Effect in Kinetic World.** Cyber-warfare is not relevant unless it affects someone or something in the non-cyber world Cyber-warfare can affect objects in the physical world such as shutting down the power grid or transport services. Cyber-warfare in its most subtle form can affect the minds of decision-makers in the physical world. The former is analogous to kinetic warfare. The latter is more purely a form of information warfare, in which one's opponent is presented with information that leads to wrong decisions. Examples of affecting decision-makers include both tactical and strategic decision-makers. Tactical decision-makers can be misled about the location and size of enemy and friendly forces. At an operational level, the time of arrival and amount of reinforcements can be manipulated to cause bad decisions such as attacking with insufficient ammunition or withholding attack through fear of lack of supplies. Strategic decision-makers may be fooled by attributing actions to other countries or groups than the actual attacker.[9]

9 http://www.periwork.com/peri_db/wr_db/2004_May_11_11_30_41/DOCS percent20WEBREVIEW/PrinciplesCYBER percent20WARFARE.pdf

(b) **There are no Laws of Behaviour in the Cyber World.** There are no laws of behaviour in the cyber world except those that require a physical world action to change. In the physical world, one can expect that a bullet will act in a certain way when fired. The bullet's path can be predicted with ballistics. Every time that one fires the bullet, it will act the same, within a variance due to minor physical causes. In the cyber world, nothing can be taken for granted in this way. It can and does change in ways that seem chaotic. Software may fail, hardware may fail, programs may run faster than expected, and a thousand other variations can cause the unpredictability of the cyber world. In cyber-warfare, this principle translates to attacks that do not always behave the same way. The only aspects of the cyber world that do not change are those things that require a physical world change. For example, the performance of software cannot exceed the capacity of a computer's processing power unless a physical world person changes to a faster processor. The bandwidth of communications is limited by the telecommunications infrastructure and can only be changed by replacing one physical layer with another. An example of real-world experience that supports this occurs during sniffing of packets. We frequently see one set of connections and packet streams during discovery only to find a different set when we attempt our attack.[10]

(c) **The Tools of Cyber-warfare are Uniquely Dual-use.** The tools of kinetic warfare are primarily used for a single purpose. Weapons are used to attack and sensors are used to detect the enemy. During actual warfare, one does not test own defences by shooting own troops. The commander of an ambushing unit uses his night vision gear to look for the enemy. He can, but rarely does, walk out to where he expects the enemy to be and look at his own troops with that night-vision gear. In cyber-warfare, tools are used by both the attacker and the defender. The attacker uses vulnerability scanners to look for exploit opportunities as part of an attack. The defender uses the same vulnerability scanners to look for weaknesses in their own

10 Ibid.

systems. Packet capture devices originated because network administrators had to see the actual packet traffic to diagnose network problems. Attackers use them for discovery. Specific exploits are collected by defenders to test their own systems, since those systems can regain vulnerabilities from poor vendor upgrades.[11]

(d) **Physical Limitations of Distance and Space do not Apply to the Cyber World.** In cyber world, physical distance is not an obstacle to conducting attacks. A cyber-attack can be executed with equal effectiveness from the other side of the earth as from the next room. In kinetic warfare attacks are carried out by physical objects that must traverse a distance. These types of attacks are limited to those that possess the technology to make that object traverse that distance. The acquisition of appropriate mass in the kinetic world has physical limitations. The creation of mass in the cyber world does not have this limitation.[12]

(e) **Information Superiority/Dominance.** Wars, if fought, will have an overwhelming application of cyber assets which will spread across to the other four domains as well. These assets will provide better situational awareness through intelligence (Stuxnet type viruses), sensors, analysis of vast amount of data and faster dissemination of information which would result in increased pace of operations and faster resolution of conflict. Information Superiority/Dominance will therefore help reduce, what Clausewitz said "fog of War", and enable commanders to correctly comprehend the battle situation and hasten decision making.

(f) **Public Opinion.** In the environment of internet information virtually flows in real time. Social networking sights such as Facebook, Twitter Disseminate information in near real time as was witnessed when US Naval Seals were carrying out their operation in Abbottabad to eliminate Osama-Bin Laden, when a young student, on hearing the sound of chopper had tweeted on

11 Ibid.

12 Ibid.

his site. It is very important to carry the public opinion in fovour as it will have a definite bearing on the launch, conduct and termination of operations. Media management will play a key role. The Israelis have recommended image and legitimisation as a Principle of War. Only China lists political mobilisation as one of the Principles of War.

Conclusion

The Principles of War not only apply to the cyber-domain, but also lead us to a better understanding of the very nature of cyber war. Cyber brings new operational capabilities that commanders can leverage to achieve mission success. In order to integrate cyber-assets into their operations, commanders need a better understanding of their capabilities and limitations.

The Principles of War are an effective means of providing clarity and insight into the operational capabilities of cyber assets. Cyber-assets allow commanders to focus on the "aim" using more resources, maintain an "offensive" spirit that further disrupts the enemy's morale and degrades his decision cycle, to "concentrate" additional effects in conjunction with traditional methods, to "economize the use of force" while saving lives and conventional resources, and to "surprise" the enemy with an instant first strike capacity. Additionally, the Principles of War highlight the fact that commanders' must still retain unity of command in the cyber- domain, take adequate "security" measures to protect his force, and maximize the coordination of cyber operations through "simple" and logical courses of action.

CHAPTER 4

CYBERSPACE STRATEGIES AND CAPABILITIES OF NATIONS

Introduction

A military strategist once said," Attaining one hundred victories in one hundred battles is not the pinnacle of excellence. Subjugating the enemy's army without fighting is the true pinnacle of excellence". It fits aptly into the scenario of information age.

Computer networks control important functionalities and institutions. The attacker would seek to gain control over key information/knowledge or disrupt key infrastructure systems. Identification of the attacker remains as elusive as never before. While in other forms of warfare enemy could be identified and retaliated, attribution remains one of the biggest problems on the internet when it comes to cyber warfare. How do you hold a nation responsible for attacks if you cannot determine whether the activity was state sponsored? The attack on Estonia is a perfect example.

It is understood that at least five countries – US, China, Russia, Israel and France now have offensive cyber warfare capabilities and have moved from a defensive posture to a more offensive posture. Other countries are slowly trying to follow suit. However, achieving the desired capability is one thing and conceiving and putting into practice a time tested doctrine is another. This aspect of cyber warfare merits some discussion.

Difficulties in Conceiving Military Doctrine and Rules of Engagement for Cyber War [1]

In theory, cyber warfare might be a good thing for the world if it makes future conflicts shorter and costs fewer lives, which could

1 DCAF HORIZON 2015 WORKING PAPER No. 7 "On Cyber Warfare" by Fred Schreier

facilitate economic recovery and post-war diplomacy. However, it may be more difficult to conceive *a military doctrine* for many aspects of cyber conflict that are *truly revolutionary.* As examples of the many revolutionary aspects existing, the following ones can be listed to consider:-

(a) The Internet is an artificial environment that can be shaped in part according to national security requirements.

(b) The blinding proliferation of technology and hacker tools makes it impossible to be familiar with all of them.

(c) The proximity of adversaries is determined by connectivity and bandwidth, not terrestrial geography.

(d) Software updates and network reconfigurations increase the unpredictability of the battle space of cyber conflict with little or no warning.

(e) Contrary to our historical understanding of war, cyber conflict favours the attacker.

(f) Cyber-attacks are flexible enough to be effective for information warfare and propaganda, espionage, and the destruction of critical infrastructure.

(g) The difficulty of obtaining reliable attack attribution lessens the credibility of deterrence, retaliation, and prosecution.

(h) The 'quiet' nature of cyber conflict means a significant battle could take place with only the direct participants knowing about it.

(j) The dearth of expertise and evidence can make victory, defeat, and battle damage assessments a highly subjective undertaking.

(k) There are few moral inhibitions to cyber-attacks, because they relate primarily to the use and abuse of data and computer code. So far, there is little perceived human suffering.

Top military thinkers can help the armed forces to fill the holes in their cyber defences. But it will take many years to incorporate all the revolutionary aspects of cyber conflict into military doctrine. The same is true for rules of engagement (ROEs). Developing appropriate rules for the use of cyber weapons is very difficult. ROEs are supposed to be developed prior to the need for use of these weapons, so that war fighters have proper guidance under operational circumstances. That means that various contingencies must be anticipated in advance. However, it is difficult to imagine all possible contingencies before any of them happen. As examples of some of the problems to be solved, the following ones can be listed to consider: -

(a) ROEs must be developed to cope with the fact that several dimensions of cyber-attacks span a wider range than those encountered in the classical war fighting domains.

(b) Cyber-attacks may range from being non-lethal to destructive on a society-wide scale.

(c) The impacts of cyber-attacks may be easily predicted in some cases, but may have a higher uncertainty than the impacts of kinetic weapons in other cases.

(d) The set of potential targets that may be adversely affected by cyber-attacks is likely larger than the corresponding set of potential targets for other weapons.

(e) A cyber-attack conducted for offensive purposes may well require authorization from higher levels of command than would a technically similar cyber-attack conducted for defensive purposes.

(f) The adversary might not react at all to a cyber-attack, or might even react with weapons of mass destruction.

(g) The adversary may range from being an individual hacker to a well-funded nation-state.

It is thus unrealistic to try to craft a single ROE that attempts to cover all uses of cyber-attack. Rather, it will be necessary to tailor an array of ROEs that are applicable to specific kinds of cyber-attack and for likely specific circumstances. And it will be more difficult to craft ROEs for missions involving cyber-attacks than for missions involving other kinds of weapons. The following issues illustrate the complexity of developing ROEs in advance by just looking at the question under what circumstances governed by what authority a retaliatory cyber-attack might be launched to neutralize an immediate or ongoing threat:-

(a) Who should influence and who should develop ROEs for active threat neutralization?

(b) What level of impact must an incoming cyber-attack have to justify active threat neutralization?

(c) How far are the intent and the identity of a cyber-attacker relevant?

(d) How does the proportionality principle apply to active threat neutralization?

(e) How far down the chain of command should delegation of authority for neutralization be carried?

(f) How should the scope, duration, and intensity of a neutralization action be calibrated?

A further level of complication in developing ROEs is that the factors above cannot be assessed independently.

While cyber-attack is an important capability for states to maintain, the acquisition and use of such capabilities raise questions which either do not exist or pose more difficult problems to solve than in the traditional war fighting domains. Such questions show other differences existing at the operational and tactical level between cyber war and traditional war fighting. Some countries have undertaken studies on what differentiates cyber-attacks from the use of other weapons, and on the implications of their acquisition of cyber weapons. The findings of these studies may serve as an indicator of many other differences existing between cyber war and traditional war fighting.

We shall limit our discussion to US and China as US is undoubtedly way ahead of others and China being a rising power.

US

The United States' cyber security strategy is based largely on two documents: the Comprehensive National Cyber security Initiative (CNCI) and the Cyberspace Policy Review. Both documents include important initiatives and recommendations for the U.S. government as it is creating a national cyber security strategy.

There are three major goals listed in CNCI:-

(a) To establish a front line of defence against today's immediate threats.

(b) To defend against the full spectrum of threats.

(c) To strengthen the future cyber security environment.

Each of these goals is supported by a number of key initiatives. The CNCI calls on the government to manage the Federal Enterprise Network as a single network enterprise with Trusted Internet Connections, which includes consolidating the Federal Government's external access points. The government must also deploy an intrusion detection system of sensors across the Federal enterprise which will help to identify when unauthorized users have accessed government networks. The CNCI further recommends that the government pursue deployment of intrusion prevention systems across the Federal enterprise, which is part of the Einstein 4 program from DHS, and will allow the government to identify and stop malicious network traffic entering or leaving government networks.

The CNCI also calls for better coordination of research and development efforts funded by the US government. The US also needs to connect current cyber ops centers and enable better information sharing in order to enhance situational awareness. The report calls for the development of a government-wide cyber counterintelligence plan, and for increased security on classified networks. The report also discusses the need for expanded cyber education and an adequately established Federal cyber security career field. The CNCI says that the US government must define and develop new technologies, strategies and programs as well as enduring deterrence strategies. The U.S. also needs a multi-pronged approach to global supply chain risk management, and a better definition of the federal role in critical infrastructure defence.

The Cyberspace Policy Review, a 60-day review of federal cyber security efforts ordered by President Obama, also has several recommendations for the government. The report calls on the government to appoint a cyber-security policy official responsible for coordinating national cyber security policies, and also designate cyber security as one of the president's key priorities including performance metrics. The report also calls for better cooperation among federal agencies including information sharing and collaboration on cyber security. The report calls for a public awareness and education campaign that will promote cyber security. The report also discussed the need for an international cyber security policy framework that will help to improve international partnerships and deter cyber-attacks. The government was also asked to prepare a cyber-security incident response plan, and address privacy and civil liberty issues (www.whitehouse.gov/assets/cyberspace_Policy_Review_final.pdf).

As a consequential step for meeting the imperatives given above US created US Cyber Command. **United States Cyber Command** (USCYBERCOM) is an armed forces sub-unified command subordinate to United States Strategic Command. The command is located in Fort Meade, Maryland and led by General Keith B. Alexander. USCYBERCOM centralizes command of cyberspace operations, organizes existing cyber resources and synchronizes defence of U.S. military networks.

Mission is stated as - "USCYBERCOM plans, coordinates, integrates, synchronizes and conducts activities to: direct the operations and defence of specified Department of Defence information networks and; prepare to, and when directed, conduct full spectrum military cyberspace operations in order to enable actions in all domains, ensure US/Allied freedom of action in cyberspace and deny the same to our adversaries." The command is charged with pulling together existing cyberspace resources, creating synergy and synchronizing war-fighting effects to defend the information security environment. USCYBERCOM is tasked with centralizing command of cyberspace operations, strengthening DoD cyberspace capabilities, and integrating and bolstering DoD's cyber expertise. USCYBERCOM is an armed forces sub-unified command subordinate to United States Strategic Command.

Organization. USCYBERCOM is an armed forces sub-unified command subordinate to United States Strategic Command. U.S. Cyber Command is composed of several service components, units from military services who will provide Joint services to Cyber Command. They are given below:-

- Army Cyber Command/2nd Army (Army)
- Army Network Enterprise Technology Command / 9th Army Signal Command
- Portions of 1st Information Operations Command (Land)
- United States Army Intelligence and Security Command will be under the operational control of ARFORCYBER for cyber-related action
- United States Army Intelligence and Security Command will be under the operational control of ARFORCYBER for cyber-related actions.
- Fleet Cyber Command/10th Fleet (Navy)
- Naval Network Warfare Command
- Navy Cyber Defence Operations Command
- Naval Information Operation Commands
- Combined Task Forces
- Air Forces Cyber Command/24th Air Force (Air Force)
- 67th Network Warfare Wing
- 688th Information Operations Wing
- 689th Combat Communications Wing

- United States Marine Corps Forces Cyberspace Command (Marine Corps)

Initial operational capability was attained on May 21, 2010. General Alexander was promoted to General and took charge of US Cyber Command in a ceremony at Fort Meade that was attended by Commander of U.S. Central Command Gen David Petraeus, and Secretary of Defence Robert M. Gates. Maj Gen Suzanne M. "Zan" Vautrinot was assigned as Director of Plans and Policy, responsible for the development and coordination of issues as related to cyberspace operations policy, doctrine, organization, capabilities and requirements. USCYBERCOM reached full operational capability on October 31, 2010 (US Cyber Command – Wikipedia).

A natural fallout of the creation of Cyber Command was the expression of serious concerns that Pentagon will overshadow civilian cyber defence efforts. These were however allayed when it was clarified that the Org will restrict to defence of DOD networks and the civil part would remain with Department of Homeland Security. However in the event of cyber hostilities it could assist Department of Homeland Security.

On 25 Jun 2010 the draft National Strategy for Trusted Identities in Cyberspace was hosted on the White House web site for comments by the public. One of the near term action items of the President's Cyberspace Policy Review was to develop a "cyber security-focused identity management vision and strategy." The National Strategy for Trusted Identities in Cyberspace (NSTIC) answers that requirement. The need for such a strategy was due to the rising tide of identity theft, online fraud and cyber intrusions, the proliferation of usernames and passwords that individuals must remember, and the need to deliver online services more securely and efficiently. The draft was posted on www.nstic.ideascale.com for public review and input. The Department of Homeland Security supported the National Security Staff (NSS) who has led an interagency writing team to develop the draft strategy through a very transparent, open, and collaborative process during public review period.

The scope of the strategy was focused on improving the ability to identify and authenticate the organizations, individuals, and underlying infrastructure (e.g., routers, servers, desktops, mobile devices, software, data, etc.) involved in an online transaction.

It is a reasonable assessment that cyber-attacks will be a significant component of future conflicts. More than thirty countries are creating cyber units in their militaries and it would be unrealistic to believe that each one will limit its capabilities to defence.[2] US must therefore guard against the possibility of a cyber-strike from a potential adversary.

Department of Defence has developed a strategy for operating in cyberspace that has five pillars: treating cyberspace as an operational domain; employing active defences to stop malicious code before it affects their networks; protecting commercial networks that operate the critical infrastructure that the military relies upon; joining with allies to mount a collective cyber defence; and mobilizing industry to redesign network technology with security in mind.[3]

In Nov 2011, Pentagon laid out its most explicit cyber warfare policy to date, stating that if directed by the commander-in-chief, it will launch "offensive cyber operations" in response to hostile acts against the US or its facilities. Those hostile acts may include "significant cyber-attacks directed against the US economy, government or military." The US Defence cyber terrorism policy states that: "When warranted, we will respond to hostile to hostile attacks in cyberspace as we would to any other threat to our country. We reserve the right to use all necessary means – diplomatic, informational, military and economic- to defend our nation, our allies, our partners and our interests," the report stated.

US President Obama delivered a public address in the Pentagon on 05 Jan 2012 while introducing the "Defence Strategic Review." The doctrine will focus on cyberspace supremacy. The US Department of Defence's technical research branch, the Defence

---

2 The Pentagon's Cyberstrategy, One Year Later- www.foreignaffairs.com 28 Sep 2011

3 The strategy is available at www.defence.gov/home/features/2011/0411_cyber strategy/

Advanced research Projects Agency (DARPA) is currently working on National Cyber Range: a miniature version of the internet meant as a testing ground for cyber intelligence and warfare. The cyber range is intended for testing new tactics and techniques through cyber war games, as well as for training cyber troops. The new strategy also includes developing new cyber weapons and tools, such as passive viruses, cyber beacons etc.

The 2011 US Cyberspace Policy Review focuses on the civilian aspect of cyber security, and many of the goals revolved around establishing communication and management strategies for preparing for and warding off cyber-attacks, including increasing interagency cooperation and public awareness. The 2012 US defence review mentions the cyber threat in several places: deterring and defeating aggression in all spaces, including cyberspace; projecting power despite anti access measures by implementing the joint Operational Access Concept, a cross domain capability sharing instrument; and by operating effectively in cyberspace by investing in advanced network defence and operation capabilities. US hopes to preserve internet freedom by dissuading and deterring potential aggressors by removing the benefit of waging an attack.

The Department of Defence has chosen to be rather vague in publicly defining what an attack warranting a military response will look like and the precise rules of engagement for cyber war. Reports suggest that development for the next strategy is already in progress. The field is complex, and perhaps there is a fear that a scenario no one has planned a contingency for will occur. For the US, then, a publicly declared strategy will likely limit the number of politically viable responses it could wage against a cyber-attacker. In the remaining opaque in where it intends to draw the line in the sand, the US is remaining flexible, fighting asymmetric threats by being asymmetric itself.[4]

DoD, in its July 2011 report "Department of Defence Strategy for operating in Cyberspace"assesses challenges and opportunities in cyberspace and sets a strategic approach for DoD's cyber-mission.

4 The state of Cyberwar in the US by Shawnna Robert edited by Charles Rault 06 Feb 2012- DiploNews

The report lists five strategic initiatives:-

(a) **Strategic Initiative 1.** Treat cyberspace as an operational domain to organize, train, and equip so that DoD can take full advantage of cyberspace's potential.

(b) **Strategic Initiative 2.** Employ new defence operating concepts to protect DoD networks and systems.

(c) **Strategic Initiative 3.** Partner with other U.S. government departments and agencies and the private sector to enable a whole-of-government cyber security strategy.

(d) **Strategic Initiative 4.** Build robust relationships with U.S. allies and international partners to strengthen collective cyber security.

(e) **Strategic Initiative 5.** Leverage the nation's ingenuity through an exceptional cyber workforce and rapid technological innovation.

These five strategic initiatives offer a road map for DoD to operate effectively in cyberspace, defend national interests, and achieve national security objectives. Each initiative is distinct, yet necessarily connected with the other four. Across the strategy, activities undertaken in one initiative will contribute to DoD's strategic thinking and lead to new approaches in the others. DoD, through this strategy, expects to capitalize on the opportunities afforded to the Department by cyberspace; defend DoD networks and systems against intrusions and malicious activity; support efforts to strengthen cyber-security for interagency, international, and critical industry partners; and develop robust cyberspace capabilities and partnerships. This strategy, the Department hopes, will guide defence of U.S. interests in cyberspace so that the United States and its allies and partners may continue to benefit from the innovations of the information age.

US lawmakers have already developed new legislation regulating government and military activities aimed at securing America's cyberspace supremacy. One of the significant trends is simplified decision making for offensive cyber warfare operations and activities. In the past, launching a cyber-attack required stage by stage authorization from the Joint Chiefs of Staff, and then the US President. Under the new rules, decision making on such an action will take no more than 10 minutes. This primarily concerns psychological operations targeting any specific audience of internet users.[5]

US has announced $489 billion cut in defence budget and this does not include cyber warfare gear. Leon Panetta, US Defence Secretary has stated" As we reduce overall defence budget, we will protect our investments in special operations forces, new technologies, unmanned systems, space and cyberspace capabilities and our capacity to quickly mobilize. The US forces need to be smaller and leaner, but its strength will be that it is more agile, flexible, ready to deploy, innovative and technologically advanced."[6]

Senior US military leaders are now recommending that the Pentagon's two year old cyberwarfare unit be elevated to full combatant command status, sending a signal to adversaries that the US military is serious about protecting its ability to operate in cyberspace. The elevation would give the nation's top cyberwarriors more direct access to Dempsey and Panetta, allowing them more clout in the struggle for resources. US Cyber Command employs about 750 people- far fewer than most combatant commands and reports to Strategic Command, based in Omaha. US feels that establishment of a combatant command for cyberwar fits the administration's multipronged cyber-strategy by projecting military force as a deterrent. Importantly it shortens the chain of command up to the President and Secretary of Defence. It sends a signal that it's a four- star general's job to advocate for the cyber mission.[7]

Conclusion. No nation dominates the cyber battlefield today.

5 Supremacy in cyberspace: Obama's Stars Wars'? –www.rt.com/politics/cyberspace-defence-us-panarin-543/ published 11 Jan 2012

6 Obama, officials lay out new Defence Strategy- Defence systems 05 Jan 2012-defencesystems.com/Articles/2012/01/05/Obama-Panetta-defence-strategy-briefing

7 Military leaders seek higher profile for Pentagon's Cyber Command unit by Ellen Nakashima in Washington Post accessed on 04 May 2012.

Cyberspace is also the domain that, as of now, the US stands the greatest chance of ceding to another nation. Countries such as China and Russia have similar capabilities to defend and attack in cyberspace. The US however has taken the lead in moving forward in a coherent and focused manner towards evolving a comprehensive cyber space policy and creating organizations to handle the threat.

China

The Chinese Communist Party has added a high tech dimension to its vaunted tradition of "democratic proletarian dictatorship" which is cyber dictatorship. During the last few years, the state security forces have smashed thousands of "illegal" web sites and locked up hundreds of Net based dissidents and editors. The much publicized cyber-attacks against Google and other high profile companies and efforts by China based hackers to infiltrate other nations government agencies have placed China in an unwanted focus.

China has made clear its intention to become a leading player in the fields of information and cyber warfare, and began publishing theories, doctrine and policies more than 20 years ago. In fact China's focus on cyber warfare is an extension of Sun Tzu strategy of "overcoming the superior with the inferior" (i.e., asymmetric warfare) and Mao Zedong's concept of "People's War". It is intimately connected to the country's broader geopolitical strategic interests: regime survival; dominance in Asia/Pacific region; growing influence on a global level; and prevention of Taiwan's independence and its ultimate assimilation into the PRC. Since the mid-1990s the Chinese army has implemented a modernization program guided by the concept of 'informationization' (which translates as dominance over information technologies and cyberspace)." The Central Military Commission Committee of the Chinese Communist Party has also endorsed the concept of 3 Warfare, which includes psychological warfare, media warfare and legal warfare. China also has several military training centers that provide cyber-war training programs. These centers and the Chinese military conduct information warfare exercises show that China is transitioning to practicing cyber capabilities, although their information warfare and cyber warfare capabilities are still unknown.

US campaign in Iraq exemplified the triumph of technology and demonstrated how it provided control over battlefield and was the key to military success, victory and power. The RMA (Revolution in Military Affairs) concept and the following Transformation, guided the new strategies of evolution in Chinese military affairs. Hence, since 1990s the concept of Information Warfare acquired greater consideration among military experts in China. A great number of publications have defined the concept and strategies of Information Warfare in China.

In 1995 the General Wang Pufeng, considered as the "father" of Chinese doctrine of Information Warfare, said that:-

(a) The goal of Information Warfare is no longer the conquest of territories or the destruction of enemy troops, but the destruction of the enemy's will to resist.

(b) Information Warfare is a war in which the ability to see, to know and to strike more accurately before the adversary, is as important as firepower.

In 1997, Colonel Baocun Wang added that: -

(a) Information Warfare can be conducted in times of peace, crisis and war.

(b) Information Warfare consists of offensive and defensive operations.

(c) The main components of Information Warfare are C2 (Command and Control), Intelligence, Electronic Warfare, Psychological Warfare, Hackers Warfare and Economic warfare.

In 1999, Colonels Qiao Liang and Wang Xiangsui in their famous "Unrestricted Warfare", a book concerning the art of asymmetric warfare between terrorism and globalization, emphasized that "*technological progress has given us the means to strike at the enemy's nerve centre directly without harming other things, giving us numerous new options for achieving victory, and all these make people believe that the best way to achieve victory is to control, not to kill*". That form of modern warfare, called "unrestricted", means that the weapons, techniques are now multiple, that the battlefield is everywhere, that there will be no longer borders between War time and Peace time. "*The battlefield is next to you and the enemy is on the network*", and the information war is the war where the computer is used to obtain or destroy information.

People's Liberation Army Daily, the official paper for PLA and the primary medium for announcing top-down policy, in 2006 defined information warfare as:-

(a) A process to take advantage over the enemy in a war under conditions of informationization.

(b) A process which finds its strongest expression in our ability or inability to use several means to obtain and ensure an efficient flow of information.

(c) The ability or inability to make full use of the permeability of information space to share and connect information and information systems, to merge materials, energy, and information and create a combined fighting force.

(d The ability or inability to weaken the information superiority of the enemy and operational effectiveness of the enemy's computer equipment.

The Chinese People's Liberation Army (PLA) is actively developing a capability for computer network operations (CNO) and is creating the strategic guidance, tools and trained personnel necessary to employ it in support of traditional war fighting disciplines. Also PLA has not openly published a CNO strategy with the formal vetting of the Central Military Commission (CMC), China's foremost body for doctrine and strategy development. The Chinese military modernization is guided by the concept of "informationization" which means developing a network architecture allowing the coordination of military operations in all dimensions. The strategy of information warfare is contained in the Chinese concept of iNEW (Integrated Network Electronic Warfare), defined by General Dai Qingmin in the early 2000's. iNews is the integration of electronic warfare (EW), computer network attacks (CNA) in the offensive side, and in the defensive role in protecting networks (CND – Computer Networks Defence), and intelligence operations (CNE – Computer Networks Exploitation). The joint action of CNA and EW against C4ISR and logistic systems networks of the adversary constitutes the basis of offensive Chinese Information Warfare.

China's military strategists describe cyber capabilities as a powerful asymmetric opportunity in a deterrence strategy. Analysts consider that an "important theme in Chinese writings on CNO is the use of computer network attack (CNA) as the spear point of deterrence. CNA increases the enemy's costs to become too great in warfare in the first place, which Chinese analysts judge to be essential for deterrence. This could, for example, leave China with the potential ability to deter the United States from intervening in a scenario concerning Taiwan. CNO is viewed as a focal point for the People's Liberation Army, but it is not clear how the actual capacity functions or precisely what conditions it works under. [8] Martin C Libicki of RAND Corporation, a well-known figure in cyber world, in a presentation before the US China Economic and Security Review commission on 27 Jan 2011 talked of two scenarios involving Taiwan as examples to illustrate the strategic choices facing China and the US in cyber war. He concludes to say that the threat of strategic cyber war is probably overblown and that US needs to take the prospect of operational cyber war seriously enough to understand imaginatively and great detail how it would carry out its missions in the face of a full-fledged attack.[9]

The Chinese Military Encyclopedia defines cyber strategy as "the analytical judgment of such factors as international conditions, hostilities in bilateral politics, military economics, science and technology, and geography as they apply to the preparation and direction of the overall military/war plan." Achieving information dominance is therefore one of the key goals for the PLA at the strategic and campaign level. Seizing control of the adversary's information flow and establishing information dominance are

8 China's Use of Cyber Warfare: Espioage Meets Strategic Deterrence by Magnus Hjortdal, 2011, Journal of Strategic Security

9 Chinese use of Cyber war as an Anti-Access Strategy- Two Scenarios by Martin C Libicki Jan 2011, RAND Corporation

essential requirements in the campaign strategy. The haste in making the transition from a mechanized to an informationized force is driven by the perception that winning local wars against adversaries such as US may only be possible with strong information warfare capability to first control enemy access to its own information.[10]

As China seeks to occupy an exalted place in its quest for global dominance and challenge US its political leadership is steadily heralding China in the right direction. President Hu Jintao has put expansion of PLA's cyber warfare capacity as a top priority for defence and security forces this decade. Significantly while visiting Shanghai last year, Hu gave a pep talk to computer and telecom engineers. "We must win a prominent place in global telecommunications through acquiring technologies that are based on domestic research and development'" Hu said. "We must assiduously attain breakthroughs in more critical core technologies." In internal speeches, Hu and his advisers have expressed the optimism that in 10 years China can close the gap with US in the field of IT warfare.[11]

China, for some time now has been mandating the use of a UNIX variant operating system, developed in China, called Kylin. Its earlier move to encourage government and civil organizations to switch to Linux had failed for variety of reasons. First and foremost was that most windows operating systems being used by government and non-government organizations were pirated and were infected. Second windows are widely pirated in China and one can use number of pirated software on windows. Third was that more games run on windows. The move to switch over has thus gained a sense of urgency as China knows that while its cyber war forces are capable of launching attacks over internet their own computers that are using windows and are ridden with viruses and worms. China has subsidized development of Kylin UNIX based server software. Kylin is a shareware and is designed to be secure. China seems to be getting success in server software but the real

10 Capability of People's Republic of China to conduct cyber warfare and computer network exploitation by Northrop Grumman,2009

11 Cyber Warfare another key to China's global ambitions -//thejakartaglobe.com/opinion/cyber-warfare-another-key-to-chinas-global-ambitions/354491

problem is PCs.[12]

While China's offensive capabilities on the Internet are widely recognized, it is now discovering the other edge of the sword. China is facing a paradox as it tries to manipulate and confront the growing capabilities of Internet users. Recent arrests of Chinese hackers and People's Liberation Army (PLA) pronouncements suggest that China fears that its own computer experts, nationalist hackers and social media could turn against the government. While the exact cause of Beijing's new focus on network security is unclear, it comes at a time when other countries are developing their own defences against cyber-attacks and hot topics like Stuxnet and Wikileaks are generating new concerns about Internet security.

On 02 Nov 2010, the People's Liberation Army Daily recommended the PLA better prepare itself for cyber threats, calling for new strategies to reduce Internet threats that are developing "at an unprecedented rate." While the report did not detail any strategies, it quoted a PLA order issued for computer experts to focus on the issue. The Chinese government also enforces the infamous "Golden Shield" which is a filter that blocks politically sensitive material from entering or leaving China. In the West, the information block is referred to as the "Great Firewall of China," but this shield may give China an advantage in a future cyber war. Possibly this could provide the government control over information and its tight relationship with Internet service providers could help China better coordinate a defence against online attacks. Also if China ever did use viruses as a military tool, it could use the Golden Shield to prevent collateral damage. Further China could also use an Internet kill switch to completely isolate the Chinese Internet in case of a cyber-war.[13] China with its aggressive and sophisticated interception technology can block the flow of information between an internet user inside China and the information source outside China.

---

12 Running for Linux at www.strategypage.com/htmv/htiw/articles/20110109.aspx

13 International Cyberspace Strategies by Kathryn Stephens and Larry K Mckee Jr, 28 Jun2010 – National Security Cyberspace Institute, Inc. (NSCI),Virginia.

The 02 Nov 2010 PLA announcement is part of a long trend of growing network-security concerns in China. In 2009, Minister of Public Security Meng Jianzhu emphasized that the development of the Internet in China created "unprecedented challenges" in "social control and stability maintenance." In June 2010, the State Council Information Office published a white paper on the growing threat of cybercrime and how to combat it. Clearly, these challenges have been addressed this year. The Ministry of Public Security (MPS) announced on 30 Nov that it had arrested 460 suspected hackers thought to have been involved in 180 cases so far in 2010. This is part of the MPS' usual end-of-year announcement of statistics to promote its success. But the MPS announcement also said that cybercrime had increased 80 percent this year and seemed to blame the attacks only on hackers inside China.

China's highly developed hacking capabilities, more offensive than defensive, include Internet censorship measures like the infamous Great Firewall, and the official police force run by the MPS specifically to monitor Chinese Internet traffic and censor websites is 40,000 strong. China also has developed two unofficial methods of censorship. First, operators of private websites and forums must follow certain government regulations to prevent statements critical of the government from being disseminated, which encourages private operators to be their own censors. Second, there is a veritable army of nationalistic computer users in China that include "hacktivist" groups such as the Red Hacker Alliance, China Union Eagle and the Honker Union, with thousands of members each. They became famous after the 1999 "accidental" bombing of the Chinese Embassy in Belgrade, which prompted China-based hackers to attack and deface U.S. government websites. The Chinese government, state-owned enterprises and private companies also engage public relations firms to hire, deploy and manage what have become colloquially known as "Party of Five Maoists." These are individuals who get paid half a yuan (5 mao) for every positive Internet post they write regarding government policy, product reviews and other issues.

As China's Internet-using population over 500 million, with nearly 160 million using social networking, Beijing recognizes the risk of all this spiraling out of control. Censors have not been able to keep up on the social-networking front. Even with limited or banned access to sites like Twitter and Facebook, their Chinese versions, Weibo and Kaixin, for example, are expanding exponentially. While the government may exercise more control over the Chinese-based sites, it cannot keep up with the huge number of posts on topics the CPC considers disharmonious. The recent announcement of Liu Xiaobo's Nobel Peace Prize is an example of news that was not reported at first in Chinese media but through social networking sites, and thereafter spreading like wildfire. And the censorship is not exclusive; even non-dissidents can be censored, such as Prime Minister Wen Jiabao when he recently called for limited political reform.[14]

China's large Internet population will not all be nationalists. The possibility of dissidents resorting to hacking, Beijing would consider them a serious threat. The Internet presents exactly the type of tool that could pose a major threat to the CPC because it spans regions, classes and ethnicities. Most social grievances are local and economic or ethnic-based. The potential for one opposition group to be united nationwide over the Internet is one of Beijing's gravest concerns. It has realized that a weapon it once wielded so deftly against foreign powers and business entities can now be used against Beijing.[xxiv]

Conclusion. China with its $ 5.5 trillion economy is becoming increasingly assertive as it seeks not only a dominant role for itself in Asia Pacific but in the world order. It fancies itself as the closest rival to US. Hence its strategy is shaped by these considerations. It already has well developed offensive capability but has some way to go before it develops matching defensive capability.

14 China and its double-edged cyber-sword by Sean Noonan, 09 Dec 2010 – www.stratfor.com

CHAPTER 5

OFFENSIVE CYBER WARFARE

Introduction

The world today finds itself enmeshed in a new zone of warfare. Military strategies and doctrines that were enunciated with the advent of the industrial revolution are now facing a dire need for change in to enable the nations to face the challenges posed by cyber technology. While the earlier forms of warfare was based on the premise that the enemy is visible in all the four domains of warfare i.e., land sea, air and space it is the fifth domain of cyberspace in which the enemy is not visible and hence the need for new principles and polices. Interestingly this fifth dimension of warfare is man-made and happens to be the most complex. As nations reap the fruits of IT they becoming increasingly dependent upon cyber space, not in the realm of military but more so in all spheres of vital national activity, they are becoming frightening vulnerable to exploitation by adversaries and terrorist organizations.

Cyber war exists in the military and intelligence realm and refers to conducting military operations according to information-related principles. It means disrupting or destroying information and communications systems. It also means trying to know everything about an adversary while keeping the adversary from knowing much about oneself. Cyber war is a warlike conflict in virtual space with means of information and communication technology (ICT) and networks. As other forms of warfare, cyber war aims at influencing the will and decision making capability of the enemy's political leadership and armed forces in the theater of *Computer Network Operations* (CNO).

Three forms of Computer Network Operations can be

distinguished:-

(a) Computer Network Attack – operations designed to disrupt, deny, degrade, or destroy information resident in computers and computer networks, or the computers or networks themselves.

(b) Computer Network Exploitation, which means retrieving intelligence-grade data and information from enemy computers by ICT means.

(c) Computer Network Defence, which consists of all measures necessary to protect own ICT means and infrastructures against hostile Computer Network Attack and Computer Network Exploitation. Thus conceptually, Computer Network Operations cover only a narrower section of all cyber-attacks. However, the potential for damage that cyber-war can inflict on national and economic security of a state could be large.

Computer Network Attack, or the deliberate paralyzation or destruction of enemy network capabilities, is only one of many instruments in the framework of military missions. While the importance of Computer Network Attack will certainly increase in the coming years, with regard to the state of developments in offensive cyber-war capabilities, there is still a lack of established knowledge about Computer Network Attack capabilities already available. There are very few case studies, and most information lies outside the public domain. And most organizations are still unsure about the state of their own cyber security. Thus, some of the estimates in this area seem exaggerated, particularly those linked to the expectation that the future will bring not only an arms race in cyberspace, but also strategic cyber-wars. Conducting an 'information operation' of strategic significance would not be easy, but neither is it impossible. However, cyber alone is still unlikely to win wars. Given the intrinsic difficulties of operating surgically in cyberspace, and since it is, with few exceptions, still not possible today to conduct precisely targeted cyber-attacks, great doubts remain as to whether strategic cyber-war is really feasible.

One important aspect of this is that uncontrollable blow back effects in the highly networked virtual space constitute considerable risks for an attacking state. This factor is all the more relevant since the states that are most likely to develop the technological know-how for strategic cyber war are also the most dependent on their own infrastructures, thus highly vulnerable in a cyber-war. Due to uncontrollable side-effects, a cyber-war would also undermine trust in cyberspace over the long term, with possible detrimental effects for the global economy, and thus for all parties involved. Strategic cyber war, by itself, would probably annoy but not disarm an adversary. And any adversary that merits a strategic cyber war campaign to be subdued also likely possesses the capability to strike back in ways that may be more than annoying. The fact remains that no one really knows how destructive a strategic cyber- attack in a conflict conducted in the virtual realm would be. It may well be less decisive.

If a strategic cyber-attack is less likely to be decisive, then cyber warfare capabilities at the operational level for actions against military targets during a real war might become more important. Operational cyber war may have the potential to contribute to warfare. How much is unknown and, to a large extent, still unknowable. Because a devastating cyber-attack may facilitate or amplify military operations, and because an operational cyber war capability seems relatively inexpensive, it may well be worth developing. It is obvious that for operational cyber war to work, its targets have to be accessible and offer vulnerabilities. These vulnerabilities have to be exploited in ways the attacker finds useful, the result of which he can only assess if the effects can be monitored – what may still be an inconclusive endeavour.

The present day warfare has entered the information age as was evident by the attacks on Estonia, Georgia and South Korea. Cyber warfare issues are of growing interest and concern and urgently need to be incorporated in the military doctrine and strategy. Many of the challenges of traditional warfare are magnified in the cyber realm. Chief among these is the challenge of situational awareness. Cyberspace is a vast, incredibly complex and rapidly changing battlefield. In the kinetic realm, the "fog of war" is a term derived from Clausewitz to refer to uncertain knowledge about one's adversary and even one's own position in the midst of an operation. While situational awareness is a major challenge in traditional warfare, the fog of cyber war threatens to be so thick that it can become the primary impediment to victory. As Sun Tzu said, "If you know the enemy and know yourself, you need not fear the results of a hundred battles." Developing the techniques and tools for cyber situational awareness is paramount to achieving strategic and tactical advantage in this new domain.

Nations face the possibility of losing the cyber war, without ever getting to know the identity of the enemy. An offensive cyber capability enabled enemy could disrupt or play havoc with the financial institutions, telecommunications, power and other critical functionalities of the government institutions and important private sector companies of the unsuspecting adversary.

Although cyberspace is agnostic to politics and ideology, state and non-state actors can use this power to achieve objectives in cyberspace and the physical world. Low cost, high potential impact and general lack of transparency make cyber power attractive to both powerful and less powerful actors. The former can combine cyber power with existing military capabilities, economic assets, and soft-power means. Less powerful actors can gain asymmetrically in cyberspace by inflicting damage on vulnerable targets. The virtual terrain of cyberspace is said to favour the offense because cyber- attacks are inexpensive and conducting them rarely has consequences. These two facts are a major reason why cyber-attacks have become ubiquitous, increasing in scope, and at a scale far greater than national resources to respond and defend can handle.

Along with many other countries, India is under constant assault in cyberspace and currently witnessing large scale cyber-attacks (Appendix B to D refers). Some of these incidents may be what is generally known as "Advanced Persistent Threats", which is commonly used to refer to cyber threats, in particular that of Internet enabled espionage, but is primarily used in reference to a long-term pattern of targeted sophisticated hacking attacks aimed at governments by well-resourced state actors, or agents affiliated with nation-states. Such attacks have targeted governments around the world, global oil, energy, and petrochemical companies, the mining sector, military contractors, the science and technology sector, critical infrastructure, and many additional sectors. Ever more they are also targeting high-tech companies that could enable future targeting.

Targets of Cyber War

Cyber War puts resources of the nation at risk that includes all of the components of national infrastructure that depend on information technology. There are three basic steps of Cyber War:-

(a) **Gain Control over the Opponent's Network**. The basic first step of military strategy to secure yourself against the enemy is to first know who your enemy is. The methodology is a simple one where the enemy scans the network for a specific weakness finds it, exploits it through automated tools and then gains complete control. Most of the tools they use are automated, requiring little interaction. Once in control, the enemy redirects, stops, or disables the systems from operating effectively.

(b) Disrupt financial Systems to cause chaos among the people.

(c) Take over the control of important utilities such as telecommunication systems, power grid systems and other critical infrastructure facilities.

Once the enemy is able to accomplish above actions successfully, the nation stands vanquished.

The New Paradigm of Warfare

Analysts define four factors facilitating the use of cyber weapons. They determine key directions of research concerning the combat use of cyber weapons.

(a) **Freedom of Access to Information Systems.** Development of information networks leads to the emergence of new challenges. A competent swindler has a potential opportunity to gain immediate access to a wide range of national strategic targets making the global information infrastructure. Under these circumstances, inter-connected computer networks may become a victim of many threats initiated by skilled individuals, non-state actors and states possessing well-trained personnel for combat operation in cyberspace.

(b) **Transparency of State Boundaries.** One of the most significant aspects of global information infrastructure (and consequently national infrastructures) is the elimination of traditional borders. The growing interdependence of national and global systems inevitably undermines national sovereignty. One of the most serious aspects of such transparency of borders is the lack of distinction between internal and external threats and diminishing difference among various forms of action against the state – from regular crime to military operations. Without clear distinction of external and internal threats, it is difficult to identify traditional espionage, crime, or war.

Some countries that lack sufficient military and economic power may try to profit from this situation and attack the enemy infrastructure through the cyberspace by using individuals or international criminal community.

(c) **Perception Management.** As a result of development of information systems, diminishing costs of access to the information and undermining of national sovereignty there are expanding opportunities for manipulations with information that enable to shape the perception. For instance, the Internet maybe used for dissemination of propagandistic materials from different sources. Political groups may use the Internet to mobilize political support.

It is quite possible that facts describing certain event may be distorted with the help of text, graphics and video techniques. This will enable a broad range of individuals and groups concerned to affect public perception and organize large propagandistic campaigns in order to undermine people's trust in the government. Such campaigns cause serious problems not only for the government, but for the mass media, which are supposed to disseminate objective information. The direct consequence of such use of cyber weapons is deception of the leadership and the society.

(d) **The Lack of Intelligence Data.** In the conditions of transparent borders and free access to information, the intelligence service face serious problems in providing the government with reliable and timely strategic information concerning current and prospective threats of cyber warfare. It becomes more difficult to identify the objects for intelligence. The classical geo-strategic approach (focusing on specific state – a source of threat) is now nearly obsolete. The targets for intelligence are transnational non-governmental and criminal organizations and non-state actors. The significance of information challenge will depend on the assessment of capabilities and intentions of potential enemies in the cyberspace and vulnerability of targets.

Tools of Cyber Warfare

Cyber weapons can be considered as weapons of mass destruction. Cyber weapons may be defined as computer programs that are developed for destruction of confidentiality, integrity and availability of computer data systems. Cyber weapons may be classified as offensive, defensive and dual use weapons. Some of the basic weapons in the cyber arsenal are given in the table below (See Appendix A for details):-

Attack	Description
Denial-of-Service Attacks	
Flooding	Sending extraneous data or replies to block a host service

Synchronize/reset flooding	Exploiting limited cache in IP stack to block connections
Smurfing	Using the IP broadcast system and IP spoofing to multiply floods
Out of band/fragment attacks	Exploiting vulnerabilities in IP stack kernel implementations
Nuking	Using forged messages to reset active connections
Specific denial of service	Generating requests that block one specific vulnerable service
Malicious Software Attacks	
Back door	Program feature allowing remote execution of arbitrary commands
Worm	Program that spawns and spreads copies of itself
Virus	Code that self-reproduces in existing applications
Trojan	Program-in-a-program that executes arbitrary commands
Exploiting Vulnerabilities	
Access permissions	Exploiting read or write access to system files
Brute force	Trying default or weak login/password combinations
Overflow	Writing arbitrary code behind the end of a buffer and executing it
Race conditions	Exploiting temporary, insecure conditions in program
IP Packet Manipulation	
Port spoofing	Using commonly used source ports (entry points) to avoid filtering rules
Tiny fragments	Using small packets to bypass firewall protocol/port/size checks

Blind IP spoofing	Changing source IP to access password services without a password
Name-server ID "snoofing"	Blind spoofing with calculated false ID numbers name-server-caches
Sequence-number guessing	Calculating TCP sequence/acknowledge number to spoof a trusted host
Remote-session hijacking	Using spoofing to intercept and redirect connections
Insider Attack	
Backdoor daemons	Opening a port for further remote access
Log manipulation	Removing traces of attacks and unauthorized access
Cloaking	Replacing system files to hide unauthorized access
Sniffing	Monitoring network data to find sensitive data (e.g. passwords)
Nonblind spoofing	Monitoring network to hijack active or to make forged connections

Computer Viruses and Worms. Viruses are harmful software programs secretly introduced into an IT system with the characteristic feature of being able to generate and distribute multiple copies of it, thereby spreading throughout the system. Viruses piggyback on programs already resident in a computer. Each virus has a destructive payload that is activated under certain conditions. When activated, a virus can corrupt, alter, or destroy data, generate bogus transactions, and even transfer information. 136 Worms are programs in their own right, which hide within a computer and stealthily propagate themselves onto other machines. Viruses do not spread on the network, worms do, and a virus can be their payload. Moreover, so-called polymorphic and metamorphic malware can automatically mutate in an attempt to avoid detection by anti-virus technology.

There are many other types of software weapons enabling

software vulnerability exploitation, such as information blockades, rootkits, malicious embedded code, key loggers,[1] IP spoofing,[2] logic bombs, sniffing, spamming, backdoors,[3] and video morphing. There are also dual-use technologies like port vulnerability scanners and network monitoring tools. New types of weapons are being developed at a rapid pace and existing weapons are transforming.

Unlike nuclear or other weapons of mass destruction, cyber weapons and cyber-attacks require less infra-structure, and no restricted materials or knowledge which is in short supply. Cyber weapons have be come easier to obtain and to use, much more powerful, and ever more sophisticated. Botnets,[4] for instance, which are used for launching Distributed Denial of Service Attacks (DDoS), are comprised of advanced remote exploitation capabilities within as many computers as a hacker can compromise all over the world. These programs, mostly well-disguised, have several advanced capabilities. The characteristics of the 'Storm' worm, for example, a Trojan horse spread through email, include self-morphing – it changes code to evade anti-virus; self-defending – if you try to delete it copies itself; self-replicating – it identifies and infects other computers; self-encrypting – it can encrypt and decrypt itself to elude signature detection; and self-cloaking – it changes its communications path to inhibit tracking. The vast Storm botnet first detected in 2007, running on anything from 20 to 115 million computers, has increased its capacity constantly as more and more

1 Keystroke logging, or key logging, is the action of tracking the keys struck on a keyboard, typically in a covert manner so that the person using the keyboard is unaware that his actions are being monitored. There are numerous methods, ranging from hardware and software-based approaches to electromagnetic and acoustic analysis.

2 IP spoofing refers to the creation of Internet Protocol (IP) packets with a forged source IP address, called spoofing, with the purpose of concealing the identity of the sender or impersonating another computer system.

3 A backdoor in a computer (or cryptosystem or algorithm) is a method of bypassing normal authentication, securing remote access to a computer, obtaining access to plain text, and so on, while attempting to remain undetected.

4 A botnet (robot network) refers to multiple computers infected with remote-controlled software that allows a single hacker to run automated programs on the botnet behind the users' back. The remote-controlled software or rootkit is clandestinely installed in each computer, hiding its presence and tracks, making detection difficult. The hacker can use the botnet for many purposes: distributing spam, spreading Trojan horses, perpetuating phishing scams, or gathering information for identity theft or fraud, etc.

computers have become compromised. 2010 saw a sharp escalation in the scale, frequency, and severity of DDoS attack activity on the Internet. For the first time an attack of 100 Gbps bandwidth was reported. This represents a dramatic escalation in the amount of information that is piled up on a network in order to shut it down. Over 50 percent of the observed Internet attack traffic in the last quarter of 2010 originated from 10 countries, with the US, Russia, and China accounting for 30 percent. The global average Internet connection speed is now about 2 Mbps. Therefore, to deliver a 100 Gbps attack would take some 7,000 to 50,000 bots. The Dutch police found a 1.5 million-node botnet. Estimates suggest that the botnet can generate more instructions per second than many of the world's top supercomputers. With so much power, attacks can be launched with devastating consequences.[5]

Offensive Cyber War

Sun Tzu had propagated that to win the war one must confuse the enemy, disrupt their plans, cut off their lines of communications and finally throw them off balance. As military planners write the doctrine for offensive cyber warfare two aspects stand out. First is the near total dependence of modern armies (particularly those of technologically advanced countries including India) on computer networks and information systems present new vulnerabilities which can easily be exploited by the attacker. Second is the heavy dependence on *dual use infrastructure* – those owned by private sector but is used both by military and society which are not geared up to withstand cyber-attacks. These could include financial institutions, telecommunications, power infrastructure and media.

It appears, in all probability, that in future the first battle between warring nations will be fought in cyber space irrespective of whether the nation states are technologically advanced or otherwise. Estonia and Georgia are perfect examples of this. While Estonia ranked 33rd in the world for internet usage with 62 percent population using it, Georgia had only 8 percent penetration. Cyber war thus becomes very attractive compared to kinetic warfare

5 DCAF HORIZON 2015 WORKING PAPER No. 7 "On Cyber Warfare" by Fred Schreier.

particularly in the case of Estonia. Some of the notable features which favour cyber warfare are given below:-

(a) **Low Entry Cost.** Anyone with a computer and internet connection and freely available tools on the internet can conduct cyber warfare operations.

(b) **Blurred Physical Boundaries**. The attacker may sit launch the attack sitting hundreds of miles away. Cyber warfare creates its own 'fog and friction of war.'

(c) **Lack of Intelligence**. It is extremely difficult to gather intelligence on the impending cyber attack until it actually launched.

(d) **Difficulty in Assessment.** It is difficult to assess whether the attack is from an adversary state or it is a handiwork of some hackers. Even the attack on Estonia was not labeled as Cyber-attack by a nation by NATO or UN.

(e) Inadequate Defences against cyber-attacks.

(f) Availability of non-state actors.

(g) Tools for attack are cheap and openly available on the Internet. The proliferation of such tools happens without any control.

(h) There are no technological, financial or legal hurdles to overcome against that proliferation.

(j) There is an advantage for the attacker who can profit from the latest and newest innovations.

(k) Cyberspace gives disproportionate power to small and otherwise relatively insignificant actors.

(l) Operating behind false IP addresses, foreign servers and aliases, attackers can act with almost complete anonymity and relative impunity, at least in the short term.

(m) Cyber war may help to avoid the need to engage in combat operations and thus saves lives.

(n) Cyber war leads to the ability to disrupt the adversary rather than destroy his forces.

(o) Inherent in cyber wars are the difficulties of tactical warning and attack or damage assessments.

(p) Cyber war enables actors to achieve political and strategic goals without the need for armed conflict.

(q) Cyber war does not require the traditional battlefield. Systems that people rely upon, from banks, the electric power grid to air defence radars, are accessible worldwide from cyberspace and can be quickly taken over or knocked out without even defeating the country's traditional forces.

(r) Cyber war happens at almost the speed of light. As photons of attack packets stream down fiber-optic cables, the time between the launch of an attack and its effects is barely measurable, thus creating more risks for decision makers, particularly in a crisis.

(s) The victim of an attack has to invest considerable resources into neutralizing the threat, which requires teams of dedicated software and hardware experts with specific skill sets. Such persons, for the military, are difficult to recruit and to retain as private industry offers more attractive terms for their talent.

(t) The vulnerabilities of countries increasingly dependent on complex, interconnected, and networked information systems will only increase over time, thus providing adversaries with a target rich environment.

The most unique feature of cyber-attacks is the difficulty in identifying what constitutes the attack itself. Second whether it is a handiwork of some thrill seeking hackers or is state sponsored is difficult to attribute. These two factors pose a serious dilemma to nations under attack and on the contrary this precisely makes it attractive to the attacking nation. UN charter clearly outlines what constitutes an act of aggression. Cyber-attacks do not qualify the definition though however, one may argue that a SCADA type attack which causes death and destruction may indeed be called an attack.

There is subtle difference between cyber warfare and cyber-attacks. Clausewitz had stated that war is a continuation of politics by other means. This implies war involves two states in conflict. The difficultly in attribution makes it difficult to distinguish it as an act of attack by an individual or war by a state. Cyber-attacks occur every day and every minute over cyber networks with blurred boundaries.

Cyber-attacks have tactical, operational, and strategic applications. They can be used against deployed forces or against strategic targets in an opponent's homeland, for instance, against those that contribute to the ability to wage war. Their range is practically unlimited, and targets can be attacked anywhere the global network extends. Cyber-attacks have a variety of delivery options: over networks or from dedicated ground, sea, air, and space platforms. The tools are relatively cheap. Cyber-attacks may become more expensive as they depend ever more on time and effort for reconnaissance of network targets to find vulnerabilities. And this reconnaissance must be periodically refreshed as networks change and new equipment or software is added or reconfigured. While the preparation for a cyber-attack may be lengthy, the speed of the actual attack is measured in seconds irrespective of the distance from the target. Surprise and stealth are normal attributes of cyber-attacks.

In limited cyber war, the information infrastructure is the medium, target, and weapon of attack, with little or no real-world action accompanying the attack. As a medium of attack, the information infrastructure forms the vector by which the cyber-attack is delivered to the target – sometimes through interconnections between the enemy and its allies, using links for sharing resources or data, or through wide-area network connections. Alternatively, insiders might, in collusion or unwittingly, place malware directly on the own networks or IT systems.[6]

As a target of attack, infrastructures are the means for some operations, which might expose additional vulnerabilities." In addition, degrading data on a network might force the enemy to question the quality of the information to make decisions thereby delaying the decision making which is very crucial. As the weapon of attack, infrastructures could even be perverted to attack themselves, either via implantation of multiple pieces of malware, or via deliberate actions that exploit existing weaknesses. Limited cyber war could either be used to slow an opponent's preparation for military intervention, as part of an economic warfare campaign, or as part of the maneuvering that typically accompanies a crisis or confrontation between states.

Unrestricted cyber war would certainly be more serious, since it is a form of warfare that has three major characteristics: - [7]

(a) It is comprehensive in scope and target coverage, with little or no distinctions between military and civilian targets or between the home front and the fighting front.

(b) Unrestricted cyber war can have physical consequences and may cause casualties, some of which would result from attacks deliberately intend to create mayhem and destruction. And some of which would result from the erosion of civilian command and control capabilities in areas such as air-traffic control, emergency-service management, water resource management, and power generation.

(c) The economic and social impact could be profound, in addition to damage and loss of life. Ultimately, unrestricted cyber war may have the potential to result in economic and social degradation of a state. The great unknown and thus danger of unrestricted cyber war is the unintended secondary and tertiary consequences an attack may have on uninvolved third parties, or even for the attacker.

---

6 DCAF HORIZON 2015 WORKING PAPER No. 7 "On Cyber Warfare" by Fred Schreier.

7 Ibid.

Cyber-attacks on hospitals, for example, could produce casualties by manipulating data, through erasing, replacing, or adding ones and zeros; by changing prescriptions or turning off life-support and other critical systems; by causing radiation overdose, etc. While terrorists may find such attacks attractive, for states they would be a violation of the laws of war. It is certain that causing harm to non-combatants is not likely to produce any military advantage. However, an opponent still might do it. Attacks on critical national infrastructures, for example the electric power grid, might also disrupt medical services and produce casualties, but would not necessarily be contrary to the laws of war if there would have been some prior considerations as to whether the value of the target outweighed the risk of non-combatant casualties. This fact alone might justify calling for adaptation of the Geneva Conventions.

To effectively manage a cyber-conflict, it may have to be categorized into various levels of intensity. A low intensity cyber conflict involves the legitimate use of cyber resources to undermine the adversary. Examples are psychological or information warfare, a usual precursor of an armed conflict. A medium intensity cyber conflict comprises low intensity conflict and sporadic cyber-attacks, as well as intrusions to gather intelligence or to harass or destabilize the adversary. A high intensity cyber conflict consists of conflicts of low and medium intensity, plus cyber-attacks resulting in the destruction or damage to infrastructure, injuries and even the loss of human lives.[8]

Critical national infrastructures are normal targets for military planners with the mission of gaining a strategic advantage. Cyber-attacks could potentially produce the same disruptions, and possibly at lesser cost compared to any military force. This is different from strategic attacks against manufacturing or other critical infrastructures where the intent is not to gain immediate operational advantage, but to benefit from the degradation of the opponent's capacity for sustained resistance. In this erosion of the capability to resist, the utility of cyber-attacks may be open to question. However, the ability to interfere with communications

8 DCAF HORIZON 2015 WORKING PAPER No. 7 "On Cyber Warfare" by Fred Schreier.

and logistics for operational or tactical advantage is not. Thus, for a number of conflict scenarios, an opponent could reasonably be expected to use cyber-attacks to interfere with efforts to move, deploy, and supply forces.[9]

Offensive cyber operations can thus be broadly classified under following categories:-

Active	Active attacks include attempts to circumvent or break protection features, introduce malicious code, or steal or modify information. These attacks may be mounted against a network backbone, exploit information in transit, electronically penetrate an enclave, or attack an authorized remote user during an attempt to connect to an enclave. Active attacks can result in the disclosure or dissemination of data files, denial of service, or modification of data.
Close-in	Close-in attack consists of a regular individual's attaining close physical proximity to networks, systems, or facilities for the purpose of modifying, gathering, or denying access to information. Close physical proximity is achieved through surreptitious entry, open access, or both.
Insider	Insider attacks can be malicious or nonmalicious. Malicious insiders intentionally eavesdrop, steal, or damage information; use information in a fraudulent manner; or deny access to other authorized users. Nonmalicious attacks typically result from carelessness, lack of knowledge, or intentional circumvention of security for such reasons as "getting the job done."

9 DCAF HORIZON 2015 WORKING PAPER No. 7 "On Cyber Warfare" by Fred Schreier.

Distribution	Distribution attacks focus on the malicious modification of hardware or software at the factory or during distribution. These attacks can introduce malicious code, such as a backdoor, into a product to gain unauthorized access to information or a system function at a later date.

Cyber espionage is also a very effective tool in conducting cyber warfare. Many nations, particularly China has been accused for conducting cyber espionage by US. Duqu is an example of this wherein a nation may use military-technological espionage to gain military knowledge and industrial espionage to gain economic advantage.

Deception in Cyber Attacks. Deception can be employed in cyber-attacks as in conventional attack. Privilege escalation is a subtle form of identity deception in which the attacker gains access to a system through a vulnerable account, and then exploits vulnerabilities to gain privileges that of system administrator. Spoofing can be used as a deception tool wherein it can screen or camouflage the origin of attack.

Cyber War- A Real Possibility

In the recent conflicts no nation has openly carried out full blown cyber war though nations have come close to using large-scale cyber warfare techniques. In Iraq, US had drafted plans to restrict access to funds by Saddam that were never used. It was primarily so because by the time they were authorized it was too late for them to have any bearing on the outcome of war. The delay was probably due to the concern that due to the interconnected nature of banks that the efforts would bring down some banking operations in Europe. Last year, New York Times reported that US considered using cyber warfare to tamper with Libya's electronic warning systems such as air defence radars. Indeed there are three reasons why military leadership would be negligent if they did not ask about cyber options. The first is that cyber capabilities are new, classified and uneven. Commanders and their staff are broadly unfamiliar with cyber capabilities and their effects. Commanders state their objectives and then their staff determines what capabilities the military services or intelligence agencies might have developed or could develop in time. Secondly, Cyber capabilities might provide a commander another means to win the battle but not put his men in any danger. Thirdly, military commanders according to Geneva Conventions must limit the number of civilian deaths. If cyber capabilities could disable Libyan air defences without killing anyone, then a commander is obligated to use them.

Cyber capabilities are not nuclear weapons, to be used as a last resort. It is said that critics shot down the idea because of, among other reasons, the fear that such an action might set a precedent for other nations to follow suit. However what has been missed out in the discussion is the word NATO. The cyber capabilities discussed in NYT story are US only and would have been conducted as a separate operation to support NATO but outside of its formal chain of command.[10]

US CYBERCOM held a simulation exercise early in Dec 2011, in which 300 cyber specialists designated as CYBERCOM elements and the enemy practicing offensive and defensive tactics and coordination. The simulated US cyber defence operation was centered at the Air Force's Nevada Test and Training Range at Nellis, Nevada while the designated aggressors sought to penetrate the American cyber network from remote locations. The exercise served to try out various real time scenarios based on the probable actions and counter action of a potential adversary.

Conclusion. Cyber war offers a low cost option with maximum dividends with little risk of attribution. The success is assured as cyber war favours the attacker. Also there are no rules of engagement. Geneva conventions are only applicable to kinetic warfare and do not cover cyber war. Until nations put the right conventions to govern the cyber conflict, it will continue to favour the attacker.

10 Why the US explored cyber war against Libya, and why it backed down by Jason Healey, 18 Oct 2011- www.acus.org

CHAPTER 6

DEFENSIVE CYBER WARFARE

Introduction

In the present day scenario it is felt that cyber war alone may not defeat the enemy, it may weaken its resolve to resist having been plunged into a state of utter chaos. Kinetic war has to be launched in case the enemy is to be physically defeated. Cyber warfare can be used as supporting form of warfare.

Certainty in predicting the effects of cyber-attacks is undermined by the same complexity that makes cyber-attacks possible in the first place. Investigations may reveal that a particular system has a particular vulnerability. But predicting what an attack can do requires knowing how the system and its operators will respond to signs of dysfunction, and knowing the behaviour of processes and systems associated with the system being attacked. Even then, operational cyber war operations may rarely harm individuals directly, nor do they, with some exceptions, destroy equipment. At best, such operations are more likely to confuse and frustrate operators of military systems, and then only temporarily because, due to the exponential innovation, even the best cyber-attacks have a limited shelf life. Thus, cyber war at the operational level may well only be a support function for other elements of warfare. "Attempting an operational cyber-attack in the hopes that success will facilitate a combat operation may be prudent; presuming the operation's success on achieving a particular goal may not be."

Cyber defence remains the most important activity for the armed forces in cyberspace. The vast majority of attacks about which concern has been expressed apply only to Internet-connected computers. As a result, systems which are stand-alone or communicate over proprietary networks or are air-gapped from the Internet should be safe from these. Victims of cyber security lapses and cyber-attacks include many civilian systems, and for this reason the value of a purely military approach to cyber security defence is limited. The armed forces have an important role in protecting their own systems and in developing potential offensive capabilities. Although most of what it takes to defend military networks can be learned from what it takes to defend civilian networks, the former differ from the latter in important ways. Hence, the armed forces must think hard as they craft their cyber defence goals, architectures, policies, strategies, and operations.

Early warning is the key to thwart attack in any form. Cyber warfare is no exception. Technology will be critical for early identification and tracking of cyber-attacks. Military doctrine defines three major areas of Computer Network Operations (CNO): computer network defence (CND), computer network attack (CNA), and computer network exploitation (CNE). Nations tend to invest more in improving and maintaining network defences. CND remains neglected. This in effect contributes to slowing down of R & D effort in protecting our networks.

Only US, France, China, Russia, Israel and North Korea have established military cyber commands which employ cyber warriors to ward off cyber-attacks and conduct full scale of cyberspace operations. On 04 Nov 2010 EU carried out its first ever cyber-attack desk exercise to find weak spots in the way their governments might behave when faced with real attack (Techworld, Nov 10).

External Threats

Cyber-attacks can be launched from outside the network, using hackers, or from the inside, using agents and rogue components. External hacking is by far, the most common path that a state would take, particularly if going after civilian targets. Militaries and intelligence agencies, however, cannot completely ignore insider attacks. At the syntactic level, again, where hacking tends to take place, Cyber-space is hedged with authorities. A person who owns a computer can normally do whatever he or she wishes to do. For the most part, the user should expect to retain full control over the computer, even when it is exposed to others via networking. Computers in an enterprise setting tend to come under more control by system administrators, and parts of such systems are closed to mere users.

To hack a computer is to violate these authorities. A hacker may send a user a rogue email or lure a user to a rogue site from which bad code is downloaded. Some types of code steal information on such machines. Other types permit the hacker to issue subsequent commands to machine, thereby "owning" it (at least for such purposes).[1]

Hackers can also enter enterprise systems by linking to them and successfully masquerading as legitimate users with the rights and privileges of any other user. In some cases, hackers go further; fooling the system into thinking they have the privileges of system administrator. As a system administrator, a hacker can arbitrarily change nearly everything about a system, not least of which are the privileges other users enjoy. Once hackers have wormed their way into a system and appropriated enough privileges, they can perpetrate many additional forms of mischief.[2]

The most common aim of hacking is to steal data. When states steal data from other states, it is called Computer Network Exploitation (CNE). Corporations might also steal data (intellectual property) from other corporations. Individuals also steal data, from or, more often, about other individuals, often for the purpose of

1 A hacker is said to own a machine if it can get it to do what he or she wants. This is an unfortunate use of the term *own*, which normally implies exclusivity: If one owns something, others do not (co-ownership is a different matter). Rarely does so-called hacker-ownership prevent users from using their own machines. They may not even notice that their machines are doing something they did not authorize. Alas, computers are always doing something users are unaware of and would not necessarily approve of if they did know.

2 Two of the other forms of mischief, not discussed in detail here, are theft of service and unauthorized advertisement. *Theft of service* occurs when hackers run their programs on another computer's processors, ride on another network's capacity, or store materials within another computer (pornography or jihadist propaganda are two noted types of data). With everything about systems become cheaper by the year, few people worry about theft of service. *Unauthorized advertisement* (not to be confused with spyware, which leads to data theft) can be annoying but is otherwise harmless.

identity theft. Each may steal from the other. Because stealing data does not prevent users from enjoying free use of their own systems, there may be few signs that they are being tapped into. Detection is possible, if a user notices an unexpected exfiltration of data packets; notices anomalous activities or activity patterns; notices rogue code resident on a system; or observes the consequences of a specific intrusion.

Unauthorized access, however, can lead to more dastardly possibilities: disruption and corruption. Disruption takes place when systems are tricked into performing operations that make them shut down, work at a fraction of their capacity, commit obvious errors, or interfere with the operation of other systems. It is very rare that hacker attacks on code can break physical objects, but at least one laboratory demonstration of bad code caused a turbine to self-destruct. Corruption takes place when data and algorithms are changed in unauthorized ways, usually to the detriment of their correct functioning. Despite the lack of hard-and-fast distinctions between disruption and corruption, a good rule of thumb is that the effects of disruption are drastic, immediate, and obvious, while the effects of corruption are subtle and may linger or recur. It is relatively easy to tell that a system is not working. It is harder to tell that it functions but generates wrong information or makes bad decisions.

Hackers intent on causing later mischief often facilitate their efforts by dropping rogue computer code into systems for later use. What can be termed implants often lie dormant, only to be activated either by events on the target machine (e.g., the appearance of a new information which the hacker might be interested in) or by commands from the hacker. In some cases implants operate autonomously, searching for computers on the network that lack such implants and making sure they do not lack for long.

Regardless of what the hacker intends to do to steal information—disrupt systems or corrupt them—the first, and often the most difficult step, is, in fact, getting inside (that is, receiving the privileges of a system's user or administrator). For this reason, the early phases of a CNE look the same as the early phases of a computer-network attack. As a corollary, those with the best capability to get inside another system tend to be best qualified to carry out a computer-network attack.

Because the syntactic layer rests on the physical layer, one can confidently assert that there is no forced entry in cyberspace. If someone has got into a system from the outside, it is because that someone has persuaded the system to do what its users did not really want done and what its designers believed they had built the system to prevent. Nevertheless, in any contest between a computer's design and use-model (e.g., a user's intuition that email is information, not instructions) on the one hand and its software code, on the other, the code always wins. Whoever gets into a system gets into it through paths that the software permits. The software may have flaws (most would be inadvertent, but some may be deliberate; see below) or may have been misconfigured (e.g., the permissions the administrator established differ from the permissions that the administrator thought had been established), ut a system is what it is, not necessarily what it should be.[3]

---

3 There is one exception to the rule that computer attacks arise from host-system vulnerabilities. In a *flooding attack*, a hacker generates such a high volume of packets destined for a particular network location that legitimate information does not get to the affected network, cutting it off from the rest of the world. These days it is very difficult for one computer to flood another.

Floods today thus tend to arise from DDOS attacks, generally caused by thousands or millions of unwitting computers (bots) that have come under the control of hackers. There is currently a thriving business in creating large numbers of bots (by subverting third-party computers), organizing them into botnets, and renting their services to others, such as spammers. The first well-known DDOS attack occurred in February 2000, when several e-commerce sites were taken down for periods ranging up to several hours. The attack on Estonia was of this type. By one estimate, up to one in ten packets over the Internet is part of some bot attack.

DDOS attacks are difficult to defeat precisely because they can target otherwise well protected networks. The programs that convert third-party computers into bots only need to work against the least well-protected Internet-linked computers to take them over. Spamming aside, most bot attacks affect people in shady businesses, so there is little political will to shut down access to machines whose innocent owners have unknowingly let them be converted into bots. This could change if DDOS attacks become a far more serious problem to the Internet than they have been to date. Conceivably, Internet service providers could be ordered by law to cut off service to users whose machines demonstrate an unusual pattern of outgoing packets. Internet service providers could force users to demonstrate the presence of antivirus software before allowing them on the networks. To work, however, such solutions would have to be applied worldwide—an unlikely prospect.

Such a divergence, when it has security implications, is a vulnerability. Whatever the methods, manual or automated, hackers' use, an attempt to take advantage of a vulnerability to gain access to a system or to get it to accept rogue instructions is called an *exploit*. A system's integrity dictates how badly a system can be hurt by attacks in cyberspace. One might even argue that a system's integrity is a more important determinant of success than the quality of the adversary's exploits—after all, no vulnerabilities, no exploits; no exploits, no cyber-attacks.

Thus, in theory, all computer mischief is ultimately the fault of the system's owner—if not because of misuse or misconfiguration, then because of using a system with security bugs in the first place. In practice, all computer systems are susceptible to errors. The divergence between design and code is a consequence of the complexity of software systems and the potential for human error. The more complex the system—and they do get continually more complex—the more places there are in which errors can hide. Every information system has vulnerabilities—some more serious than others. The software suppliers themselves find a large share of these vulnerabilities and issue periodic patches, which users are then supposed to install—which some do more expeditiously and correctly than others. Hackers find some vulnerabilities and then spring corresponding exploits on unsuspecting users who have otherwise done everything correctly. Literally thousands of exploits are sitting around. Many of the more-devious ones require physical access to the target system. Most of the ones that reach the news do not work on well-patched systems.

In a sense, cyber-attacks rely on deception—persuading systems to do what their designers do not want them to do. Fortunately, deception can be its own undoing. An exploit, if discovered, shows system administrator that something is not right. With good logs, system administrator may be able to determine where something unusual took place in the interaction between the hacker and the

---

Thus, for the time being, DDOS attacks are likely to remain a threat. Fortunately, DDOS attacks cannot corrupt or, these days, crash systems, and they do not affect traffic internal to server-restricted spaces.

system. Changes in files (data or instructions), or the presence of unexpected files can also be telling. The process is hardly perfect; it is possible to determine a specific vulnerability and miss the broader design flaw of which the specific vulnerability is just an instance. Furthermore, individual system administrators almost never have direct visibility into packaged software and cannot fix vulnerabilities of which the software vendor is himself unaware. Nevertheless, any one system administrator can take advantage of an international community with a common interest in minimizing outstanding vulnerabilities.

In contemplating cyberspace, it may help to differentiate the peripheries of the system. The peripheries may be said to contain user equipment; that is, equipment whose function and parameters are established by users. Peripheries, if not air gapped or protected via consistent encryption, tend to be repeatedly vulnerable largely because users are rarely trained in or focused on information security.[4] User systems and privileges can be taken over through password cracking, phishing, social engineering, downloads from bad Web sites, use of bad media (e.g., corrupted zip drives), etc. Sadly, the security of the periphery as a whole is often no better than the security of the most feckless user. The core, by contrast, is what system administrators' control— monitors, routers, management devices, machinery (such as weapons), and databases. System administrators are (or should be) trained and sensitive to security issues; they also set the terms by which users (and their systems) interact with the core. Although it is good personnel practice to sensitize users to security issues, it is good engineering practice to assume that users will not always be sensitive. While it is possible to protect the core from insecure users, it is less clear whether networks can function when enough user systems are compromised badly enough, even though network administration is a function of system administrator. In general, it is hard to compromise the core

4 An *air gap* is the lack of an electronic connection between the system and the rest of the world. A true air gap also requires that the system not any have RF links (or at least not ones that are powerful enough to be picked up beyond the protected perimeter), and that no media (such as thumb drives) cross the perimeter (such as by being removed from a computer).

in the same precise way twice, but the periphery is always at risk.

Internal Threats

States have two other methods of gaining access to systems; in fact, these are the only ways to get into truly closed systems. One is to recruit insiders, who, with varying degrees of help, can introduce mischief into systems (especially if they are system administrator themselves). The other is to toy with the supply chain so that target systems contain components that appear benign but contain code that responds to a state's directions or at least priorities.[5] Unlike computer hacking, many of whose techniques are published on the Web and in print, the insider and component methods are essentially the province of state intelligence agencies and therefore highly protected. It is unclear how well they have worked.

Insiders

Unlike operating a system connected to the rest of the world, which is known to contain hackers, operating one from the inside to create mischief tends to violate explicit trust conditions. System operators capable of doing so must go through much more comprehensive security processes to achieve any given level of security in the face of an insider threat.

The insider threat has always been a staple of computer security, not least in the banking industry. Most well-managed systems therefore make it difficult for rogue employees to do a great deal of damage and, in some cases, limit how much material they can access (even when any individual item is available). As a general principle, a rogue employee presents risks similar to those of a feckless user in the periphery of an open system. Rogue system administrators are a much deeper headache but, again, one that banks deal with constantly. Insider recruitment can produce unexpectedly sharp pain but does not lend itself to nationwide effects very easily. Such an attack cannot be duplicated at will, as an exploit can (unless used as a launch point for a hacker or malware attack that cannot otherwise

5 Although the components themselves are often hardware, it is almost always the software that is altered.

work as well). Revealing one turncoat can lead to investigations that could unravel entire recruitment networks.

Supply Chain

Many countries are worried that China's growing presence in component manufacturing provides it plenty of opportunities for mischief— which it may not be shy about taking advantage of.

Unless and until purchasers get access to all the code in the electronics they buy, a supply-chain attack is difficult to defend against. Such components can fail and perhaps bring down the rest of the system at a pre-specified time or in response to some system state. Yet there are also limits to what rogue components can do if installed in a truly air gapped system: They cannot respond to a signal unless the system can receive messages from the outside, and they cannot exfiltrate information unless the system can generate messages. A component attack is a sporty move. The discovery of lead paint contamination on Chinese toys led to major tremors in China—and that was just sloppiness. Consider what damage a deliberately corrupted component would have on China's reputation, much less the reputation of the guilty supplier. One discovery may create the incentive to recycle everything acquired from the now-suspect source.

Cyber-attacks and cyber exploitations are possible only because IT systems and networks are vulnerable. Most vulnerabilities existing are introduced accidentally through design or implementation flaws as described below. As long as nations rely on IT systems and networks as a foundation for military and economic power, and as long as these are accessible from the outside, they are at risk of being attacked.[6]

6 DCAF HORIZON 2015 WORKING PAPER No. 7 "On Cyber Warfare" by Fred Schreier.

Vulnerabilities	Description
Software	Applications or system software may have accidentally or deliberately introduced flaws the use of which can subvert the intended purpose for which the software is designed.
Hardware	Vulnerabilities can be found in hardware, including microprocessors, microcontrollers, circuitboards, powersupplies, peripherals such as printers or scanners, storage devices, and communications equipment such as network cards. Tampering with such components may secretly alter the intended functionality of the component or provide opportunities to introduce malware.
Seams between hardware and software	An example of such a seam might be the reprogrammable read-only memory of a computer (firmware) that can be improperly and clandestinely reprogrammed.

Vulnerabilities	Description
Communications channels	The communications channels between a system or network and the 'outside' world can be used by an adversary in many ways. An adversary can pretend to be an authorized user of the channel, jam it, and thus deny its use to the adversary, or eavesdrop on the channel to obtain information intended by the adversary to be classified or kept secret.
Configuration	Most systems provide a variety of configuration options that users can set based on their own trade offs between security and convenience. Because convenience is often valued more than security, many systems are – in practice – configured insecurely.
Users and operators	Authorized users and operators of a system or network can be tricked or blackmailed into doing the bidding of an adversary, or sell their services.
Service providers	Many computer installations rely on outside parties to provide computer-related services, such as maintenance or Internet service. An adversary may be able to persuade a service provider to take some special action on its behalf, such as installing attack software on a target computer.

Defensive Cyber Operations

Cyber operations will favour the attacker in the short term. However, as nations strive to invest in protection of their cyber assets, the defender may get parity in the long run. This is not to say that new attack tools will not develop in future, in fact they will even more deadly than what exist today. The argument is primarily based on the fact that nations are showing urgency in evolving early warning, detection, monitoring and analysis tools which will help them to face the attacks and thwart them off in real time.

As a direct corollary to cyber-attacks not being restricted to military targets alone, the cyber defensive operations will have to cover both military and non-military assets. The primary objective would be to ensure protection of critical infrastructure and the ability to operate them with complete freedom. However, no cyber war has been fought till date to draw lessons or test the efficacy of protection systems available today. The policy makers and military planners therefore face a daunting task which becomes even more complex because of the following:-

(a) It is man made domain unlike the other four domains.

(b) It is highly technical and a dynamically changing environment.

(c) It is to a large extent owned and operated by commercial entities.

(d) It is likely to have disastrous kinetic consequences ex SCADA.

National cyberspace policy must include the ability to defend critical networks outside the boundaries of their owned infrastructure. It is because though physical boundaries are defined, network boundaries are not. Hence, Proactive Cyber Defence would be the key planning consideration factor. This implies acting in anticipation to oppose the cyber-attack. It represents the dynamic between offensive and defensive action, interdict and disrupt an attack or preparation to attack, either pre-emptively or in self-defence. Effective cyber defence should prevent from an attack taking place. This would require real time situational awareness. Any other approach would simply be reactive.

Cyberspace is a vast, complex and rapidly changing battle space. The key to prevailing in a hostile cyber-space environment may lie in the ability to generate a comprehensive picture of that environment. In the kinetic realm, the fog of war is a term derived from Clausewitz referring to uncertain knowledge about the adversary, and the position and activities of the own forces in the midst of an operation. While situational awareness is a major challenge already in traditional warfare, the fog of cyber war may well be so thick that it could become the primary impediment to victory. Thus, developing the techniques and tools for cyber situational awareness would be paramount to achieving strategic, operational, or tactical advantage in this novel domain.

A fundamental obstacle in the cyber domain is the difficulty of determining the own defensive posture in the continuous process of safeguarding computers and networks: the continuum of protect, detect, respond, and recover that helps organizations to anticipate dangers, neutralize, limit the impact of those dangers, and react quickly and effectively in the event of an attack. Two aspects make situational awareness difficult in cyberspace: its vast complexity and its incredible rate of change. Traditional manual techniques for gaining situational awareness of the own defensive posture are quickly over-whelmed by these effects. The complexity of cyberspace stems from several factors. One is that today's ICT systems, based on distributed computing concepts, are so intricate. Functionality is spread across a multitude of computer systems that are tied together in global networks. Every element in these architectures must be assessed, monitored, and protected: applications, databases, webservers, host computers, networking gear, etc. Even basic knowledge such as the number of ICT systems deployed and how they are connected can be a challenge for those attempting to achieve situational awareness in these networks.

Military ICT systems are mostly built to insure availability even if individual components fail. To achieve a high degree of availability, they have built-in redundancy, offering backup systems and failover network paths. While redundancy is important for availability, it also greatly enhances the complexity of security. A typical network offers many possible paths to connect a user to an application.

If any single path is available, the application is available. But vulnerabilities in any of these paths also enable security breaches. "While availability is a function of the strongest link in the chain, security is a function of the weakest."

In addition to the complexity of cyberspace, situational awareness is made very challenging because of constant and dynamic change. Even if the own position is accurately defined and assessed at a given time, the assessment can be quickly out of date because unrelenting change is an inherent characteristic of cyberspace. There are different aspects of change. One is in the ICT systems themselves, which are constantly deployed, decommissioned, integrated, and updated with new software and hardware. This sort of change is fundamental to the power of distributed computing. It enables great flexibility, rapid reaction time, and rapid innovation, all of which are essential to effective and efficient mission support. While steps can be taken to manage this change, there are limits to how much control can be imposed without compromising the advantages that cyberspace offers.

Cyber Defence Objectives. Following four aspects may be considered as objectives for cyber defence:-

(a) **Protected Environment.** This will ensure availability of own systems. Apart from protective measures, reducing the surface area for attack, segregation of critical networks and data may be beneficial.

(b) **Detection.** Detect attack at the earliest by so configuring the systems.

(c) **Reporting.** It implies truthful and immediate reporting of incident and restoration of system.

(d) **Response.** This implies responding to the attack in appropriate manner.

Cyber Denial or Deterrence

Deterrence is a fundamental element of defensive strategy. Threat of retaliation, is an effective tool of defence for achieving deterrence.

Deterrence is a fundamental element of defensive strategy. However, for deterrence to be effective, potential adversaries must be convinced that they will be identified, and punished swiftly and severely. Nuclear deterrence is a case in point where this policy has succeeded. However, for this policy to succeed the attacker has to be identified. This poses the real challenge in case of cyber warfare.

The need for timely and unequivocal identification of attackers is essential for deterrence to be effective. Unfortunately, the technical basis for such identification has not received much attention of nations and the research and development community. Intrusion detection and monitoring systems will require to provide monitoring in real time and trace the trail back to the attacker will irrevocable evidence. Further, the antivirus software available today is useful at thwarting cyber-attacks for stand-alone computers. However, they are inadequate for defending a network of thousands of computers from attacks orchestrated by groups of expert programmers as well as solitary hackers.

Cyber denial would require preventive systems to be put in place. Here the comparison between cyber offense and defence becomes interesting for two reasons. First, defensive measures are very expensive and second they require less coordination than offensive measures. While basic defensive tools have been put in place by states they cannot withstand the attacks by nations or organized groups. While militaries require more stringent protection mechanisms civil organizations will require them at a lower scale depending upon their criticality. It is imperative that nations invest in evolving tools for denial so that prevent the attacks from happening in the first place.

One of the suggested concepts for cyber defence is "Cyberspace hot pursuit" which implies having the capability to trace the incident back to the attacker. This capability requires laws which authorize agencies to conduct cyberspace pursuits and since these pursuits will invariably take the trace out the nation, necessary agreements with foreign countries will have to put in place. Other concept is for the development of a tamper-proof, aircraft-like "black box" recording device to ensure that when an incident occurs and is not detected in real time, the trail back to the perpetrator does not become lost. Detailed discussion on cyber denial or Deterrence is out the scope of the present paper and we shall limit to what has been discussed above.

Defensive Measures

Internet today is a major medium for information exchange and has therefore become the major source of concern. Today the world has graduated from the thrill seeking or sole hacker to a group of qualified professionals who define attack strategies with specific results. Protection against cyber warfare therefore implies being aware about happenings in cyberspace and continually be a step ahead to stand the attacks. The defensive approach must encapsulate the following considerations:-

(a) **Active Cyber Security.** Protective measures like firewall and antivirus are not enough. It is not to say they are not relevant but it is to emphasize that they are not adequate in themselves to protect the systems. Similarly the concept of air gap between the networks which are physically isolated is no guarantee to safeguard the network. A simple UBB drive is enough to bring down the network. Hence there is the requirement for moving from passive defence to active cyber security. This implies detecting the threat before it enters the network.

(b) **Coordination between State and Industry.** While the state lays down the policy and spell out the qualitative requirement of protection systems, it would be the industry which will develop them. This would continuous interaction over prolonged periods, unlike in other systems, to continuously upgrade them to new evolving and anticipated threats.

There are three classes of systems for defensive posture management, which can be classified by when they operate in relation to an attack: after, during, and before. Forensic systems help organizations investigate attacks after they have occurred to understand both their impact and their root causes. The core of these solutions is historical logs that record activity on each aspect of the infrastructure, from software to network devices. These logs can be analyzed manually to determine the sequence of events that have led to an intrusion or disruption. But the volume and complexity of this data is enormous. Thus, organizations now implement log management systems that collect, store, and analyze that data automatically. These systems correlate information from multiple systems to identify patterns, and put together a timeline of the incident. Using this information, the armed forces can remediate the problems that enabled the breach, and identify, evaluate, and address the damage done.[7]

The next better class of situational awareness systems helps the forces to detect and respond to an attack in progress. Such systems rely on sensors and intrusion detection systems deployed throughout the infra-structure to identify suspicious behaviour, deviation from normalcy, and to raise alarms. An alarm can be analyzed manually, but an intrusion may raise too many such alarms as it moves through the infra-structure. And sorting out a true attack from the normal background noise of false alarms is an extremely complex endeavour. To address this, systems for security information and event management can be deployed which collect events, analyze them on an infrastructure-wide basis, and identify where an exploit is occurring at that point in time. With information thus gained, incident response teams can take action to prevent the intrusion from progressing any further. [8]

The last and most important class of situational awareness systems is designed to operate before an attack begins, focusing on stopping attackers before they gain entry. Consequently, defences that block malicious software and unauthorized access are crucial. In addition, baseline configuration standards must be established and monitored to prevent deviation and noncompliance that can create vulnerabilities in the system. This requires systems which identify vulnerabilities, misconfigurations, and other risks in the infrastructure. Like forensic and event-based systems, these systems are equipped with components that assess individual

---

7 DCAF HORIZON 2015 WORKING PAPER No. 7 "On Cyber Warfare" by Fred Schreier.

8 Ibid.

devices such as vulnerability scanners. Scanners and similar tools identify vast numbers of potential device issues, most of which are effectively mitigated by the defence-in-depth architectures of security. Security posture management solutions can be deployed that analyze the configurations and vulnerabilities of the various devices and hosts throughout the infrastructure, correlate them together, and identify the system-wide security issues that exist in the infrastructure. Using this information, those responsible for security can then prioritize and address problems to remediate before they are exploited by adversaries.[9]

The aim of defensive cyber operations should be to ensure the following:-

(a) Confidentiality of information- disclosed to authorized personnel only.

(b) Availability of information to authorized personnel.

(c) Authentication before granting access.

Cyber war will see the information infrastructure of the nation as the target as the adversary will attempt to disrupt or deny it. In order to avoid this, nations will need to put in place defensive measures that deflect these attacks. Some of the measures are given below:-

(a) Encryption of data before it is sent.

(b) Network Security - It implies safety of network infrastructure and policies that control the network.

(c) System Security - It refers to security of individual systems from unauthorized access, theft etc.

(d) Intrusion Detection and Monitoring.

Deception in Cyber Defence. Like in conventional warfare, deception can be employed to confuse the attacker in cyber warfare. Honeypots are the best known example of defensive

9 Ibid.

deception in cyberspace. They are computer systems meant for collecting data about attacks on them and have no legitimate user other than the system administrator. The defender can also employ disinformation, deceptive delays and deceptive lies to confuse the attacker. Disinformation implies planting information deliberately for the attacker to discover. Deceptive delay is a useful tactic when a defender needs time to assemble a defence or await reinforcement. It implies gaining time by giving information to the attacker to read before he proceeds. Detailed discussion on cyber deception is out of the scope of present book.

Conclusion. Cyber-attack will come hard and fast at the victim nation and in all probability may cause threat to human life. Further, with the inability of present protection systems to trace the attacker it becomes vitally important to adopt measures that deny access to unauthorized users. Security awareness among personnel handling sensitive systems is equally important.

CHAPTER 7

CYBER DETERRENCE

Introduction

The advent of nuclear weapons disrupted the historical logic of war completely. Deterrence theory emerged after the United States and the Soviet Union created enough military firepower to destroy human civilization on our planet. From that point forward, according to the American military strategist Bernard Brodie (1946), the purpose of armies shifted from winning wars to preventing them.

Deterrence in foreign affairs, as Bernard Brodie (1959) wrote in his seminal work, is nothing new.[1] In the simplest sense, deterrence means using the threat of military action to compel an adversary to do something, or to prevent them from doing something, that another state desires. Deterrence theory gained increased prominence as a military strategy during the Cold War with regard to the use of nuclear weapons. And, it took on a unique connotation during this time as an inferior nuclear force, by virtue of its extreme destructive power, could deter a more powerful adversary -- provided that this force could be protected against destruction by a surprise attack. A credible nuclear deterrent, Brodie wrote, must be always at the ready, yet never used.

In Thomas Schelling's (1966) classic work on deterrence, the concept that military strategy can no longer be defined as the science of military victory is presented. Instead, it is argued that military strategy was now equally, if not more, the art of coercion, of intimidation and deterrence.[2]

---

1 Brodie, Bernard (1959), "The Anatomy of Deterrence" as found in Strategy in the Missile Age, Princeton, pp. 264–304

2 Schelling, T. C. (1966), The Diplomacy of Violence, New Haven: Yale University Press, pp. 1–34

Thomas Schelling goes on to explain the foundations of deterrence theory based on diplomacy. Diplomacy between states is defined as a form of bargaining that seeks outcomes for each state that though not ideal for either party, are better for both than other alternatives. In order for diplomacy to succeed, there must be some common interest, if only in the avoidance of mutual damage. Traditionally in military strategy, mutual pain and suffering are among the results of warfare; however they have also been incidental and not the primary purpose. In the development of military strategy however, Schelling (1966) argues the capacity to hurt another state is now used as a motivating factor for other states to avoid it and influence another state's behaviour. In order to be coercive or deter another state, violence has to be anticipated and avoidable by accommodation. It can therefore be summarised that the use of the power to hurt as bargaining power is the foundation of deterrence theory, and is most successful when it is held in reserve.

The concept of deterrence can be defined as the use of threats by one party to convince another party to refrain from initiating some course of action.[3] A threat serves as a deterrent to the extent that it convinces its target not to carry out the intended action because of the costs and losses that target would incur. In international security, a policy of deterrence generally refers to threats of military retaliation directed by the leaders of one state to the leaders of another in an attempt to prevent the other state from resorting to the threat of use of military force in pursuit of its foreign policy goals.

As outlined by Huth,[4] a policy of deterrence can fit into two broad categories:-

(a) Preventing an armed attack against a state's own territory (known as direct deterrence); or

(b) Preventing an armed attack against another state (known as extended deterrence).

3 Huth, P. K. (1999), "Deterrence and International Conflict: Empirical Findings and Theoretical Debate", Annual Review of Political Science **2**: pp. 25–48

4 Ibid.

Situations of direct deterrence often occur when there is a territorial dispute between neighbouring states in which major powers do not directly intervene. On the other hand, situations of extended deterrence often occur when a great power becomes involved. It is the latter than has generated the majority of interest in academic literature. Building on these two broad categories, Huth goes on to outline that deterrence policies may be implemented in response to a pressing short-term threat (known as immediate deterrence) or as strategy to prevent a military conflict or short term threat from arising (known as general deterrence).

A successful deterrence policy must be considered in not only military terms, but also in political terms. In military terms, deterrence success refers to preventing state leaders from issuing military threats and actions that escalate peacetime diplomatic and military cooperation into a crisis or militarized confrontation which threatens armed conflict and possibly war. The prevention of crises of wars however is not the only aim of deterrence. In addition, defending states must be able to resist the political and military demands of a potential attacking nation. If armed conflict is avoided at the price of diplomatic concessions to the maximum demands of the potential attacking nation under the threat of war, then it cannot be claimed that deterrence has succeeded.[5]

Rational Deterrence Theory[6]

The predominant approach to theorizing about deterrence has entailed the use of rational choice and game-theoretic models of decision making. Deterrence theorists have consistently argued that deterrence success is more likely if a defending state's deterrent threat is credible to an attacking state. Huth[7] outlines that a threat is considered credible if the defending state possesses both the military capabilities to inflict substantial costs on an attacking state in an armed conflict, and if the attacking state believes that the defending state is resolved to use its available military forces.

5 http://en.wikipedia.org/wiki/Deterrence_theory

6 Ibid.

7 Ibid

Huth goes on to explain the four key factors for consideration under rational deterrence theory:-

(a) The military balance.

(b) Signaling and bargaining power.

(c) Reputations for resolve.

(d) Interests at stake.

The Military Balance

Deterrence is often directed against state leaders who have specific territorial goals that they seek to attain either by seizing disputed territory in a limited military attack or by occupying disputed territory after the decisive defeat of the adversary's armed forces. In either case, the strategic orientation of potential attacking states is generally short term and driven by concerns about military cost and effectiveness. For successful deterrence, defending states need the military capacity to respond quickly and in strength to a range of contingencies. Where deterrence often fails is when either a defending state or an attacking state under or overestimate the others' ability to undertake a particular course of action.

Signaling and Bargaining Power

The central problem for a state that seeks to communicate a credible deterrent threat through diplomatic or military actions is that all defending states have an incentive to act as if they are determined to resist an attack, in the hope that the attacking state will back away from military conflict with a seemingly resolved adversary. If all defending states have such incentives, then potential attacking states may discount statements made by defending states along with any movement of military forces as merely bluffs. In this regards, rational deterrence theorists have argued that costly signals are required to communicate the credibility of a defending state's resolve. Costly signals are those actions and statements that clearly increase the risk of a military conflict and also increase the costs of backing down from a deterrent threat. States that are bluffing will be unwilling to cross a certain threshold of threat and military action for fear of committing themselves to an armed conflict.

Reputations for Resolve

There are three different arguments that have been developed in relation to the role of reputations in influencing deterrence outcomes. The first argument focuses on a defending state's past behaviour in international disputes and crises, which creates strong beliefs in a potential attacking state about the defending state's expected behaviour in future conflicts. The credibilities of a defending state's policies are arguably linked over time, and reputations for resolve have a powerful causal impact on an attacking state's decision whether to challenge either general or immediate deterrence. The second approach argues that reputations have a limited impact on deterrence outcomes because the credibility of deterrence is heavily determined by the specific configuration of military capabilities, interests at stake, and political constraints faced by a defending state in a given situation of attempted deterrence. The argument of this school of thought is that potential attacking states are not likely to draw strong inferences about a defending states resolve from prior conflicts because potential attacking states do not believe that a defending state's past behaviour is a reliable predictor of future behaviour. The third approach is a middle ground between the first two approaches. It argues that potential attacking states are likely to draw reputational inferences about resolve from the past behaviour of defending states only under certain conditions. The insight is the expectation that decision makers will use only certain types of information when drawing inferences about reputations, and an attacking state updates and revises its beliefs when the unanticipated behaviour of a defending state cannot be explained by case-specific variables.

Interests at Stake

Although costly signaling and bargaining power are more well established arguments in rational deterrence theory, the interests of defending states are not as well known, and attacking states may look beyond the short term bargaining tactics of a defending state and seek to determine what interests are at stake for the defending state that would justify the risks of a military conflict. The argument here is that defending states that have greater interests at stake in a dispute will be more resolved to use force and be more willing to endure military losses in order to secure those interests. Even less well established arguments are the specific interests that are more salient to state leaders such as military interests versus economic interests.

Furthermore, Huth[8] argues that both supporters and critics of rational deterrence theory agree that an unfavourable assessment of the domestic and international status quo by state leaders can undermine or severely test the success of deterrence. In a rational choice approach, if the expected utility of not using force is reduced by a declining status quo position, then deterrence failure is more likely, since the alternative option of using force becomes relatively more attractive.

Cyber War and Deterrence Theory

Nothing compares to the destructive power of a nuclear blast. But cyber-attacks loom on the horizon as a threat that is best understood as an extraordinary means to a wide variety of political and military ends, many of which can have serious national security ramifications. For example, computer hacking can be used to steal offensive weapons technology (including for weapons of mass destruction) or to render an adversary's defences inoperable during a conventional military attack. In that light, attempting proactively to deter cyber-attacks may become an essential part of national military strategies.

Cyber deterrence, like all other deterrence, succeeds when an adversary decides not to act aggressively. This decision follows two separate assessments: whether the costs of cyber aggression outweigh its benefits and whether the benefits of restraint in cyberspace outweigh its costs. These assessments are made partly rationally, partly irrationally. To be completely rational, the decision makers would need both perfect information about the scenario of potential conflict and the willingness to make a decision only on

8 Ibid.

the basis of its strategic implications. In real life, decision makers have incomplete information, which is rife with inaccuracies, and consider many factors (personal emotions and interests, domestic politics, etc.) when making decisions. Therefore, continual dialogue, in the form of a regular exchange of deterrent messages, is the first necessary condition to deter cyber aggression. During the Cold War, the United States and the Soviet Union famously created channels for crisis and noncrisis communications (for example, "the Hotline") to engender this exchange of deterrent messages.

Thus the efficacy of cyber deterrence relies on the ability to impose or raise costs and to deny or lower benefits related to cyber-attack in a state's decision-making calculus. Credible cyber deterrence is also dependent on a state's willingness to use these abilities and a potential aggressor's awareness that these abilities, and the will to use them, exist. The ability of a state to deter cyber-attacks is a subset of its overarching defence strategy comprised of all instruments of national power. Effective cyber deterrence in cyberspace will employ a comprehensive scheme of offensive and defensive cyber capabilities supported by a robust international legal framework.

Advances in technology are normally evolutionary, but they can be revolutionary- artillery reached over the front lines of battle; rockets and airplanes crossed national boundaries; today, cyber-attacks can target political leadership, military systems, and average citizens anywhere in the world, during peacetime or war, with the added benefit of attacker anonymity. Political and military strategists now use and abuse computers, databases, and the networks that connect them to achieve their objectives.

However, the real-world impact of cyber conflict is still difficult to appreciate, in part because there have been no wars between modern, cyber-capable militaries. But an examination of international affairs over the past two decades suggests that cyber battles of increasing consequence are easy to find. Since the earliest days of the World Wide Web, Chechen guerilla fighters, armed not only with rifles but with digital cameras and HTML, have demonstrated the power of Internet-enabled propaganda. In 2001, tensions between the United States and China spilled over into a non-state, "patriotic" hacker war, with uncertain consequences for national security leadership. In 2007, Syrian air defence was reportedly disabled by a cyber-attack moments before the Israeli air force demolished an alleged Syrian nuclear reactor. In 2009, the entire nation-state of Kyrgyzstan was knocked offline during a time of domestic political crisis, and Iranian voters, in "open war" with state security forces, used peer-to-peer social-networking websites to avoid government restrictions on dialogue with the outside world. Such a quick evolution in the use of cyber tools and tactics suggests that they will play a lead role in future international conflicts.[9]

Some experts feel that the "attribution problem" totally demolishes the rationale to think about cyber deterrence strategy. While this would be true in some cases thereby making deterrence and retaliation redundant. Researchers are already working in this direction; Japan is reportedly developing a "good virus" to resolve the problem.[10] In future there are likely to be cases, involving major powers such as US, China and others, in which adversaries

---

9 http://www.ccdcoe.org/articles/2010/Geers_Cyberpercent20Attackpercent20Deterrence. pdf

10 The Japanese Defence Ministry is developing a computer virus aimed at seeking and destroying cyber-attacks launched against the country.

The malware-fighting cyber weapon, which is being created by defence contractor Fujitsu for an estimated $2.3 million, has the ability to identify the source of a cyber-attack with a high level of accuracy, then replicate itself from computer to computer, cleaning up viruses across the network.

The cyber weapon, which has been in development since 2008, has been tested in a closed network environment and was developed for defence, but Japanese lawmakers must create new legislation allowing for its use because it would appear to violate current Japanese law.

News of the effort comes amid growing concern over cyber-attacks in Japan. Last year, Japan's parliament, Japanese defence contractor Mitsubishi Heavy and several of Japan's overseas diplomatic missions were targeted by hackers, according to local media.

Japan's development of a cyber-weapon is part of what some experts see as a growing cyber arms race. The Stuxnet computer virus, which damaged Iran's nuclear program in 2010, was one of at least five cyber weapons developed on a single platform, according to Russian computer security firm Kaspersky Lab. Security experts believe the United States and Israel were behind Stuxnet, though the two nations have not accepted responsibility. Source http://www.huffingtonpost.com/2012/01/04/fujitsu-cyberweapon-japan_n_1183462.html

will use the threat of cyber-attacks (or actual attacks) as a means to a larger political end or to exert coercive leverage on them. In these circumstances, the adversaries will be willing to make their identities known, or alternatively, their identities can be reliably inferred from the surrounding strategic circumstances. Deterrence mechanism can be applied to such "attributable"attackers.[11]

Richard L Kugler in his essay on "Deterrence of Cyber Attacks" included in the compilation, "Cyber Power and National Security", edited by Franklin D Kramer, Stuart H Starr and Larry Wentz, argues that major cyber-attacks should not be seen in isolation, but in the context of larger global security affairs. While some attacks may launched purely for the purpose of causing damage, other attacks could be launched by adversaries whose political and strategic agenda extends beyond cyber domain, in addition to allowing their identities to be determined, this larger context can set the stage for determining how multifaceted US efforts to deter them can be forged. Second, endeavouring to deter cyber-attacks is a matter both of assembling the physical capabilities for defending against them and of employing offensive capabilities-cyber, diplomatic, economic, and military tools- for inflicting unacceptable damage in retaliation. Equally important, cyber deterrence also involves a psychological and cognitive component like other forms of deterrence, it requires the capacity to influence the motives, cost-benefit calculations, and risk taking propensities of adversaries, in order to convince them that launching a cyber-attack would not serve their interest and objectives and that the costs and risks would outweigh any sensible calculation of benefits.

Deterrence in general comes in many forms. Some forms are singular, while others have to be repeated. Some are asymmetric and some are symmetric (among peers).[12]

Nuclear deterrence is singular and symmetric. It is singular in that the point is to make the prospect so frightening that no one dares invoke it. If nuclear retaliation ensues, by the time retaliation

11 Cyber Power and National Security edited by Franklin D Kramer, Stuart H Starr and Larry Wentz,pp.310

12 Cyber Deterrence and Cyber War by Martin C. Libicki, RAND Corporation,2009

and counter-retaliation has run its course, the (literal) landscape and hence the strategic circumstances underlying the deterrence are likely to have become quite different. One or both parties may have been eliminated, lost their freedom of action, or been rendered powerless. The nature of deterrence the second time will also be different. The same largely holds true for heavy conventional deterrence: If retaliation is invoked, it too is likely to run its course and lead to a major war, which one or another regime also may not survive.[13]

Criminal deterrence is repeatable and asymmetric. It has to be repeatable because many first-time offenders become second-time offenders. The prospect of counter-retaliation from criminals, meanwhile, is not a serious problem in the developed countries in general. Police and other officials of the justice system are rarely at personal risk, thanks in large part to the legitimacy they are accorded and their latent ability to mass force and the force of law against criminals. Communities in which this is not the case (e.g., drug-infested states in the rest of the Americas, formerly insurgent dominated precincts in Iraq) are clearly troubled. There, criminal justice has been rendered ineffective, and the rule of the jungle prevails.[14]

Cyber deterrence has to be repeatable because no feasible act of cyber-retaliation is likely to eliminate the offending state, lead to the government's overthrow, or even disarm the state. Thus, a state could attack, suffer retaliation, and live to attack another day. But cyber deterrence is also symmetric because it takes place among peers. The target state (the potential retaliator) does not, a priori, occupy a higher moral ground than the attacker. There is also no reason to believe that the target can win any confrontation with the attacker if things go too far. Thus, the retaliator always has to worry about counter-retaliation (as it does in nuclear conflict) and cannot help but shape its deterrence policy with that in mind.[15]

Cyber deterrence is not unique in being repeatable and

13 Ibid.

14 Ibid.

15 Ibid.

symmetric. Such deterrence typically characterizes interactions among quarreling states (or quarreling tribes for that matter), each on guard against depredations from the other side and each willing to defend itself against small slights. Deterrence in such situations does not necessarily keep the peace; in an anarchic system, violence is endemic. Fights, in retrospect, often look like they have no larger issues than themselves.[16]

Role of Cyber- power

Cyber-power contributes significantly to the strength of a nation in global politics. As countries, earlier impoverished acquire greater economic strength, owing partly to cyber-power, they will acquire greater diplomatic and political influence, allowing them to pursue more assertive strategic agendas in their regions and beyond. Expertise of modern networks will also enable them to acquire greater military strength by equipping their forces with tools for modern doctrine and operations, even without the expensive ground, air and naval platforms used by advanced nations. These nations, thus with their enhanced strategic clout, will get motivated to seek greater influence in pursuit of their national interests.[17]

Some countries might also pursue cyber-power as an instrument of state policy to intimidate and coerce its neighbours and adversaries. As a strategic tool, cyber-power is both, attractive and advantageous as it can be acquired cheaply and can be used in concert with other traditional tools of kinetic warfare or alone. This explains why over 105 countries are engaged in seriously developing the cyber- power capability and interestingly all these countries are not necessarily rich, advanced or have the traditional military might. Since cyber-power can provide nations with potential leverage that would far exceed their traditional strength, the future may see a fast proliferation of cyber predators.

The notion that lack of attribution renders deterrence redundant is misplaced. Most of the attacks are not likely to be

16 Ibid.

17 Cyber Power and National Security edited by Franklin D Kramer, Stuart H Starr and Larry Wentz,pp.316

conducted in a political vacuum. In fact, they will be conducted with an explicit political or strategic goal as a means to an end rather than to exert pressure, intimidation, and coercion on an adversary to induce it to acquiesce in the larger agenda being pursued by the attacker. Such attacker would not like to conceal identity as it render the effort redundant thereby diluting the prospect of an acquiescent response. On the flip side one can say that by revealing the identity, the attacking nation exposes itself to the targeted nations deterrent mechanism and retaliatory steps.

Cyber Deterrence

Military leaders have begun to look beyond reactive, tactical cyber defence to the formulation of a proactive, strategic cyber defence policy, which may include international military deterrence. However, two challenging aspects of cyber-attacks – attribution and asymmetry – will be difficult to overcome. In theory, nations have two primary deterrence strategies:-

(a) Denial.

(b) Punishment.

Both strategies have three basic requirements:-

(a) Capability.

(b) Communication.

(c) Credibility.

Cyber Attack Deterrence by Denial

Deterrence by denial is a strategy in which an adversary is physically prevented from acquiring a threatening technology. This is the preferred option in the nuclear sphere, because there is no practical defence against a nuclear explosion; its heat alone is comparable to the interior of the sun, and its blast can demolish reinforced concrete buildings kilometers away. The abhorrent nature of nuclear warfare makes even a theoretical victory difficult to imagine. Deterrence by denial is a philosophy embodied in the Non-Proliferation Treaty (NPT).

Denial: Capability

Despite the diplomatic efforts of NPT, the well-funded inspection regime of the International Atomic Energy Agency (IAEA), and unilateral military operations such as Israel's destruction of nuclear facilities in Iraq in 1981 and in Syria in 2007, the size of the world's nuclear club is growing. In addition to the five permanent members of the United Nations Security Council, de facto members now include India, Israel, Pakistan, and North Korea.

Cyber-attack tools and techniques are not nearly as dangerous as their nuclear counterparts, but they are by comparison simple to acquire, deploy, and hide. More sensitive hacker information can be kept secret, physically transported on a miniscule hard drive, or sent encrypted across the Internet. A nuclear weapons program is difficult to hide; a cyber-weapons program is not. Cyber-attacks can be tested discretely in a laboratory environment or live on the Internet, anonymously. Further, it appears increasingly common to outsource the illegal business of hacking to a commercial or criminal third party.

A major challenge to cyber-attack tool anti-proliferation is how to define malicious code. A legitimate path for remote system administration can also be used by a masquerading hacker to steal national secrets. Even published operating system and application code is difficult for experts to understand thoroughly, as there are simply too many lines of code to analyze. The dynamic and fast-evolving nature of cyber-attack technology contrasts sharply with the fundamental design of nuclear war-heads, which, with the exception of the neutron bomb, has not changed much since the late 1950s.

Finally, in nuclear warfare, one of the most important considerations is the retention of a second-strike capability. Following a surprise attack, is it still possible for the victim to fight back? In nuclear and conventional warfare, this is a constant worry among strategic planners. A unique characteristic of cyber-attacks is their ability to be launched from anywhere in the world, at any time. During the cyber-attacks on Estonia in 2007, most of the compromised and attacking computers were located in the United States.

Cyber-attacks can be set to launch under predetermined conditions or on a certain date in the future. Discovered attack tools can also be difficult to remove from a computer net-work completely, even by forensic experts. With cyber-attack technology, it seems impossible to know for sure that all adversary attack options have been eliminated.

Both denial and penalty measures feed into an adversary's calculation of whether or not the costs of cyber aggression outweigh the benefits. By taking cyber-attack targets offline, by making them impenetrably secure, or by making attacks impossibly futile, denial measures diminish the benefits of a possible cyber-attack. Denial, however, is not in itself sufficient to deter aggression in cyberspace. Adversaries must also face some threat of penalty—which raises the costs of cyber-attack—for deterrent messages to take effect. If adversaries do not face penalties, they will continue to mount unsuccessful cyber-attacks until they find an effective approach. While denial admittedly cannot stand alone, strong denial measures coupled with a reasonable expectation of penalty will go a long way toward deterring cyber aggression.

In addition to strong denial measures, classical deterrence theory demands that penalty measures be certain, severe, and immediate; however, cyber deterrence emphasizes certainty more so than severity or immediacy. Because of the dire consequences involved, nuclear deterrence necessitated that mutually deterring states be able to quickly and overwhelmingly counterattack. But cyber-attacks typically involve less-serious consequences, less-identifiable attackers, and a wider variety of tools for counterattack. With less-serious consequences, counterattacks do not need to involve overwhelmingly severe (and disproportionate) retaliation. Neither does the counterattack need to come immediately, for unlike a surprise nuclear first strike, few, if any, cyber-attacks can render a victim state completely impotent to respond. For these reasons, neither severity nor immediacy is ultimately necessary for cyber deterrence penalty measures—only certainty.

Denial: Communication

Cyber-attacks now have the attention of the world's national security planners. However, cyber warfare is a new phenomenon; national and international norms have yet to be established. Different approaches are under consideration. One is to broaden international law enforcement coordination. Objections to this strategy include the possible infringement of national sovereignty by foreign law enforcement agencies. Another approach is to prohibit the development of cyber weapons via international treaty, such as that negotiated for chemical weapons. Articles to such a treaty might ban supply chain attacks, the disruption of non-combatant networks, and increase international management of the Internet. One objection to the second approach is that it does little to improve cyber attack attribution.

Denial: Credibility

Deterrence theory states that capability and communication alone are insufficient. The threatened party must believe that the threat of retaliation, or of a preemptive strike, is real. This third requirement of deterrence is the most difficult for national security leadership to assess, because it involves evaluating human psychology, rationality, the odds of miscalculation, and foreign political-military affairs.

It is still not likely that nation-states will sacrifice much to prevent the proliferation of cyber-attack tools and techniques. Although it is indisputable that cyber-attacks cause enormous financial damage, that world leaders increasingly complain of cyber espionage, and that Internet-connected critical infrastructures are now at risk, deterrence theory was created for nuclear weapons. In terms of their destructive power, nukes are in a class by themselves. Cyber-attacks per se do not cause explosions, deadly heat, radiation, an electro-magnetic pulse (EMP), or human casual-ties.

A future cyber-attack, by causing any of the above effects, could change this perception. Worldwide technological convergence is constantly expanding what hackers call the "attack surface." In theory, the successful conquest of an adversary's Internet space could equate to assuming command and control of the adversary's military forces, and firing their own weapons against their own cities.

Cyber Attack Deterrence by Punishment

The aim of deterrence is to create disincentives for starting or carrying out further hostile action. The target threatens to punish bad behaviour but implicitly promises to withhold punishment if there are no bad acts or at least none that meet some threshold. At a minimum, it requires the ability to distinguish good behaviour from bad. False positives and false negatives are both bad for such a policy, but the former is worse. Undeserved punishment lacks legitimacy: If the presumed attacker is innocent, the retaliator may have made a new enemy. Even if the presumed attacker deserved punishment for other bad behaviour, its incentive to behave well may be attenuated: If punishment follows both innocence and crime, why avoid crime? Failure to punish the guilty weakens deterrence but does not necessarily eliminate it; much depends on the likelihood and consequences of getting caught. People are inhibited from committing crimes even though the odds of getting caught are less than 100 percent—if they figure that the consequences of getting caught greatly exceed the criminal gains. To some extent, if the odds of getting caught are low, the potential retaliator can keep the expected cost of being caught constant by keeping punishment high. This is true, however, only if punishment is within reason: Rare severe punishments tend to be perceived as disproportionate and hence less legitimate. If one is operating within a peer-level system, outsized response may be interpreted as aggressive acts of escalation.[18]

Deterrence also requires the adversary to be able to distinguish being punished from not being punished. In most realms this is not a problem—not so in cyberspace. Both the retaliator and the attacker be unable to predict the effect of retaliation, neither may be entirely certain of what effect retaliation did have. If the potential retaliator doubts whether its planned retaliation will have

18 Cyber Deterrence and Cyber War by Martin C. Libicki, RAND Corporation,2009

the desired effect, it may be better off pretending that no attack occurred (quite possible in some cases) than making a big deal of the attack, revving up the retaliation machine, and having little or nothing to show for it.[19]

Deterrence by punishment is a strategy of last resort. It signifies that deterrence by denial was not possible or has failed, and that Country X possesses the technology it needs to threaten Country Y or its government. The goal of deterrence by punishment is to prevent aggression by threatening greater aggression, in the form of painful and perhaps fatal retaliation. For the strategy to work, Country X must be convinced that victory is not possible, even given the option of using its new technology.

Two key aspects of cyber-attacks present challenges to national security planners who would seek to deter them by punishment:-

(a) Attribution.

(b) Asymmetry.

The first challenge undermines a state's capability to respond to a cyber-attack, and the second undermines its credibility.

Punishment: Capability

All nations with robust military, law enforcement, and/or diplomatic might theoretically have the power to punish a cyber-attacker in some way, either in cyberspace or in the real world. And if a known attacker is beyond the reach of physical pursuit, the victim could at least present incriminating evidence in an international forum. But in practice, for punishment to be a viable option, the victim must know for sure who the attacker is, and be able to prove it.

In cyber warfare, the attacker enjoys a formidable advantage: anonymity. Proof in cyberspace is hard to come by. Smart hackers hide within the maze-like architecture of the Internet. They route attacks through countries with which the target's government has poor diplomatic relations or no law enforcement cooperation, and exploit unwitting, third-party networks. Cyber investigations

19 Ibid.

typically end at a hacked, abandoned computer, where the trail goes cold. Plausible deniability is also a concern. Because hackers obscure the true origin of an attack by hopping through a series of compromised computers to reach their target, the real attacker could always claim that her computer had merely been hacked and used in someone else's operation. This aspect of cyber-attacks also makes "false flagging," or intentionally trying to pin the blame on a third party, an attractive option.

Even in the event that cyber-attack attribution is positively determined, deterrence by punishment is still inherently less credible than deterrence by denial. It requires decision-makers to make more difficult choices. A proactive law enforcement strategy is easier to justify than the use of military force, which can cause physical destruction, human casualties, or other collateral damage. At the very least, there will be serious diplomatic consequences.

One important decision facing decision-makers in the aftermath of a cyber-attack would be whether to retaliate in kind or to employ more conventional weapons. It may seem logical to keep the conflict within cyberspace, but a cyber-only response does not guarantee proportionality, and a cyber-counterattack may lack the required precision. A misfire in cyberspace might adversely affect critical national infrastructure such as a hospital, which could result in a violation of the Geneva Convention and even bring war crimes charges against national authorities. The Law of Armed Conflict states that the means and methods of warfare are not unlimited: commanders may use "only that degree and kind of force ... required in order to achieve the legitimate purpose of the conflict ... with the minimum expenditure of life and resources.

Punishment: Communication

Whereas deterrence by denial relies on a criminal law framework for support, the foundation of deterrence by punishment lies in military doctrine. When bombs begin to fall on adversary targets, diplomatic and law enforcement options have normally run their course. Military doctrine serves at least two important purposes: to prepare a nation's military forces for conflict and to warn potential foes of the consequences of war.

It should not be surprising that the advent of an open and ubiquitous communications medium like the Internet demands a reassessment of military strategy, tactics, and doctrine. In 2006, a secret Israeli government report argued for a "sea change" in military thinking: the national security paradigm of army versus army was under assault by suicide bombers, Katyusha rockets and computer hackers, none of whom has to have direct ties to government or even be susceptible to political pressure. In China, the potential impact of computer network operations on the nature of warfare is thought to be strong enough even to have transformed 2,500 years of military wisdom; the Chinese military has almost certainly quit the defensive depth of the Chinese countryside to conquer international cyberspace.

Cyber doctrine must address how military and civilian authorities will collaborate to protect private sector critical information infrastructure. Even cyber-attacks that strike purely military sites are likely to traverse civilian networks before reaching their target. In fact, the destruction of civilian infrastructure may be the cyber attacker's only goal. A further challenge is that private sector enterprises such as banks have been reluctant to disclose successful cyber-attacks against them for fear of an impact on their bottom line. This dynamic could make it difficult for national security leadership even to know that an attack on its national territory – in violation of its national sovereignty – has occurred. Thus, proactive cyber-attack deterrence by government to defend civilian infrastructure will be difficult to achieve, and any national response may be too little, too late.

The dynamic nature of cyber-attacks could ensure that defenders never see the same attack twice. Therefore, decision makers will need a range of diplomatic and military options to consider for a punitive response. In terms of military doctrine, one possibility might be the delineation of red lines in cyberspace. Propaganda and low-level computer network exploitation (CNE) may trigger the first line of passive cyber defence, while the manipulation of code in an operational weapons system could be grounds for real-world retaliation. Finally, to support a deterrence strategy, cyber doctrine must be clearly written. An adversary should have no doubt what the consequences will be if the red lines are crossed.

Punishment: Credibility

As we have seen, the credibility of cyber-attack deterrence by denial is low. The political will and even the capability to attempt such a denial are lacking. Therefore, a strategy of cyber-attack deterrence by punishment is a more likely scenario.

The trouble with a punishment strategy, however, is that governments are always reluctant to authorize the use of military force. Deterrence by punishment is a simple strategy but one that demands a high burden of proof: a serious crime must have been committed, and the culprit positively identified. The challenge of cyber-attack attribution, described above, means that decision-makers will likely not have enough information on an adversary's cyber capabilities, intentions, and operations to respond in a timely fashion.

But there is another characteristic of cyber-attacks that undermines the credibility of deterrence by punishment even more: asymmetry. At the national level, some countries are more dependent upon the Internet than others. Some governments possess sophisticated computer network attack programs while others have none at all. Non-state actors such as a lone hacker or a terrorist group may not possess any computer network or other identifiable infrastructure against which to retaliate. The asymmetric nature of information technology and cyber warfare thus manifests itself in many ways.

Evolving Credible Cyber Deterrence: Indian Model

The efficacy of cyber deterrence policy practiced by any nation state to withstand sustained cyber-attacks by a determined adversary is yet to be successfully tested. The adversary could a nation state whose agenda would be governed by explicit motives, goals, cost benefit calculus, the risk of identification and consequent retaliation by the targeted nation and finally its own ability to withstand counter attacks. The same logic is applicable to non-state actors also who too are guided by their strategic goals and self- preservation besides their ideology. One can argue that cyber-attacks are not deterreable because the attacker enjoys impunity due to attribution problem but this situation is likely to change soon with the development of new deterrence mechanisms such as "good virus" explained earlier, and other related research in this field.

A worthwhile goal of cyber deterrence strategy would be to transform medium-sized attacks into low-probability events and to provide practically 100 percent deterrence of major attacks.[20] A forceful cyber deterrence strategy would, in effect, contribute immensely in boosting the instruments of national power simply because the targets are both civil and military. As a nation, for example, India should be forceful and explicit in stating its intentions to deter major cyber-attacks and respond to them decisively and, if required, respond with all instruments of power.

Indian government is finally looking at the above aspect seriously. Recent article in "The Times of India" said," India is set to take steps to protect its cyber infrastructure and designate agencies for carrying out offensive cyber-attacks on other countries. The move comes at a time when proof shows countries launching cyber-attacks — not only for intelligence gathering — and many nations describing the attacks as an act of war."[21]

---

20 Cyber Power and National Security edited by Franklin D Kramer, Stuart H Starr and Larry Wentz,pp.326

21 According to sources, the National Security Council NSC) headed by Prime Minister Manmohan Singh would soon approve the comprehensive plan and designate the Defence Intelligence Agency (DIA) and National Technical Research Organization (NTRO) as agencies for carrying out offensive cyber operations, if necessary. All other intelligence agencies would be authorized to carry out intelligence gathering abroad, but not offensive operations, sources said.

The detailed policy for national cyber infrastructure protection is presently before the NSC awaiting its approval. The policy would identify all government agencies that would have a role in the protection of Indian cyber infrastructure and define their roles.

The move to not just define defensive mechanism but also designate agencies for offensive operations comes as New Delhi tackles repeated waves of cyber intrusions, though all of them are aimed at gathering information from critical networks. But the next stage, of an adversary carrying out offensive cyber-attack, of bringing down a power grid, stalling air traffic control systems, or manipulating controls of a dam are

India is situated in a rather troubled and instable region. China is a belligerent neighbour, Pakistan –a declared adversary providing safe haven and support to terror groups inimical to India, Bangladesh- a vacillating neighbour whose attitude depends upon the government of the day, Nepal- an erstwhile reliable and friendly state which is slowly leaning towards China under the influence of Maoists who are calling the shots in the government, Sri Lanka- which recently quelled LTTE and was abused of human rights in UN in which India voted has a peaceful albeit uneasy relationship and Myanmar- its military junta has been kept engaged by India which has shown definite signs of leaning towards China. India is the only country in the world which is surrounded by two inimical nuclear capable countries. Further, terror groups directing their activities against India enjoy all weather support of Pakistan, China and to a lesser extent Bangladesh- the present regime has not allowed anti-India activities.

China has acquired fairly advanced cyber warfare capability and Pakistan is also following suit, as we have seen earlier. Dissuading adversaries or terror groups against launching cyber-attacks is not

---

now believed to be a real possibility.

Stuxnet, the cyber worm created by US's National Security Agency and Israeli military and specifically targeted at Iran's nuclear enrichment center at Natanz, was found to have infected Indian systems. "It was probably unintentional, but an intentional attack on India's critical infrastructure cannot be ruled out," says a senior official. "We haven't yet seen a cyber-attack, but only intelligence gathering. An attack that can debilitate our infrastructure is what we must be prepared for," he said.

CERT-IN (Computer Emergency Response Team India) would be responsible for protection of most of the cyber space, while NTRO would be tasked to protect the critical infrastructure such as important government networks. NTRO would be tasked to create the National Critical Information Infrastructure Protection Centre (NCIPC), which would be a command and-control centre for monitoring the critical infrastructure. It would be a round-the clock centre, providing real time response to cyber security breaches.

The proposal before NSC also envisages creation of sectoral CERTs in order to respond quickly to protect power distribution networks, Air Traffic Controls, traffic networks and other areas that heavily dependent on networked systems, and thus are susceptible to attacks.

The policy suggests that the defence forces would be responsible for their own networks' protection. NTRO and Intelligence Bureau (IB) would primarily be responsible for security of various government networks. While NTRO would operate through NCIPC, IB would be mainly looking at the physical security of networks. State polices, CBI, NIA etc. would be tasked to do follow up action, if any intrusions are detected.

Times of India 11 June 2012

going to be an easy task. To have that capability, India will have to invest heavily in building the technical expertise required. Successful deterrence will depend upon the capability of India to project its resolve, cyber capability in sufficient strength and most importantly its political will to convey to its adversaries that retribution is going to be swift, hard and very costly.

That the Indian cyber deterrence policy should primarily focus on influencing the adversary's decision making process in a decisive manner in order to deter it to launch cyber-attacks, there is no doubt. While this is true for external adversaries, it is the internal threat- terror groups, which have an external dimension as well, home grown insurgency- which may or may not have an external dimension and lastly the most potent of all- the Maoist insurgency. It is now a well known fact that the terror groups and Maoists have technically qualified people in their ranks and their intent to leverage cyber-attacks to cause damage or strike a bargain is a distinct possibility. While gathering kinetic weapons require immense resources in terms of money and sources, cyber provides them the alternative which is both low in money and sources.

How does India, as a nation state deter these elements? They have no strategic assets, unlike a nation state, which can be targeted. While deterrence by denial can be advocated, how do you punish those who resort to cyber-attacks. Attribution again will be the problem. Then how does the nation deal with these insurgents to deter them from inflicting cyber-damage? Does it imply that the law enforcement agencies should monitor internet traffic in real time or there is any other solution? Either way it is debatable and implementation is going to be tedious and heavy on resources.

Recent reports suggest Britain is introducing a bill on these lines. British authorities unveiled an ambitious plan to log details about every email, phone call or text message in the UK — and in a sharply-worded editorial the nation's top law enforcement official accused those worried about the surveillance programme of being either criminals or conspiracy theorists.[22]

22 Officials insist they're not after content. They promise not to read the body of emails or eavesdrop on phone calls without a warrant. But the surveillance proposed in the

Shri Rajeev Chandrasekhar, Member of Parliament wrote in Times of India, "An Assault on Freedom- India's proposal in the UN for government control of internet endangers free speech and privacy." He was commenting on the proposal by the HRD Ministry to pre-screen content on Google and facebook.[23]

---

government's 118-page draft bill would provide British authorities a remarkably rich picture of their citizens' day to-day lives.

Home office secretary Theresa May said in an editorial published ahead of the bill's unveiling that only evildoers should be frightened.

"Our proposals are sensible and limited," she wrote in The Sun. "They will give the police and some other agencies access to data about online communications to tackle crime, exactly as they do now with mobile phone calls and texts. Unless you are a criminal, then you've nothing to worry about."

Yet plenty of people were worried, including a senior lawmaker from May's ruling Conservative Party.

"This is a huge amount of information, very intrusive to collect on people," David Davis, one of the proposal's most outspoken critics, told BBC radio. "It's not content, but it's incredibly intrusive."

The bill would force communications providers to gather a wealth of information on their customers. Providers would log where emails, tweets, Skype calls and other messages were sent from, who they were sent to, and how large they were. Details of file transfers, phone calls, text messages and instant conversations would also be recorded.

The bill also demands that providers collect IP addresses, details of customers' electronic hardware, and subscriber information including names, addresses, and payment information.

Even physical communications would be monitored: Address details written on envelopes would be copied; parcel tracking information would be logged as well.

All the data would be kept for up to a year or longer if it was the subject of legal proceedings.

The measure remains a draft bill, which means it's subject to change before it is presented to Parliament.

The Times of India, Delhi, 15 June 2012.

23 If you were a tad worried about the government's intentions to censor free speech by controlling the internet and monitoring your access to the Web through a vague and draconian legal framework – 'IT Rules, 2011', followed by an attempt to pre-screen content on Google and Facebook – you haven't seen anything yet.

In mid-2011, the success of the internet and social media in bringing down dictatorships in Egypt and Libya was being celebrated. The speed at which anti-corruption protesters were collecting at various locations from June through December 2011 had dazzled citizens around the world. Against this background, and without any prior consultation or as much as a whisper in Parliament, the Indian government moved a proposal at the 66th session of the UN General Assembly on October 26, 2011, proposing a 50-member intergovernmental (read bureaucrats and politicians) UN Committee on Internet Related Policies (CIRP).

This body would control the internet, regulate it through treaties, and oversee all bodies responsible for the technical and operational functioning of the internet. CIRP is proposed to be funded by and reporting to the UN General Assembly. In short, all internet control to be placed in the hands of a 50-member body run, funded, owned and reporting to the governments of the world. In the process, India proposed to turn on its head the current multi-stakeholder internet governance process, which has brought 2.5 billion users to the Net thus far, with half a million new users joining each day.

The reason? It is argued that the current governance process is too close to the US government and within the jurisdiction of US law. While this system has served internet users' needs reasonably well thus far, it is certainly far from ideal. No one government should have excessive influence, but that should mean strengthening the multistakeholder governance process. Civil society, media, private sector, governments, international organisations, academics, engineers, and students should all play their rightful roles, rather than handing internet governance over to a bunch of governments – a large majority of which are imperfect or occasional democracies or downright authoritarian. Worried yet? Here is what else is wrong with India's proposal.

CIRP, with 50 governments in control, will undoubtedly have representations from governments such as China, Iran, Bahrain, Russia, Sudan, Uzbekistan, Cuba, and Kazakhstan – to name a few. Imagine writing a common treaty which will regulate the internet and govern censorship, including issues such as website blocking and access for Indian citizens based on what these countries consider 'appropriate'. In short, imagine negotiating definitions of free speech, freedom of expression and privacy – values that our Constitution guarantees as fundamental rights – with authoritarian states, some with a track record of enhanced internet censorship, Web blocking, and in extreme cases, death sentences for netizens and bloggers.

Secondly, internet governance is a highly complex issue – run through a multi-stakeholder model which derives significant benefits from equal access to decision-making. A top-down, centralised international governmental overlay is fundamentally against the very architecture of the internet. No government, let alone an intergovernmental body, can dream of making engineering and economic decisions in lightning-fast internet time. The proposal will be hurtful as engineering and business decisions relating to the growth of the internet become politically paralysed within a global regulatory body.

Research shows that India's effort as part of the government advisory council to the current internet governance process has been dismal. It is ill-represented and made no effort to strengthen and improve the existing process before an attempt to destroy it through a bazooka called the CIRP. The government is perhaps trying to piggyback on US-bashing and project itself as the saviour of global internet governance, never mind its abysmal policy failure in internet and broadband penetration.

In spite of cautions, the Indian government, during meetings in Geneva last month on the issue of internet governance, persisted with its proposal for intergovernmental control of the internet. This time, India's statement paraded India's proposal as advancing the mandate enshrined in the Tunis Agenda, 2005. A simple but careful reading of 'India's Statement proposing UN Committee for Internet Related Policy – UN, New York, October 2011' alongside 'Tunis Agenda for the Information Society – WSIS,

The author has raised some very pertinent issues which cannot be brushed aside and hence his suggestion that the government should "seek wide and transparent stakeholder consultations and then resubmit an enlightened plan which can safeguard the internet" needs serious consideration.

However, despite all the conflicting views, it is vitally important that under the pretext of debate and transparency the urgency to enact safeguards is not lost or else the price would be too heavy.

2005' will tell you that nothing could be further from the truth.

Every paragraph of the Tunis Agenda invoked in India's proposal rebels against India's claims. The agenda, finalised by over 19,000 participants representing the widest ever multi-stakeholder group, in all of its 122 paras does not even remotely suggest government oversight of the internet, leave alone the formation of a 50-member intergovernmental body.

Everyone who cares about the internet as a symbol of openness, democracy, diversity, inclusiveness, creativity and unhindered access to information and knowledge must engage and decide for himself. Any attempt to expand the government's power over the internet – however incremental, seemingly innocuous or pretending to advance democracy – should be turned back. The UN will decide on this crucial issue by November/December 2012 at meetings to be held in Dubai.

Before that, there is a need to urge the government to withdraw its proposal, seek wide and transparent stakeholder consultations and then resubmit an enlightened plan which can safeguard the internet – perhaps the one invention that has impacted our access to information, knowledge and free speech more than any other.

The Times of India, Delhi, 13 June 2012.

CHAPTER 8

LEADERSHIP IN CYBER DOMAIN

The military commander is the fate of the nation.

- Helmut Von Moltke (1800-1881)

Introduction

Leadership is a core competency of the officers, JCOs, and non-commissioned officers across the military services. A principle tenant of leadership is the professional competence in military operations. However, until recently, the defence of computer networks and the conduct of network warfare were treated as ancillary functions by the military services. The increasing cyber warfare threat against India and the recognition of cyberspace as the fifth domain of warfare by various nations, which includes India's adversaries, necessitates the study of the attributes of a successful cyber warfare leader and the leadership techniques required to successfully lead cyber warriors. While analyzing the principles of war and their application in cyber warfare it was found that while they are by and large relevant, additional principles may emerge with time as militaries acquire experience and knowledge in the cyber domain. Therefore, examination of traditional kinetic leadership principles may be taken as the starting point and analyse them to see where they fail and where new techniques may be adopted.

Leadership is not a one size fit endeavour. The capabilities and characteristics of the leader and the led, the missions proposed, combined with the impact of the operational environment, all merge to create a complex battlefield where leaders, who are flexible and capable, will adapt and succeed and less capable leaders will fail. The emergence of a new war fighting paradigm and the need to adapt is not unique to the cyber domain. Leaders are products of their development processes, which sometimes becomes out of date. A hypothetical argument would not be out of place. It is fairly common to find senior officers who flounder in the counterinsurgency domain because it is an entirely different warfare because these officers did not face this earlier in their careers. At the same time there are junior officers who, with experience in counterinsurgency warfare, excel in conducting counterinsurgency operations but have little experience with traditional kinetic warfare. These differences are to be expected. Leaders are the result of their experiences, training, education, and interaction with their colleagues. During the Charr-e-Sharif incident in 1995 in J&K, a DIG of BSF, who was from UP cadre, was totally surprised and at loss to understand how counterinsurgency operations were being carried out. He carried the concept of fighting insurgency as sending 3 to 4 policemen with a sub inspector, a legacy from his tenure of SP of Pilibhit, a district in Tarai region of UP. His tenure, thereafter, would have been a rich learning curve for him, depending upon his ability to adapt to the new challenges facing him.

Cyber Commander

Decision-making in a national security context carries significant responsibilities because lives and freedom of the nation are often at stake. Sun Tzu in "Art of War" lays emphasis on leadership.

> The Commander stands for the virtues of wisdom, sincerity, benevolence, courage and strictness.

What Sun Tzu refers to as wisdom is the professional competence in todays' environment. Good leaders not only exploit flawed adversaries but their flawed plans as well. Discipline and self-control are encouraged; emotion and personal desire are discouraged. Sun Tzu states that to avoid a superior adversary is not cowardice, but wisdom. Moreover, due to the painstaking nature of objective calculations, patience is a virtue.

Thus it is that in war the victorious strategist only seeks battle after the victory has been won, whereas he who is destined to defeat first fights and afterwards looks for victory.

Commanding a cyber-corps will require a healthy mix of these admirable qualities. As a battleground, cyberspace offers political and military leaders almost limitless possibilities for success – and failure. Behind its façade of global connectivity and influence, the Internet has a complicated and vulnerable architecture that is an ideal environment in which to conduct asymmetric and often anonymous military operations. Imagination and creativity are required skill sets. Cyber warfare also involves an enormous amount of uncertainty; even knowing whether one is under attack can be an immense challenge. And the high tempo of Internet operations may lead to a high burn-out rate throughout the ranks.

One can say that to lead cyber warriors requires a different type of leader, one who is comfortable in the inherently technical cyber domain, appreciates technical expertise, and understands the personality types, creativity, culture, motivations, and intellectual capability of cyber warriors. The present training curriculum of the military services, their employment structure, personnel evaluation, and awards systems are all focused on combat arms development for kinetic warfare and thus in their current form, are not designed to produce cyber warfare leaders.

A cyber commander must, therefore, have a minimum acceptable level of subject matter expertise in IT. The core concepts of computing, networking, and data security should be thoroughly understood before employing them in support of a national security agenda. The leader must be able to articulate the mission in a manner that everyone in the organization understands and believes in it. Another challenge in cyber warfare will be communicating with highly technical professionals, who have vastly different background, training, work ethos and personal needs than the soldiers of a traditional military element.

In all future wars, military leadership will have the challenge of coordinating and deconflicting the cyber and non-cyber elements of a battle plan. Sun Tzu gives high praise for a great tactician:-

> *Having collected an army and concentrated his forces, he must blend and harmonize the different elements thereof*

before pitching his camp. After that, comes tactical maneuvering, than which there is nothing more difficult. The difficulty of tactical maneuvering consists in turning the devious into the direct, and misfortune into gain.

As circumstances change throughout the course of a conflict, both tactics and strategy must be reevaluated and modified to fit the new environment.

He who can modify his tactics in relation to his opponent and thereby succeed in winning, may be called a heaven-born captain.

The dynamic nature of the Internet and the speed of computer network operations guarantee that traditional military challenges such as seizing the initiative and maintaining momentum will require faster decision making cycle than a traditional chain-of-command can manage. A cyber commander must have the ability and the trust of his or her superiors to act quickly, innovatively, and decisively.

Cyber warfare is an entirely different, non-kinetic problem set compared to traditional warfare. Consequently, qualified cyber leaders are rare and a mature, career long, tailored development process is non-existent. A different model for cyber warfare leaders is the need of the hour– one where the most innovative, most skilled in the cyber domain, and most effective technical problem solvers rise to the top. As discussed earlier, the underlying principles of leadership remain the same, but these principles must be adapted with the cyber warfare mission, environment, and warrior in mind. Some tried and true leadership practices may result in failure, and some principles, such as maintaining technical and tactical proficiency take on an entirely new meaning.

Differences Between Kinetic and Cyber Domains and Warriors

The difference in desirable leadership techniques and leader development stems from the people and skills required to conduct cyber warfare operations. These differences represent challenging requirements for change amidst a kinetic war fighting culture. Kinetic war fighting culture places the ability to endure physical hardship over intellectual capability.

There are both, similarities and dissimilarities between cyber warriors and kinetic warriors. The ideal cyber warrior will be required to possess high technical aptitude, be a creative problem solver, and have a hacker mindset which enjoys manipulating complex systems and using the technology in ways unintended by its designers. One of the drawbacks of hacking ethos is the temptation to conduct unethical or illegal activities, particularly as one's skills advance, which in cases may be of exploratory nature or to seek thrill rather than for material benefits. Therefore the most important key leadership challenge will be to ensure values of integrity, loyalty and duty are scrupulously practiced by the cyber warriors and the unit. Where a kinetic warrior may own a rifle or a pistol, a cyber-warrior may have his own malware analysis lab tucked away somewhere. Cyber warriors, by the nature of their training and job, are likely to be independent and would expect that their leaders are at least as bright and technically skilled. Their lifestyle is likely to revolve around updating their skills and looking for new malware. Contrast this with the physical prowess-centric kinetic warfare environment, where being the strongest in the tribe is often enough to earn the respect of the led. Hackers and cyber warriors have a RTFM (Read The Manual) culture, which expects individuals to make every effort to answer their own question before asking an expert. In the intellect-centric environment of cyber warriors, general leadership and management skills alone, without intelligence and technical competence, will not carry the day. Because of their independent streak and desire for intellectual peers (or betters) for leaders, building teams of cyber warriors is a non-trivial leadership challenge for the uninitiated. Different incentive structures may be necessary, for example pinning medal on the chest of a cyber warrior may not be valued as much as an opportunity for access to a new piece of technology or an advanced malware analysis course.

Principles of Leadership

The best leaders will adapt to the characteristics and needs of their people. The cyber warrior is different than the kinetic warrior. Examination of leadership principles, both old and new, would be appropriate to highlight these differences.

Know Yourself and Seek Self-improvement

Each leader must continually assess his strengths and weaknesses and seek self-improvement to augment future military training programs. Whereas mature professional development programs exist across the Army and other services for kinetic war fighting, cyber warfare training programs are just about emerging. At some point in the future cyber warriors will be able to lean heavily on service programs for career-long professional development. Even when these programs exist, the rapid rate of change in technology and cyber warfare tactics will necessitate that every leader maintain and extend their skills through civilian education, professional reading, guest speaker programs, research, writing, conferences/ seminars attendance etc. This implies that cyber leaders must be capable of teaching themselves unfamiliar technology. The full range of topics a cyber-warrior must understand is beyond the scope of a single article, but examples include: how a webserver works, how domain names are converted into IP addresses by the Domain Name System (DNS), the basics of a buffer overflow, and how passwords may be cracked through brute force techniques.

The urge to strive continuously and identify the gaps in knowledge and passionately pursuing professional development is a prerequisite in cyber warfare and as even the best of military training programs will provide only the basic necessary expertise. On the job experience, obtained through a series of cyber warfare assignments and self-study of emerging technologies, debates, and policies is a mandatory prerequisite for the successful cyber leader. Importantly, leaders must also know their units and facilitate subordinate's self-improvement. In kinetic world self-improvement is left to the individual. The self-improvement would imply providing opportunities for education and partnership with industry experiences, as well as opportunities to move around to other positions in the cyber warfare field. In short, leaders must seek out every opportunity to feed their subordinates knowledge. Cyber warriors would be hungry for knowledge and satiating this need will help grow more capable cyber warfare units, warriors, and leaders.

Be Technically Proficient

Technical competence is the fundamental requirement for a leader in cyberspace. It is impossible to plan and conduct cyber warfare if the leader does not understand the laws of physics as they apply to networks and automation. Adversaries may walk through walls, become invisible, move at the speed of light, change from male to female, alter history, teleport around the globe, or attack from a million locations at one time.

As an example, if an attacker were to take down a malicious webserver, complexity involved is enormous. The malicious webserver's domain name may be hosted in one country, the webserver itself could reside in another (perhaps friendly) country, and media embedded on each web page may be hosted in dozens of others locations around the globe. Even a single physical server may be an enigma for the uninitiated as the webserver may reside in a virtual machine alongside dozens of other legitimate sites, creating ample opportunity for unanticipated collateral damage. Even if a given physical server was destroyed, mirrored copies may instantly be brought online or backups of the site may be moved to another location halfway around the world in minutes.

Technical competence demands continued self-study, formal education, and professional development. Development of traditional battlefield weapons and tactics has taken decades, but significant developments in cyber warfare may occur overnight. Lack of technical literacy and an understanding of the cyber domain will produce ineffective, potentially dangerously incompetent, leaders who will not gain the respect of their personnel and who will fail in cyber war as technically adept adversaries run circles around them on the battlefield. Once technical literacy is gained, it must be maintained- at all costs. Standing still as a cyber-warfare leader will mean one is left behind, in months if not days, as current techniques, skills, and tools necessary for cyber warfare rapidly evolve.

Build a Team

Attention will have to be given to create a group of military personnel to a form an organization focused on network attack and defence. Individuals who are drawn to science and technology are, by nature, more introvert than a typical military leader, who is extrovert and exuberant. It is important that this group of largely inward looking individuals be forged into a team, but the leader must recognize that the group is not likely to interact like other teams. In other words, the team might be forged without the leader even recognizing it!

Some Army organizations forge strong teams though shared adversity, others through cooperative problem solving. The latter approach is probably more effective with a group of technologists. One must be careful, however, to ensure that the problem solving is cooperative and not a single individual trying to work through the problem on his or her own.

Leading in cyber warfare is also inherently about functioning in a team cyber environment – one that is joint, multinational and interagency. Leaders, need to develop a solid understanding of all these dynamics, but still need to understand fundamentals of joint operations to appreciate how to best integrate cyber capabilities of their team into full spectrum operations.

Employ the Team in Accordance with its Capabilities

A leader must recognize the capabilities and specific skillset of each of his subordinates and assign duties and responsibilities accordingly. In the cyber arena, perhaps more so than in other domains, leaders may often have to ignore traditional rank-based notions of who "leads" a team or organization. A jawan's skill set might make him more suited to lead a group of non-commissioned officers (NCO) than the senior NCO in a group assigned to accomplish a certain task. This is contrary to the kinetic environment – only in dire circumstances might a junior infantry squad member lead the group on an attack – but it might make perfect sense to cyber warriors whose culture is more of a group of peers with varied skills and experiences. Not only must the commander in the above example be able to assess and make such assignments, but the senior NCO must understand and be able to subordinate himself to his junior.

Other Leadership Imperatives

Apart from the application of core leadership principles to cyber leadership outlined above, there are other behaviours that may be considered to be crucial for success in this domain.

Use Physical Hardship-based Principle Sparingly

Success in some operations is determined by a leader's ability to endure sleep deprivation, eat one meal a day, and set the pace for five km runs. In the highly physical world of kinetic operations these techniques prove successful; however they should be used sparingly when dealing with cyber warriors. It is not that cyber warriors should not be fit in order to accomplish their jobs; it is that cyber warriors put a far greater emphasis on intellectual and technical prowess than physical aptitude. Unnecessary field training exercises for the cyber troops, while they may have succeeded in the past, may often prove counterproductive in building a cohesive cyber warfare unit.

Communicate Technical Issues Effectively to Non-Technical Personnel

An important quality of a cyber-leader would be his ability to communicate technical details to non-technical personnel, and vice versa. In particular, a cyber-leader must be capable of translating war fighting requirements to technologists for mission execution as well as to communicate technical capabilities and shortcomings back to war fighting organizations. However, as a leader moves up in rank and responsibility, the diversity of audiences' increases greatly. For example, it would not be uncommon for a mid-career cyber leader to communicate with tactical military forces, high-level Joint military commands, special operations units, legal professionals, hackers, academics, and computer security business leaders as well as representatives of government agencies.

Understand Cyber War Policy and Effects

Cyber warfare has profound policy implications. A mistyped keystroke could result in an attack against an entirely different country or a malicious file may propagate far beyond desired targets to non-combatants. Senior kinetic war fighting leaders will look to their cyber warriors to explain the range of authorized actions and their associated risk-benefit trade offs. The Law of Land Warfare, the Geneva Convention, and theatre rules of engagement are quite static and mature compared to the rapid change in policy surrounding cyber war. Rapid change does not negate the requirement for cyber leaders to understand current policy, it necessitates it.

Must be Operationally Involved

Mandating operational involvement for a leader may sound counterintuitive to traditional kinetic leaders, but it is possible for cyber warfare leaders to be disconnected from operational activities of those they command, not due to a one-off personal failure of an individual, but as a matter of organizational design. For example, under current structures, a company commander may have very little to do with the operational activities of his or her company. Given the evolving nature of cyber warfare units and their close intelligence community partnerships, a leader's personnel may be assigned across a large headquarters where they work for another, operational chain of command. This may change, as new cyber war fighting units are created, but currently the commander of such a unit risks becoming merely an out of touch administrative functionary isolated from the core functions of their command. In cases where operational involvement for a leader is not built into the organizational structure it is critically important to find innovate ways to stay connected.

Create a Culture of Innovation that Allows Tackling Hard Problems

Cyber warfare presents challenges that cannot be solved in a matter of days. This not unique to the cyber domain, nation building, countering improvised explosive devices, and defeating insurgencies all require long-term efforts to develop solutions. Traditionally, the individuals working on these solutions are mid-career or more senior officers. In cyber warfare the full spectrum of OR, JCOs and officer talent must be tapped to generate appropriate tactics, strategies, policy, and technology. Cyber warriors of any rank will be bright and capable of solving hard problems, but they require a creative work environment and culture of innovation that allows ideas to be heard regardless of rank. This notion runs counter to traditional military culture where the senior leader issues a directive and the unit complies. Note that research and creativity is untidy, and will sometimes lead to dead ends, but allowing your subordinates to tackle hard problems will generate surprising successes. Of course it is necessary to impose limits, lest creativity cross ethical, legal, or other boundaries, but commanders should allow space for exploration. In other words, a leader should give subordinates the desired goal, lots of latitude, and stand back. Leaders must constantly encourage initiative, power down to the lowest level, stimulate new ideas, and actively seek out people who are change agents and empower them, regardless of rank or place in organizational structure. To facilitate initiative, leaders must allow subordinates to try new things and allow them to fail, underwrite honest mistakes, and trust their subordinates. For the talented cyber warrior the ability to self-select and pursue interesting problems is a highly desirable attribute of their work environment. Creating such an environment will improve morale, increase retention, and generate solutions to pressing cyber warfare problems.

Value for the Kinetic Warfighter

Cyber warfare does not exist in a vacuum, nor does it exist at just the strategic level. For success, cyber warriors must add value to the larger Army, Navy, Air Force, and other state institutions that they support through tangible and timely contributions, or else risk becoming marginalized and irrelevant. The key to such support are the right people, with the right expertise actively seeking to add value for kinetic warfighters. Cyber warfare leaders must avoid thinking that cyber capabilities are an end unto themselves or to look with disdain on traditional kinetic personnel and missions. Adding value to the kinetic warfighter will facilitate acceptance of cyber personnel as "operators," warriors and comrades in arms.

Conclusion

The core principles of leadership remain the same, but the cyber warfare leader must adapt to the needs of the inherently different missions, personnel, weapons, and environment of cyber war. Leaders must be adept lifetime learners who maintain currency with advancing technology, threats, policy, and tactics, and inspire the same in their subordinates. The leader must create an environment which facilitates innovation and initiative by allowing creativity, underwriting honest mistakes, providing goal-oriented objectives, and boundaries upon proper behaviour. Cyber warriors have immense potential, but it is up to the qualified and prepared cyber leader to unleash this potential, and effectively execute cyber warfare missions.

CHAPTER 9

IMPACT OF ICT ON INDIAN SOCIETY

Overview

India today has the world's second largest population of mobile users with over 903 million as of January 2012.[1] It has the world's third largest internet users with over 121 million as of December 2011.[2] With its telecommunication infrastructure, by and large, as advanced and sophisticated as those in West, the foundation for rapid development has been truly laid. India is now poised to become the world's most competitive and fastest growing telecom markets. This growth story is likely to have a significant effect in shaping the lives of ever increasing Indian populace. In order to examine the impact of internet on Indian society a brief discussion on the growth Indian Telecom infrastructure would be appropriate.

Growth of Telecom Infrastructure in India

The growth of telecommunication infrastructure in India has been painfully slow. However, post liberalization the growth has picked up pace which was further spurred by launching of cellular services by coopting corporate sector which brought telephony within the common citizen, both- urban and rural. The story of growth internet in India is quite similar. Though India started before China, the latter has long ago overtaken it with the active support of state.

Telecommunication services, in true sense, began in India in 1850 when an experimental telegraph service became operational between Kolkata, then the seat of the British colonial government, and Diamond Harbor 21 miles away, a trading post of British East India Company. In 1851, it was opened for the use of the Company. Telephone services in India began with the commissioning of a

1 Highlights of Telecom Subscription data as on 31st Dec, 2011 at www.trai.gov.in

2 Internet usage in Asia at www.internetworldstats.com

manual exchange on 28 January 1882 in Kolkata.[3] The exchange was called "Central Exchange" and had a total of 93 subscribers. This was followed by exchanges at Bombay and Madras. This was less than five years after the invention of telephone by Alexander Graham Bell.[4]

India had approximately 82,000 telephone connections at the time of independence in 1947, which were less than 1300 lines per year. Post-independence , growth remained slow the number of telephones grew leisurely to 980,000 in 1971, 2.15 million in 1981, 3.05 million in 1984 and 5.07 million in 1991, the years economic reforms were initiated in the country. India's telecom network was notoriously unreliable and available to a small section of privileged households along with the corporate sector. The telecom sector was a government monopoly until 1994 when liberalization gradually took place. Cellular services were launched in August 1995 in Kolkata when the then Chief Minister of West Bengal Jyoti Basu made the call to Telecom Minister Sukhram. Interestingly, sixteen years later, in April 2012, Airtel launched 4G services in Kolkata.

The growth of telecommunication services during the British era was painfully slow despite the Government granting license to Oriental Telephone Company Limited of England in 1881 for opening telephone exchanges at Calcutta, Bombay, Madras and Ahmedabad. The foreign companies continued to operate in India till Independence when government restored its monopoly over the telecom sector. The primary reason for this slow growth, which was essentially restricted to urban India, was that the British viewed these as tools of command and control that were essential to maintain law and order in the country. During the uprising of 1857, the British authorities remained in contact with the various army formations and units by using the telegraph services. In 1883, the British combined the telegraph with postal services to

3 Dr William O'Shaughnessy, who pioneered the telegraph and telephone in India, belonged to Public Works Department, worked towards the development of these services, was the first superintendent of Electric Telegraphs in India and later became its first Director General.

4 "The Indian Telecom Industry" by Vatsal Goyal and Premraj Suman

further improve their command and control. Runners, stationed at telegraph offices, carried telegrams to remote post offices, thereby linking the British rulers with even the most distant pockets of India.[5] The thrust of growth of telecom services, therefore, was more towards serving the British interests rather than towards improving the telecom infrastructure in India. Consequently, the services were restricted to select cities and towns and there too, apart from government officials it was available to few elite in the city.

After gaining independence in 1947, the Government continued the colonial legacy, organizing post and telegraph services exclusively in the domain of the state. The socialist polices of Prime Minister Jawaharlal Nehru dedicated India to state-run, state-owned monopolies in various sectors which included telecommunications as well. Managed by slow-moving, overstaffed government machinery under the aegis of the Ministry of Posts and Telegraphs, the performance of India's telecommunications sector was slow until the mid-1990s.[6]

The main reasons for this poor growth and performance included an official view that telephones were a "luxury" than a "necessity". People in India actually endorsed this view. Telephone was seen more as a status symbol than being an instrument of utility. Family ties were strong and the joint family system was thriving both in rural as well urban India. The necessity to remain in touch was met through letters and personal visits. During the 1950s through 60s, the Government efforts towards improving education and extending its reach to the masses started paying dividends when young people from villages and towns started flocking to bigger cities in search of greener pastures. Progressive polices of the Government such as abolition of Zamindari system and Land Ceiling Act gave land to those who till the other day were working as laborers. This not only brought about prosperity but also brought about the realization of the advantages of education to the common man. By 70s a sizeable migration from the villages to towns and

5 History of Indian Telecommunications at www.indianetzone.com/42/history_indian_telecommunicatios.htm accessed on 10 May 2012

6 Ibid.

cities had taken place. Around the same time Government started a concerted drive to bring awareness about family planning. Slowly the younger generation started realizing its benefits. Towards late 70s and early 80s, the aspirations of the average citizen to remain in touch through faster means of communication started increasing. Joint family system had started breaking up and the families started becoming nuclear families.

While certain measures were taken to boost the telecom industry from time to time, like introduction of telex services in Bombay in 1953 and introduction of STD between Delhi and Kanpur in 1960, these measures were too few to have any significant impact. The first wave of changes were set going by US based NRI, Sam Pitroda in the eighties who was brought to India in 1981 by Prime Minister Indira Gandhi.

The Growth Story

The entire evolution of the telecom industry can be classified into three distinct phases:-

(a) Phase 1 : Pre- Liberalisation Era (1980-1989)

(b) Phase 2 : Post Liberalisation Era (1990-1999)

(c) Phase 3 : Post 2000

Until the late 90s the Government held a monopoly on all types of communications. The archaic Telegraph Act of 1885 was still being followed some 100 years later – a marvel of official apathy. It was only when the industry was liberalized in the early nineties with new policy initiatives by the Government that played a key role in shaping the structure and size of the Telecom industry. As a result, the Indian telecom market is one of the most liberalized markets in the world with private participation in almost all its segments.

Exhibit 1.1: Evolution of Telecom Industry

Phase - 1 (1980-89)	Phase -II (1990-99)	Phase -III (2000 onwards)
• Entry of Private Sector in telecommunications equipment manufacturing -1984 • Formation of Mahanagar Telephone Nigam Limited (MTNL) and Videsh Sanchar Nigam Limited (VSNL) -1986 • Telecom Communication was set up- 1989	• Libralisation of Indian Economy - 1990's • Private Sector Participation in provision of VAS such as cellular and paging services - 1992 • National Telecom Policy announced - 1994 • Telecom Regulatory Authority of India (TRAI) was established in 1997 • New Telecom Policy (NTP) announced - 1999	• Bharat Sanchar Nigam Limited (BSNL) established - 2000 • National Long Distance (NLD) and International Long Distance (ILD) services opened to competition • CDMA technology launched - 2000 • Internet Telephony Initiated - 2000 • Reduction of Licence Fees - 2000 • VSNL privatised - 2002 • Launch of Mobile Services by BSNL - 2002 • Unified Access Licencing (UASL) regime was introduced - 2003 • Calling Party Pays (CPP) was implemented • Broadband policy was formulated - 2004 • Intra circle merger guidelines established - 2004 • FDI limits increased from 49% to 74% - 2005 • Number portability was proposed (pending) - 2006

The Indian government was composed of many factions (parties) which had different ideologies. Some of them were willing to throw open the market to foreign players (the centrists) and others wanted the government to regulate infrastructure and restrict the involvement of foreign players. Due to this political background it was very difficult to bring about liberalisation in telecommunications. When a bill was in parliament a majority vote had to be passed, and such a majority was difficult to obtain, given to the number of parties having different ideologies.

Liberalization started in 1981 when Prime Minister Indira Gandhi signed contracts with Alcatel CIT of France to merge with the state owned Telecom Company (ITI), in an effort to set up 5,000,000 lines per year. But soon the policy was let down because of political opposition. She invited Sam Pitroda to set up a Center for Development of Telematics(C-DOT); however the plan failed due to political reasons. During this period, after the assassination of Indira Gandhi, under the leadership of Rajiv Gandhi, many public sector organisations were set up like the Department of Telecommunications (DoT), VSNL and MTNL. Many technological developments took place in this regime but still foreign players were not allowed to participate in the telecommunications business.

The demand for telephones was ever increasing. It was during this period that the Government introduced the National Telecommunications Policy (NTP) in 1994 which brought changes in the areas of ownership, service and regulation of telecommunications infrastructure. They were also successful in establishing joint ventures between state owned telecom companies and international players. But still complete ownership of facilities was restricted only to the government owned organisations. Foreign firms were eligible to 49 percent of the total stake. The multi-nationals were just involved in technology transfer, and not policy making.

During this period, the World Bank and ITU had advised the Indian Government to liberalise long distance services to release the monopoly of the state owned DoT and VSNL; and to enable competition in the long distance carrier business which would help reduce tariff's and better the economy of the country. The Government instead liberalised the local services, taking the opposite political parties into confidence and assuring foreign involvement in the long distance business after 5 years. The country was divided into 20 telecommunication circles for basic telephony and 18 circles for mobile services. These circles were divided into category A, B and C depending on the value of the revenue in each circle. The government threw open the bids to one private company per circle along with government owned DoT per circle. For cellular service two service providers were allowed per circle and a 15 years license was given to each provider. During all these improvements, the government did face oppositions from ITI, DoT, MTNL, VSNL and other labour unions, but they managed to keep away from all the hurdles.

After 1995 the government set up TRAI (Telecom Regulatory Authority of India) which reduced the interference of Government in deciding tariffs and policy making. The DoT opposed this. The political powers changed in 1999 and the new Government was more pro-reforms and introduced better liberalisation policies. They split DoT in two- one policy maker and the other service provider (DTS) which was later renamed as BSNL. The proposal of raising the stake of foreign investors from 49 percent to 74 percent was rejected by the opposite political party and leftist thinkers. Domestic business groups wanted the government to privatise VSNL. Finally in April 2002, the government decided to cut its stake of 53 percent to 26 percent in VSNL and to throw it open for sale to private enterprises.

This was a gateway to many foreign investors to get entry into the Indian Telecom Markets. After March 2000, the government became more liberal in making policies and issuing licenses to private operators. The government further reduced license fees for cellular service providers and increased the allowable stake to 74 percent for foreign companies. Because of all these factors, the service fees finally reduced and the call costs were cut greatly enabling every common middle class family in India to afford a cell phone. Nearly 32 million handsets were sold in India. The data reveals the real potential for growth of the Indian mobile market.[7]

In March 2008 the total GSM and CDMA mobile subscriber base in the country was 375 million, which represented a nearly 50 percent growth when compared with previous year.[8] As the unbranded Chinese cell phones which did not have International Mobile Equipment Identity (IMEI) numbers posed a serious security risk to the country, Mobile network operators therefore planned to suspend the usage of around 30 million mobile phones (about 8 percent of all mobiles in the country) by 30 April 2008. 5–6 years the average monthly subscribers additions were around 0.05 to 0.1 million only and the total mobile subscribers base in December 2002 stood at 10.5 millions. However, after a number of proactive initiatives were taken by regulators and licensors, the total number of mobile subscribers increased greatly to 881 million subscribers as of October 2011.

India has opted for the use of both the GSM (global system for mobile communications) and CDMA (code-division multiple access) technologies in the mobile sector. In addition to landline and mobile phones, some of the companies also provide the WLL service. The mobile tariffs in India have also become lowest in the world. A new mobile connection can be activated with a monthly commitment of US$0.15 only. In 2005 alone additions increased to around 2 million per month in 2003–04 and 2004–05.

In June 2009, the Government of India banned the import of several mobile phones manufactured in China citing concerns over quality and the lack of IMEI's which make it difficult for authorities in India to track the sale and use of such phones.[9] In April 2010, the Government was also reported to be blocking Indian service providers from purchasing Chinese mobile technology citing concerns that Chinese hackers could compromise the Indian telecommunications network during times of national emergency. A series of attacks on Indian government websites and computer

7 Economic Times.indiatimes.com 18 March 2009

8 Ibid.

9 "Government bans import of Chinese mobiles, dairy products, toys" timesofindia. indiatimes.com. Times of India 18 June 2009

networks by suspected Chinese hackers has also made Indian regulators suspicious with regards to the import of potentially sensitive equipment from China.

Growth of IT-ITeS and Financial Sector[10]

India has entered the league of countries with the most-advanced telecommunication infrastructure after the industry was deregulated. Furthermore, deregulation has stimulated India's economic growth through industry growth and through rise in investments. It is evident that a well-developed communication sector improves access to social networks, lowers transaction costs, increases economic opportunities, widens markets, and provides better access to information, health care and educational services. The growth in Indian telecom sector has been concomitant with overall growth in GDP, government revenue, employment etc. Besides, telecommunication has increased efficiency, reduced transaction costs, attracted investments and has created new opportunities for business and employment.

The NTP-99 was particularly helpful for the ITeS-BPO industry as it ended the government monopoly in international calling by introducing IP telephony. After the introduction of IP telephony, there was rapid growth in the number of data processing centres and inbound/outbound call centres, which ultimately led to the outsourcing revolution in India.

The telecom sector has been instrumental in creating jobs for a vast pool of talented and knowledge professionals in the IT and ITeS-BPO industry, which thrives on reliable telecommunication infrastructure. India has become an important outsourcing destination for the world and the boom in this sector also has transformed India's economic dynamics. The evolution of telecom sector has brought about a revolutionary change in the way some businesses operate.

Another beneficiary of the telecom revolution is the financial services industry, which has been on a growth trajectory. The

10 www.dnb.co.in/indian telecomindustry/overviewTI.asp

progress and quality of the financial sector has been a key factor that has driven the pace and diversity of the real economy. India has an extensive and well-developed financial sector with wide and sophisticated banking network. Banking in India has become service-oriented, and has matured greatly from the days of walk-in customers to the present situation when banks have migrated to a 24-hour banking platform to attract customers; however, this disintermediation in the business has led banks to be extremely prudent in terms of their internal operations and has led them to adopt newer products and delivery channels. Further, with introduction of internet & mobile banking the long queues at the banks are slowly becoming a thing of the past.

Both the financial and the IT-ITeS segments rely on good domestic as well as international network connectivity; therefore, there is a need for a sound telecommunication network.

Factors Facilitating Growth of the Sector[11]

The phenomenal growth in the Indian telecom industry was brought about by the wireless revolution that began in the nineties. Besides this, the following factors also aided the growth of the industry.

Liberalisation. The relaxation of telecom regulations has played a major role in the development of the Indian telecom industry. The liberalisation policies of 1991 and the consequent influx of private players have led the industry on a high growth trajectory and have increased the level of competition. Post-liberalisation, the telecom industry has received more investments and has implemented higher technology.

Increasing Affordability of Handsets. The phenomenal growth in the Indian telecom industry was predominantly aided by the meteoric rise in wireless subscribers, which encouraged mobile handset manufacturers to enter the market and to cater to the growing demand. Further, the manufacturers introduced lower-priced handsets with add-on facilities to cater to the increasing number of subscribers from different strata of the society. Now even

11 Ibid.

entry-level handsets come with features like coloured display and FM radio. Thus, the falling handset prices and the add-on features have triggered growth of the Indian telecom industry.

Prepaid Cards Bring in More Subscribers. In the late nineties, India was introduced to prepaid cards, which was yet another milestone for the wireless sector. Prepaid cards lured more subscribers into the industry besides lowering the credit risk of service providers due to its up front payment concept. Prepaid cards were quite a phenomenon among first-time users who wanted to control their bills and students who had limited resources but greater need to be connected. Pre-paid cards greatly helped the cellular market to grow rapidly and cater to the untapped market. Further, the introduction of innovative schemes like recharge coupons of smaller denominations and life time incoming free cards has led to an exponential growth in the subscriber base.

Introduction of Calling Party Pays (CPP). The CPP regime was introduced in India in 2003 and under this regime, the calling party who initiated the call was to bear the entire cost of the call. This regime came to be applicable for mobile to mobile calls as well as fixed line to mobile calls. So far India had followed the Receiving Party Pays (RPP) system where the subscriber used to pay for incoming calls from both mobile as well as fixedline networks. Shifting to the CPP system has greatly fuelled the subscriber growth in the sector.

Changing Demographic Profile. The changing demographic profile of India has also played an important role in subscriber growth. The changed profile is characterised by a large young population, a burgeoning middle class with growing disposable income, urbanisation, increasing literacy levels and higher adaptability to technology. These new features have multiplied the need to be connected always and to own a wireless phone and therefore, in present times mobiles are perceived as a utility rather than a luxury.

Increased Competition & Declining Tariffs. Liberalisation of the telecom industry has fuelled intense competition, especially in the cellular segment. The ever-increasing competition has led to high growth of subscribers and has put pressure on tariffs, which have seen a sharp drop over the years. When the cellular phones were introduced, call rates were at a peak of Rs 16 per minute and there were charges for incoming calls too. Today, however, incoming calls are no longer charged and outgoing calls are charged at less than a rupee per minute. Thus, the tariff war has come a long way indeed. Increased competition and the subsequent tariff war has acted as a major catalyst for attracting more subscribers. Apart from these major growth drivers, an improved network coverage, entry of CDMA players, growth of value-added services (VAS), advancement in technology, and growing data services have also driven the growth of the industry.

Outlook. The telecom industry in India has experienced exponential growth over the past few years and has been an important contributor to economic growth; however, the cut-throat competition and intense tariff wars have had a negative impact on the revenue of players. Despite the challenges, the Indian telecom industry will thrive because of the immense potential in terms of new users. India is one of the most-attractive telecom markets because it is still one of the lowest penetrated markets. The Government is keen on developing rural telecom infrastructure and is also set to roll out next generation or 3G services in the country. Under the Bharat Nirman Programme, the Government will ensure that 66,822 revenue villages in the country, which have not yet been provided with a Village Public Telephone (VPT), shall be covered. Out of the above villages, connectivity, in 14,183 remote and far flung villages will be provided through digital phone terminals.

Telecom operators are on an expansion mode and are investing heavily on telecom infrastructure. Foreign telecom companies are acquiring considerable stakes in Indian companies. Burgeoning middle class and increasing spending power, the government's thrust on increasing rural telecom coverage, favourable investment climate and positive reforms will ensure that India's high potential is indeed realised.

Growth of Internet in India and Usage

The primary objective of discussing the growth of Indian Telecom was to drive home the point that the telecom revolution took place at a time when the society was ready for it. There is no gainsaying in the fact that the Indian society has historically been quite resistant to change. The desire to remain connected was also endorsed, apart from those reasons mentioned in Para 28 above, by the elders in the family who felt lonely and to some extent insecure by breaking up of joint family system and the migration of the children to cities. Slowly and steadily the telephone had become an integral part of life and was thereafter seen as a necessity rather than a luxury.

The state-owned Videsh Sanchar Nigam Limited (VSNL) launched Internet Services in India in August 1995. For the first four years, VSNL was the sole provider of Internet Services in the Country. In the first years, broadband usage in India was growing 20 percent per month, according to the Internet Service Providers Association of India (ISPAI). Thanks to the progress in the penetration of ICT and especially, the Broadband Policy announced in 1995, the term "broadband" entered the mass lexicon and most Internet users were aware of faster Internet speeds.

In November 1998, the Government ended VSNL's monopoly and allowed provisioning of Internet Services by Private Operators. The Terms and Conditions of the ISP's License were unusually liberal with no License Fee and allowed unlimited number of players. ISPs could set their own tariffs and even their own International Gateways.

Women lead the rural Internet rush in India. In year 2004 the Internet was having a revolutionary effect on the 700 million people who lived in villages in India - and the change was led by women. A project set up by one of India's leading technology institutes put women in charge of forging the way across the digital divide as the proprietors of a fast-growing number of internet cafes or kiosks around the sub-continent. In total 80 percent of these new kiosks were run by women, many of whom have had very little or no acquaintance with technology before.[12]

12 www.internetworldstats.com/asia/in.htm accessed 15 May 2012

The growth in number of broadband connections in India has accelerated since 2006. As of December 2011, total Internet connections stood at 22.39 million, while the broadband Internet connections in India had reached 13.35 million constituting 1.0 percent of the population. India has one of the lowest penetrations of broadband connectivity in the world.□ In 2011 alone India added an estimated 2.62 million new broadband users. This translates to 24.5 percent growth in broadband connections in 2011, one of the fastest across the globe. It is also predicted that the nation is poised to become one of the top 10 countries in terms of user base the year after clinching 11th rank in the global pecking order.[13]

A number of private Internet Service Providers (ISPs) offer services in India, many with their own local loop and gateway infrastructures. BSNL and MTNL have continued to dominate the ISP market because of their existing massive copper infrastructure in the last-mile across the nation. An estimated 60 percent of Internet users were still regularly accessing the Internet via the country's more than 10,000 cybercafés.[14]

According to International Telecommunication Union, the international average broadband speed is at 5.6 Mbps, whereas in India the average speed hoovers at 256 kbit/s which is the minimum speed set by TRAI. The government declared 2007 to be "the year of broadband." Four years later, Indian broadband failed to deliver a download speed of which other developed nations delivers. South Korea led the list with an average of 43 Mbit/s, followed by Japan (10.6 Mbit/s) and United States (4.6 Mbit/s). [15]

India broadband growth is hampered by various challenges, including a complicated tariff structure, metered billing, higher charges for right of way and absence of local-loop unbundling. Average Internet speed in India is as low as 0.8Mbit/s. Out of the total Internet population 35 percent is still below 256kbit/s. To compete with international standards of defining broadband speed

13 "India's broadband base grows 24.5 percent in 2011 to 13.33 million" The Economic Times 21 Mar 2012

14 Ibid

15 Ibid

the Indian Government has taken aggressive step of proposing the $13 billion national broadband network to connect all cities, towns and villages with a population of more than 500 in two phases targeted for completion by 2012 and 2013.The network will be capable of handling speed up to 10Mbit/s in 63 metropolitan areas and 4Mbit/s in additional 352 cities.[16]

The growth of internet users in the last two years has been truly impressive. The table below depicts the growth of internet users as percentage of population.

YEAR	Users	Population	Percent Pen.	Usage Source
1998	1,400,000	1,094,870,677	0.1 percent	ITU
1999	2,800,000	1,094,870,677	0.3 percent	ITU
2000	5,500,000	1,094,870,677	0.5 percent	ITU
2001	7,000,000	1,094,870,677	0.7 percent	ITU
2002	16,500,000	1,094,870,677	1.6 percent	ITU
2003	22,500,000	1,094,870,677	2.1 percent	ITU
2004	39,200,000	1,094,870,677	3.6 percent	C.I. Almanac
2005	50,600,000	1,112,225,812	4.5 percent	C.I. Almanac
2006	40,000,000	1,112,225,812	3.6 percent	IAMAI
2007	42,000,000	1,129,667,528	3.7 percent	IWS
2009	81,000,000	1,156,897,766	7.0 percent	ITU
2010	100,000,000	1,173,108,018	8.5 percent	IWS

The two major reasons for such a growth is the increase in internet penetration in the country and availability of affordable personal computers. IAMAI's report on Internet in India (I-Cube) 2011 says that India will have 121 million users' internet users by Dec 2011. Some of the highlights of the report are given below:-[17]

16 Ibid.

17 Some of the terms used are explained below:-

Kids studying in school and above 8 years of age. They are in the age group of 8-17, although, a small portion could be over 18 years.

- Out of 121 million, 97 million would be active Internet users who access Internet at least once in a month.
- Of the 121 million internet users, 92 million (76 percent) will be from the urban cities of the country and 29 million from rural areas (23 percent).
- Of the 97 million active Internet users, 73 million (75 percent) will be from urban cities and the rest 24 million (25 percent) from rural villages.
- Of the active internet users 48 percent (46.56 million) used internet at least 4-6 times a week and 28 percent (27 million) used it daily.
- Around one third of young men and working women are heavy internet users in India.
- Most new users are light internet users.

Urban-Rural Divide

- Urban population: 302 million, 38 percent (115 million) of which know how to use a computer, of which 79 percent (90 million) use the internet at least once a month (active users).
- Rural population (aged above 12 years): 603 million, 8 percent (48 million) of which know how to use a computer, of which 36 percent (17 million) use the internet at least once a month (active users).
- More than 75 percent of the Internet usage is driven by youngsters that include young men (27 percent), school going kids (21 percent), college going kids (27 percent)
- In the 30 urban cities wherein the survey was conducted, 89 percent use it to access emails, 71 percent use it for

---

Youths studying in college (graduate, post-graduate and doctoral). Most students are in the age group of 18-25, although a small proportion will be below 18 and over 25 years.

Men in the age group of 21-35 years who are not school or college-going students. This segment includes all those who are employed as well as unemployed.

social networking activities, 64 percent access it to search education-related content, 55 percent use Internet for chatting purposes and 49 percent access videos, music and images.

- The usage pattern differs among rural Internet users. Among the survey conducted in 7 states, 46 percent use Internet for accessing music, videos and images, 38 percent use it for email and communication activities, 29 percent access it for getting general information and 27 percent use Internet to access content related to education.

Internet Access Points in India

- Cyber cafe plays an important role but home usage has grown to 37 percent.
- Mobile internet and cheaper packages from ISPs have helped the usage grow.
- Urban India has 8.7 million broadband connections, 37.1 million users who utilize broadband.
- Majority of internet connections in households are broadband connections (82 percent of 10.7 million connections)
- Household users: 54 percent have 256 Kbps, 34 percent have 256Kbps-1 Mbps, 12 percent have above 1 Mbps.
- Majority of broadband connections are wired line connections (88 percent).

It is now considered that mobile internet growth will provide impetus to internet growth in India. TRAI estimates that there will be additional 200 million new subscribers in 2012. Out of total of 898 million mobile subscribers (including 292 million in rural areas), 346 million users had subscribed to data packages, with more than half of all internet users in the country accessing the web through their mobile phones. The tablet PC "Aakash", an initiative of Government of India to provide low cost computer, has already been hailed as a huge innovation and will change the way the web can be accessed in schools.[18]

The examination of mobile internet users demographics reveal interesting facts as shown in the figure below:-[19]

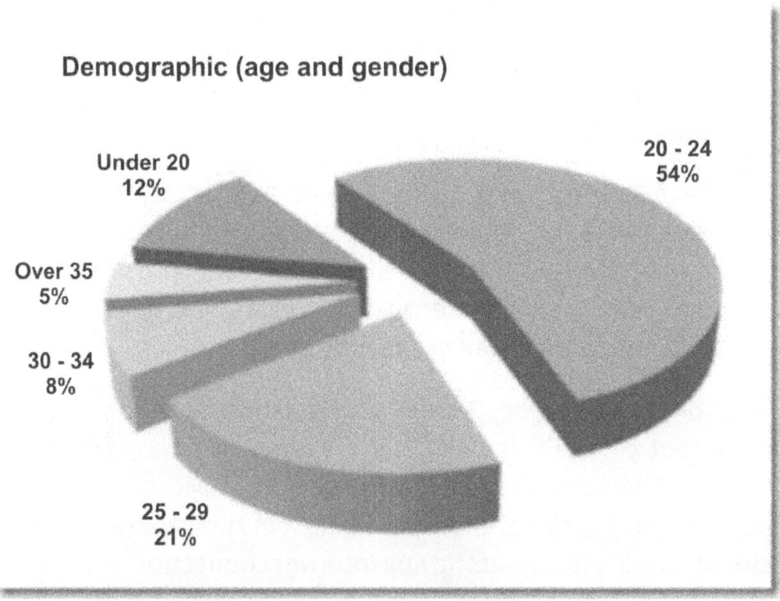

Interesting facts about Indian Mobile Internet Usage:-

- 75 percent of the mobile web users are from the age group of 20-30 years.
- Only 5 percent of the mobile internet users are aged more over 35 years.
- 89 percent of the mobile web users are male.

---

18 "Is 2012 the year for India's internet?" BBC News 03 January 2012 www.bbc.co.uk/news/business-16354076

19 The BuzzCity survey, a global roundup of recent market developments in the mobile internet, indicates that India is amongst the Top-10 countries using mobile internet; even as China plays a catch-up in the top ten lists for the first time ever. India has witnessed a high growth of 233 percent year-on-year in terms of mobile internet usage driven by cheaper data rates and much improved handsets.

- Nokia comprises 54 percent of handsets used for web surfing.

Internet revolution has bypassed rural India with less than half a per cent of families having the facility at home as against 6 per cent in cities, reveals a government survey. "At all India level only about 0.4 per cent of rural households had access to Internet at home as compared to about 6 per cent of urban households," said the National Sample Survey Organisation (NSSO) report on expenditure in 2009-10.

Reflecting the digital divide in India, the study said just 3.5 households per 1,000 families, had access to Internet services at home in rural areas in the year. However, in urban areas, Internet connectivity was much better in 2009-10 as 59.5 families out of every 1000 households had the facility at home.

Among the major States, Maharashtra was on top with the 104 out of 1,000 families had Internet in cities, followed by Kerala and Himachal Pradesh at 95 each and Haryana at 81.5. The penetration of digital services was highest in rural areas in Goa with 50 out of 1,000 households having Internet connection. Kerala came next with 34 families having such a facility at home. Among the hilly States, Arunachal Pradesh had the best reach of the Internet service in rural areas with 19 out of 1,000 households have such facility at home, followed by Himachal Pradesh at 16. The study further states that among the major states, Kerala had by far the highest proportion of households with Internet access in the rural areas at 3 per cent followed by Himachal Pradesh at 2 per cent. In cities, Maharashtra reported the highest percentage of household having access to Internet connection (10 per cent) followed closely by Kerala, Himachal Pradesh and Haryana.

Impact on Society

The Telecom revolution or mobile and internet revolution to be more precise is fast getting into the fabric of most people. People are doing multiple things online- chat, talking, working, banking etc. Research firm comScore in its findings revealed that India has the youngest internet population with 75 percent of all users under the age of 35 years while the world average stood at 52 percent. Indian users spent a total of 34.47 billion minutes on line last year which translates to over half a billion hours, the report said.

Better accessibility, easy availability of cheap mobile phones and computers, Indians are using the internet for more than just checking their e-mails. Social networking is a key driver in both the urban and rural India. Facebook is the most popular site in India; its user base grew by more than a third from July 2011 to December 2011.[20]

Facebook finds India a major growth market, where the number of users have more than doubled in the past one year, as against near-zero penetration in the neighbouring China. For Facebook, looking to raise $5 billion through initial share sale, India is a key source for future growth. The growth of 132 per cent in India has been higher than many other countries, including home market in US.

"We have achieved varying levels of penetration within the population of Internet users in different countries," Facebook has said, while noting that its penetration rate in India was estimated to be 20-30 per cent.[21]

Facebook monitors its user base through the number of Monthly Active Users (MAUs), among other metrics. An MAU is a registered Facebook user who logs in and visits Facebook, shares content or indulges in other activities in the last 30 days as of the date of measurement. "As of December 31, 2011, we had 845 million MAUs, an increase of 39 per cent from December 31, 2010," it noted.

"We experienced growth across different geographies, with users in Brazil and India representing a key source of growth," Facebook said. "... we had 46 million MAUs in India as of December 31, 2011, an increase of 132 per cent from the prior year," Facebook said. It noted that growth in the US was 16 per cent and 268 per

20 Ibid.

21 "Facebook users in India have doubled in last one year" The Economic Times 03 February 2012

cent in Brazil for the same period. Facebook has operation teams to provide support for users, developers, and advertisers in four regional centres, including one at Hyderabad in India.

Facebook had 161 million MAUs in the US and 37 million in Brazil as on December 31, 2011. According to the social networking major, it faces competition from Internet giant Google's social media platform Orkut in India, among other rivals in different countries. Listing out its strategy, Facebook said it would "continue to focus on growing our user base across all geographies, including relatively less-penetrated, large markets such as Brazil, Germany, India, Japan, Russia, and South Korea". It added, "We compete broadly with Google's social networking offerings, including Google+, and also with other, largely regional, social networks that have strong positions in particular countries, including Cyworld in Korea, Mixi in Japan, Orkut (owned by Google) in Brazil and India...".

According to ComScore study, out of four minutes spent on social network three are on Facebook. LinkedIn reaches one in eight online users whereas one in 12 users are on twitter in India.

It is interesting to note that pattern of usage of internet in rural India, which constitutes 70 percent of India's population, is strikingly different from urban India. Entertainment seems to be the primary driver of internet use in rural India according to the findings of the IAMAI Report on Internet in India (I-Cube) 2011. Out of the extrapolated sample of 7.8 million rural users 49 percent used internet to download music, videos, and photos; 38 percent used it for email and chats and 27 percent for education.

In urban India, the pattern of use was dramatically different. While email or communications continued to be the most popular use of internet, social networking seemed to be catching up father fast. 71 percent of internet users in urban India of an extrapolated sample of28 million users indulged in social networking, 89 percent used emails. Interestingly 64 percent used internet for educational purposes.

The findings by BBC News are no different. According to their findings "What Indians do online":-

- 3 hours - Average time an Indian net user spends on social media
- 13 million - Number of Indians registered on matrimonial or dating sites
- 70 percent of Indian internet users watch online videos

The IAMAI study referred above found that towns with population less than 2 lakhs collectively had a much higher number of Internet users than the top four metros put together. Interestingly the study stated that internet usage is high among people of lower economic class.[22] In 2011 the combined usage of SEC C, D and E has been more than 36 percent of the total Internet users in the country. Over the period of the last 5 years, internet users from SEC B, C, D, and E have increased from 59 percent to 68 percent. However, the core audience is the age group of 18-25 years.

Commenting on the survey, President of IAMAI, Dr Subho Ray said," Two things are absolutely clear from the survey. First, the internet density is very poor in top metros in spite of awareness, education and infrastructure. Delhi and NCR for example has only 5 million active users with a population base of 20 million. Secondly, internet is now clearly and firmly a small town phenomenon." **This is the most important deduction of our discussion as 70 percent of Indian population resides there and it is the catchment area for recruitment of soldiers in the Indian Armed Forces.**

Internet is today affecting the life of Indian netizens like never before. It is today attempting to shape the lives of Indian netizens. Indians netizens consider work and social networking, in that order, as the two most important tasks online. A survey by antivirus company Norton revealed that online socializing took up an average of 9.7 hours a week against a total of 58 hours a week spent online. After social networking came convenience of life activities like paying bills and shopping online. In fact, 83 percent of users said

22 Classification has been used in the study that indicates the affluence level of a household to which an individual belongs. SEC is defined by the education and occupation of the chief wage earner (CWE) of a household. SEC is divided into 8 categories – A1, A2, B1, B2, C, D, E1, E2 (in decreasing order of affluence).

they could not live without the internet for more than 24 hours. According to Norton, the need to stay constantly connected is a new trend among Indian net surfers. Then again, Indian netizens clearly place a high value on their personal information, says David Hall of Norton, who points out that 40 percent of India's online community has declared that they value their financial information the most, followed by 35 percent who place a premium on their online accounts, including email and social networks.[23]

Three out of four respondents to the survey said they would give up $1 million than grant a stranger full access to their computers. The survey conducted using a sample size of 500 respondents between the ages of 18 to 64 years also concluded that Indian users own an average of 2.8 devices that are connected to the Internet. While the people interviewed used multiple devices to be online, half of them had little or no understanding of online security solutions that are available to them, Hall says. And while 60 percent of users are content with basic security, the antivirus expert said it was not enough to protect them from the advanced malware and phishing attacks. **Herein lies the danger as it every computer compromised poses a threat.**

Internet users in India spend an average 58 hours a week more than half their waking hours online, a new survey has revealed. Half the netizens interviewed by anti-virus company Norton admitted that they suffered from withdrawal within the first three hours of being cut off from the web. Indians spend 12.9 hours browsing, 9.7 hours socializing and 6.1 hours on email every week, said David Hall of Norton. While Norton did not make comparisons, a 2011 survey by market research firm comScore put Canadians at 45.3 hours a week online, Americans at 38.6 hours and the British at 35.4 hours.

A recent report in The Times of India [24] shows despite the leap frogging to embrace internet the rural areas are still lagging behind. Gurgoan has high internet penetration, living up to its

23 *Times of India, Delhi, 29 March 2012.*

24 *Times of India, Delhi, 10 May 2012.*

billing as the Millennium City. More households in Gurgaon log on to the Net than any district in the country. It has even beaten India's Silicon Valley, Bangalore, in the digital race. Census 2011 says the household penetration of the internet in Gurgaon is 20.9 percent. This is way above the national average of 10 percent. Gurgaon has a better score than even IT hubs Bangalore and Hyderabad and has overtaken mega cities like Delhi and Mumbai.

The census says of the 3, 20,000 households in Gurgaon, over 1, 02,000 have computers and more than 67,000 are internet-enabled. Experts attribute Gurgaon's Net revolution to its large concentration of techies and professionals.

Most residents are employed in the IT and telecom companies and this explains the rising number of internet users, said Ibrahim Ahmed of Cyber Media, a research firm. Housing societies and residential colonies have also played their part, striking exclusive deals with internet service providers (ISPs) and offering broadband ready apartments. Realtors are partnering Net service providers to offer free installation in newly built flats, said Ahmed. Rajesh Charria, President of the Internet Service Providers of India, said 65 percent of the users are from the GenNext.

Tech pundits predict that broadband will follow the same course as mobile telephony. But ISPs and telecom firms are still struggling to tap the rural markets, where broadband penetration is very low. In rural Gurgaon, of the 88,000 registered households, only 1.8 percent are connected. The National Telecom Policy-2011 has set a target of achieving 175 million broadband connections by the year 2017 and 600 million by the year 2020. This will be at minimum 2 Mbps download speed and also making available higher speeds of at least 100 Mbps on demand. The policy intends to provide high speed and high quality broadband access to all village panchayats through optical fibre by the year 2014 and progressively to all villages and habitation. This move by the National Telecom is to increase the Internet penetration in the core rural and semi urban areas in the country that has the maximum population. Government has now launched a new scheme—Bharat Broadband Network which may be able to bridge the digital divide.

The scheme aims to connect at least 500 million users by 2020.

The private sector has also seen the potential in the rural areas. ITC Limited, a large multi business conglomerate of India, launched "e-Choupal" project in 2000 which aims to link directly with rural farmers via the Internet for procurement of agricultural and aquaculture products like soybeans, wheat, coffee, and prawns. E-Choupal was conceived to tackle the challenges posed by the unique features of Indian agriculture, characterized by fragmented farms, weak infrastructure and the involvement of numerous intermediaries. The programme involves the installation of computers with Internet access in rural areas of India to offer farmers up-to-date marketing and agricultural information.

ITC Limited has now provided computers and Internet access in rural areas across several agricultural regions of the country, where the farmers can directly negotiate the sale of their produce with ITC Limited. This online access enables farmers to obtain information on mandi prices, and good farming practices, and to place orders for agricultural inputs like seeds and fertilizers. Real-time information and customised knowledge provided by 'e-Choupal' enhance the ability of farmers to take decisions and align their farm output with market demand and secure quality & productivity. The aggregation of the demand for farm inputs from individual farmers gives them access to high quality inputs from established and reputed manufacturers at fair prices. As a direct marketing channel, virtually linked to the 'mandi' system for price discovery, 'e-Choupal' eliminates wasteful intermediation and multiple handling. Thereby it significantly reduces transaction costs.

Since the introduction of e-Choupal services, farmers have seen a rise in their income levels because of a rise in yields, improvement in quality of output, and a fall in transaction costs. Even small farmers have gained from the initiative. Customized and relevant knowledge is offered to the farmers despite heterogeneous cultures, climates and scales of production. Farmers can get real-time information despite their physical distance from the *mandis*. The farmers do not pay for the information and knowledge they get from e-Choupals; the principle is to inform, empower and compete.

There are presently 6,500 e-Choupals in operation. ITC Limited plans to scale up to 20,000 e-Choupals by 2012 covering 100,000 villages in 15 states, servicing 15 million farmers.

ITC has also benefited from the venture as mentioned below:-

- Elimination of non-value added activities.
- Differentiated product through identity preserved supply chains.
- Value added products traceable to farm practices.
- E-market place for spot transactions and support services to futures exchange.

Another path-breaking initiative - the 'Choupal Pradarshan Khet', brings the benefits of agricultural best practices to small and marginal farmers. Backed by intensive research and knowledge, this initiative provides Agri-extension services which are qualitatively superior and involves pro-active hand holding of farmers to ensure productivity gains. The services are customised to meet local conditions, ensure timely availability of farm inputs including credit, and provide a cluster of farmer schools for capturing indigenous knowledge. This initiative, which has covered over 70,000 hectares, has a multiplier impact and reaches out to over 1.6 million farmers.[25]

E-chaupal initiative has been a tremendous success primarily as it empowers the farmer who is now has all the inputs required to align his crop produce according to the market demand and then get the most optimum price for his produce. He no longer depends on the wily bania to sell his produce at a price dictated by him but is also freed his money lending clutches. Interestingly the association between the bania and the farmer was handed down from generations who grew up knowing each other. The farmer despite knowing that he was being exploited had no choice but to go to him. It is this empowerment to the simple, rustic farmer

25 http://www.itcportal.com/itc-business/agri-business/e-choupal.aspx accessed 15 May 2012.

which enthuses him to get onto internet. There is no doubt that growth of internet in India will be driven by the rural and semi urban areas. The proliferation of mobile phones among this population is growing at a fierce pace. The introduction of 4G services will offer the potential to increase internet access and provide a better, faster user experience once more compatible handsets are available in the market.

Better infrastructure and the availability if internet in the local language will further boost its proliferation in the rural areas. This boost will directly impact the Indian economy.

Ten per cent increase in internet penetration in India can increase the gross domestic product (GDP) by 1.08 per cent, says a report released Thursday by the Indian Council for Research on International Economic Relations (ICRIER).

"Indian states with higher internet penetration can be expected to grow much faster, and by 1.08 per cent for every 10 per cent increase in the number of internet subscribers," said ICRIER director Parthasarathi Shome while announcing the findings of the study. In comparison, a 10 per cent increase in mobile penetration can increase the GDP by 1.5 per cent. "States with higher penetration rates show a greater growth dividend. The developed states (with higher per capita income and level of internet penetration) will grow at 2.36 per cent for every 10 per cent increase in the number of internet subscribers," Shome added. According to the report, as the number of internet users goes up, the growth impact of internet will improve significantly. Broadband, in fact, has a bigger impact on growth.[26]

"Attaining the targets set by TRAI (Telecom Regulatory Authority of India) in the recently released National Broadband Plan could generate an additional $87 billion in GDP during the period 2012-14," according to the survey.

According to a McKinsey report titled 'Internet matters: The Net's sweeping impact on growth, jobs, and prosperity', released

26 http://articles.economictimes.indiatimes.com/2012-01-19/news/ 30642992_ 1_ internet-users-broadband-users-penetration accessed 14 May 2012.

at the e-G8 Forum held in Paris on May 24-25, 2011, internet contributed 5 per cent to the total gross domestic product (GDP) growth of India in the past five years compared with the average 3 per cent for BRIC (Brazil, Russia, India and China) economies. According to the report, companies are able to keep costs down, target customers better and bring goods and services to markets around the world much more easily.[27]

Individuals are able to compare prices, search hard-to-find items or information, communicate and learn in new, improved ways. Governments can serve citizens much more quickly and at a much lower cost through e-governance. According to the report there are 2 billion internet users worldwide and as a sector, internet related consumption and expenditure is now bigger than agriculture or energy.

The report further said that internet has a sweeping impact on growth, prosperity of a country and has created 2.4 jobs for every job that it has destroyed. "The Internet is a contributor to net job creation. While jobs have been destroyed by the emergence of internet, many more have been created during the same period, including jobs directly linked to the internet, such as software engineers and online marketers as well as more traditional jobs, logistics to deliver online purchases," the report added.

Internet is set to change the way we live today. Once addicted it becomes an integral part of our life. On any working, 64 percent users are online. Also about 2/3 households have multiple users (IAMAI data) which indicates how much internet has penetrated our daily life. India is firmly on course to become internet users powerhouse in a few years with the aspirations of its 50 percent of young population becoming the driving force for growth.

27 http://www.indiadigitalreview.com/news/internet-contributed-india percent E2 percent80 percent99s-5-gdp-growth-last-5-years-mckinsey accessed 02 March 2012.

CHAPTER 10

CYBER CHALLENGES FOR INDIA

Introduction

The Indian economy in the last decade has registered impressive growth. India recorded the highest growth rates in the mid-2000s, and is one of the fastest-growing economies in the world. The growth was led primarily due to a huge increase in the size of the middle class consumer, a large labor force and considerable foreign investments. India is the nineteenth largest exporter and tenth largest importer in the world. Economic growth rate stood at around 6.5 percent for the 2011-12 fiscal year.

Agriculture, services and manufacturing industries play a vital role in the development of the Indian economy. The IT outsourcing, software and call center/ BPO industries, in particular, have helped skyrocket India's economic development in recent years.

India is 13th in services output. The services sector provides employment to 23 percent of the work force and is growing quickly, with a growth rate of 7.5 percent in 1991–2000, up from 4.5 percent in 1951–80. It has the largest share in the GDP, accounting for 55 percent in 2007, up from 15 percent in 1950. Information technology and business process outsourcing are among the fastest growing sectors, having a cumulative growth rate of revenue 33.6 percent between 1997–98 and 2002–03 and contributing to 25 percent of the country's total exports in 2007–08. The growth in the IT sector is attributed to increased specialisation, and an availability of a large pool of low cost, highly skilled, educated and fluent English-speaking workers, on the supply side, matched on the demand side by increased demand from foreign consumers interested in India's service exports, or those looking to outsource their operations. The share of the Indian IT industry in the country's GDP increased from 4.8 percent in 2005–06 to 7 percent in 2008. In 2009, seven

Indian firms were listed among the top 15 technology outsourcing companies in the world.[1]

"India Shining" is primarily the growth story of Indian economy post liberalization. This has been possible due globalization and information revolution. Cyberspace has played a major role to the extent that today it has become a national asset. Cyberspace acts as an enabler to many Government services, corporate sector and the Armed Forces. Nations across the world are leveraging technology to transform their economy, critical national infrastructure and their Military.

Government is investing more than USD 10 billion on e-Governance through many projects that would transform government functioning. The National e-Governance Plan (NeGP), one of the most ambitious government program in the world, takes a holistic view of e-Governance initiatives across the country. It integrates the initiatives, whether at the Centre or in States, into a collective vision for a shared cause of delivering benefits to citizens in the remotest parts of the country. A massive countrywide infrastructure reaching out to the remotest of villages is evolving, and large-scale digitization of records is taking place to enable easy, reliable access over the Internet. The ultimate objective is to bring public services closer home to citizens, as articulated in the vision statement of NeGP. It aims to provide more than 1200 government services online. The NeGP comprises 27 mission mode projects (MMPs) and 8 common core and support infrastructure including State Wide Area Networks and State Data Centres.

NASSCOM-DSCI Cyber Security Advisory Group Report "Securing our Cyber Frontiers" gives out the impact of cyberspace on Indian economy. It quotes a Boston Consulting Group report which states "the Internet economy of India in 2010 was USD 70 billion (4.1 percent of GDP) and is estimated to reach USD 242 billion (5.6 percent of GDP) in 2016". Technology, according to the report, is contributing in India's development in following ways:-[2]

1 http://en.wikipedia.org/wiki/Economy_of_India

2 Securing our Cyber Frontiers - NASSCOM-DSCI Cyber Security Advisory Group Report.

(a) Development of new Infrastructure. Airports, metros, highways, etc. and augmentation of existing infrastructure - power generation, financial services, telecom, transportation, defence, etc. Nation's critical infrastructure is getting increasingly dependent on technology – power grids, air traffic controller, industrial systems, stock exchanges, banking, telecom among others are driven and controlled by ICT.

(b) e-Governance. Government is framing policies that intend to leverage power of technology to address social, economic and development challenges in the country. Government is envisaging making the Internet available to every household in India through availability of low cost devices to enable every citizen to participate in the web economy. Using technology, the government intends to improve governance by increasing transparency, curbing corruption, time bound delivery of government services and ensuring financial inclusion.

(c) **'Aadhaar'** is one of the most ambitious projects of the Indian government which is issuing 12-digit unique number to Indian residents. The number will be stored in a centralized database and linked to the basic demographics and biometric information – photograph, ten fingerprints and iris – of each enrolled resident. The Aadhaar number provides unique identity, which will become acceptable across India. The project promises that this identity will be robust enough to eliminate duplicate and fake identities through effective verification and authentication. Many of the government's social benefit programs are envisaged to be linked with the Aadhaar number. The disbursements of government entitlements like Mahatma Gandhi National Rural Employment Gurantee scheme, social security pension, handicapped old age pension, etc. are expected to be made through Aadhaar-Enabled Payment Systems (AEPS), using aadhaar number and associated personal information for authentication. The Aadhaar initiative is also expected to give a boost to government's efforts for financial inclusion by providing the means for delivery of banking services through Business Correspondents (appointed by Banks) in rural areas.

(d) e-Commerce. This industry is witnessing phenomenal growth; B2C e-commerce is expected to touch USD 10 billion– a growth of 47 percent from 20109. e-payments in India account for 35.3 percent of the total transactions in terms of volume and 88.3 percent in terms of value, card circulation - both credit and debit - was around 200 million in 2010. The e-commerce is still an untapped potential – given that the Internet penetration in India is only around 8 percent (rising exponentially) with around 120 million Internet users and India is projected to become the third largest Internet user base by 2013. With around 894 million mobile subscribers (as on December 2011), m-commerce market is a big opportunity, especially as it promises to bring rural India into the realm of e-commerce.

(e) **IT/BPO Sector**. India is the preferred global supplier for IT software and services and is emerging as the knowledge hub of the world with many global companies opening their R&D and innovation centres in India. The industry has provided job opportunities to over 10 million people through direct and indirect employment and accounts for 6.4 percent of India's GDP. It aims to grow revenues to USD 225 billion by 2020 out of which USD 175 billion will be on account of export of software and services. Domestic IT market, including telecommunications services and equipment, is expected to touch USD 110 billion by 2012. Cloud Computing is a huge opportunity for India - next wave of growth for the Indian IT industry – as worldwide cloud services revenue are expected to reach around USD 150 billion in 2014. The Indian cloud computing market opportunity is expected to reach USD 16 billion by 2020. Data protection (security and privacy) is perceived to be one of the major challenges in adoption of the cloud.

(f) **Modernization of Police and Defence**. Police agencies and Defence are making strategic use of technology to modernize. Projects such as Crime and Criminal Tracking Network and Systems (CCTNS) and National Intelligence Grid (NATGRID) are flagship projects for modernization of police. CCTNS will connect

14,000 police stations and 6,000 police officers to a centralized database. The goal of CCTNS is 'to facilitate collection, storage, retrieval, analysis, transfer and sharing of data and information at the police station and between the police station and the State Headquarters and the Central Police Organizations.' NATGRID, in its first phase, 'will network 21 sets of data sources to provide quick and secure access to information required by 10 intelligence and law enforcement agencies as part of the counter terror-related investigative processes.' Defence has also taken similar initiatives – most notably the creation of an Army Wide Area Network (AWAN) designed to connect all Army formations, units, training establishments and logistic installations in the country for secure and direct information exchange. Army also launched project 'Shakti' – a fully digitized and integrated Artillery Combat Command and Control System, which is a network of military grade tactical computers automating and providing decision support for all operational aspects of Artillery functions from the corps down to a battery level.

(g) **Social Media**. With around 45 million Indians using the social media, and the number increasing every day, social media is emerging as a very powerful phenomenon in Indian cyberspace. It is revolutionizing the way society interacts. It is growing rapidly and becoming addictive especially for young Indians who love to connect with one another, make friends, chat, and publish photographs of family and friends. Personal Information is becoming the economic commodity on which social networking is thriving. Businesses, Non-Governmental Organizations (NGOs) and even the governments are using this platform for variety of reasons – communication, marketing, branding, awareness, etc. Whole new communities that encourage people to discuss important issues and come up with innovative solutions to local problems are emerging.

The report reinforces the point that internet has impacted our lives more than any other invention in the recent history. In fact, in about five years from now the impact will be visible in almost every sphere of daily life across urban as well as rural India. Interaction with young students in the rural areas of some states indicate that they using internet and are spending time on Facebook and Twitter. While for some it is a means of social interaction, for others it provides a platform to share their thoughts. In a society which is still conventional, it has opened up a whole new world for the young population of both sexes to share their thoughts and feelings without others snooping down. Importantly for them, it gives them the freedom of thought and expression which was not realized due to their conventional upbringing. It is no longer uncommon to find a couple of PCs in the neighbourhood apart from cyber cafes as elders find no reason to deny their children something which is being taught in schools and colleges. The availability of 3G/4G mobiles in these areas will further boost the usage of internet.

The proliferation and its subsequent addiction along with increasing number of computers available which reinforces the aspect of cyber security. Users, to a very large extent are not aware of cyber security. To most of them creating a password is enough to ensure security.

Cyberspace merges seamlessly with the physical world which makes it amenable to exploitation by adversaries, both state and non-state actors. The problem of attribution and low cost, low resource effort makes it very attractive to them. Defending cyberspace is a costly affair but nations need to focus on it if they have preserve their leveraging power in the international community as was discussed earlier.

Cyberspace Problems[3]

Rosenberg, the rapporteur of a workshop on *national security threats in cyberspace*, argues that the nature of cyberspace makes threats from that domain fundamentally different from those existing in the 'real world.' At least nine factors contribute to this difference:-

(a) The span of cyberspace is global, creating conflicting and overlapping realms of control by nation-state actors with

3 DCAF HORIZON 2015 WORKING PAPER No. 7 "On Cyber Warfare" by Fred Schreier.

differing legal and cultural approaches and distinct strategic interests.

(b) The world has become so dependent upon the cyber domain that disassociation is impossible. Cyber globalization cannot be undone; neither can our reliance on cyberspace for national security functions.

(c) The now globalized production of both cyber hardware and software in many different countries makes it virtually impossible to provide reliable supply chain assurance or good product assurance.

(d) The scalability of the cyber domain makes it qualitatively different. We do not deal with kinetic force of physically limited range, but with mechanism by which operations on a global scale are controlled.

(e) Operations within the domain are controlled by a small number of people. Everyday users cannot modify or control software and hardware they use, thus only few have control of the cyber universe.

(f) Because of the inter connectedness and inter operability of cyberspace, no locus of positive control is feasible. Efforts to mitigate the threat, if possible at all, will require close international cooperation.

(g) Changes in the cyber domain occur ever more rapidly. The inter connectedness of cyberspace enhances this consequence of acceleration. But each change creates again a new cycle of vulnerabilities.

(h) The distribution of cyber assets spans all types of organizations, from closed to government controlled systems to those operated by the public, each with different resources, capabilities, and concerns.

(j) The nature of cyberspace is such that the technical capacity to attribute actions to the responsible actor with a sufficient degree of confidence is still lacking. Hence, anonymity is easily achievable.[4]

Insecurity in cyberspace is caused by three conditions that distinguish it from other domains of activity and fundamentally shape the nature of cyber threats, firstly, the architecture of the Internet; secondly, the exponential innovation, and lastly, the Internet's widespread integration into the economy, society, government, and the armed forces.

The architecture of the Internet enables nearly instant movement of information globally at low cost. The Internet has been designed to connect multiple networks, computational facilities, and institutions seamlessly and reliably. Yet it was hard to foresee the vulnerabilities that would emerge as the Internet proliferated from a Pentagon-sponsored research project into a global communications network that pervades modern life. It is the Internet's openness that carries downsides in that it makes it easier to attack applications and operating systems that are not adequately defended. Designed as a decentralized system, the users of the Internet are functionally anonymous, generating information that travels in undifferentiated packets that can be encrypted to disguise the origin. This anonymity provided by the architecture leads to an attribution challenge that renders most cyber-attacks untraceable. Establishing, let alone authenticating identity is challenging if not possible at all.

The attribution problem empowers both strong and weak actors who benefit from having their identities disguised since the online anonymity makes identifying and punishing cyber attackers extremely difficult. Interlinked individuals or groups operating from globally dispersed locations can, with no warning and only milliseconds between decision and impact, attack scores of digital targets simultaneously without revealing their identities. Those who try to locate attackers often find themselves chasing ghosts or ending up at hacked botnets when the attacks originated from a multitude of computers and servers in multiple countries.

4 *National Security Threats in Cyberspace*, a Workshop of the National Strategy Forum, Part of the McCormick Foundation Conference Series, September 2009- accessed from DCAF HORIZON 2015 WORKING PAPER No. 7 "On Cyber Warfare" by Fred Schreier.

Innovation has expanded the availability, use, and functionality of the Internet at an amazing rate. Today, there are more than 2 billion Internet users globally, a vast increase from the 361 million users online in 2000. The spread of mobile devices, which surpassed 5 billion subscriptions worldwide in 2010, gives an even greater number of people access to the Internet as mobile devices continue to offer better functionality, particularly for the developing world. Ever-growing processor speeds and improved algorithms continue to facilitate greater reliance on the Internet, which adds trillions of dollars to the global economy each year. Global e-commerce activity totalled 10 trillion dollars in 2010, and is expected to amount to 24 trillion dollars by 2020.

Thus, continued innovation offers increasing opportunities for productive use of the Internet. However, it also aids all those with malicious intent by providing more targets and tools for attack. Cyber security is time consuming and expensive. Moreover, the pressure security companies feel to unveil innovative products quickly leads to introduction of technologies that are less secure than they would be if more time were devoted for bolstering their security. McAfee identified more than 20 million new pieces of malware in 2010, or an average of nearly 55,000 per day, each one representing a new weapon for attackers. It also reported increases in targeted attacks, in their sophistication, and in the number of attacks on the new classes of devices in 2010.

The architecture has facilitated Internet's integration into almost every aspect of modern life. While this has yielded most remarkable advances in productivity and efficiency, it has also created vulnerabilities that exceed understanding of the potential consequences. The integrated nature of cyberspace increases the chances that any disruption will ripple far beyond the original incident. Network disruptions resulting from cyber- attacks can lead to damage and even potential loss of life through cascading effects on critical systems and infrastructure.

Cyber Threats

Cyber threats, depending upon the motive, can primarily be

classified under following four heads:-

(a) Cybercrime.

(b) Cyber terrorism.

(c) Cyber espionage (also known as Computer Network Exploitation).

(d) Cyber-attacks.

The vulnerabilities of cyberspace offer many alternative tools to the actors who seek to exploit them. Cyber criminals may be young students who hacks the system to hone his skills or they be serious criminals who may be working alone or be a part of a group. Terrorist group are also using cyberspace not only to hack and disrupt the networks of target state but also to exchange information, command and control, generate funds and propagate their ideals.

Mumbai terror attacks of 2008 spurred the Indian Government into enacting laws dealing with cyber terrorism. The Indian parliament passed amendments to the IT Act, with emphasis on cyber terrorism and cybercrime, with a number of amendments to existing sections and the addition of new sections, taking into account these threats. Information Technology Act (IT Act) was enacted in year 2000 to provide legal recognition for transactions carried out by means of electronic data interchange and other means of electronic communication. The IT Act was amended in year 2008, resulting in establishment of a robust cyber security and data protection regime in the country. The IT (Amendment) Act, 2008 provides a comprehensive definition of the computer system, and tries to ascertain liability based on the type of cybercrime committed – hacking, spamming, tampering, identity theft, impersonation, cyber terrorism, pornography, child pornography, etc. It introduces the concept of 'sensitive personal information', and fixes liability of the 'body corporate' to protect the same through implementation of 'reasonable security practices'.

The rules issued under the Act, also require body corporates to follow privacy principles such as notice, choice and consent, access and correction, disclosure to third party, etc. On the other hand, the amended Act provides provision for legal action against a person for the breach of confidentiality and privacy, under lawful contract. Critical systems can be declared as 'protected systems' under the Act; security breaches of such systems attract higher prison sentences.

The IT (Amendment) Act, 2008 is an omnibus and comprehensive legislation which includes provisions for digital signatures, e-governance, e-commerce, data protection, cyber offences, critical information infrastructure, interception & monitoring, blocking of websites and cyber terrorism.[5] The government, in the process of enacting this bill, treaded a fine balance between the fundamental rights to privacy under the Indian Constitution and national security requirements.

Computer Network Exploitation (CNE) or espionage needs to be distinguished from cyber-attack. Firstly, CNE does not deprive the user of the full benefits of his machine. The user does not suffer any harm other than the data being stolen. Secondly, CNE is very difficult to detect and hence deterrence policy may useful sparingly. Thirdly, the law of war rarely recognizes espionage as a *casus belli,* and the case for changing this may be made in future through UN, as the means of espionage have changed. Fourthly, both state and non-state actors do it, albeit, with different motives. A great deal of state sponsored CNE is going on.

IDSA Task Force Report on India's Cyber Security Challenge, released recently by National Security Advisor Shri Shiv Shanker Menon, states that "thousands of megabytes of data and intellectual property worth millions being exfiltrated from the websites and NWs of both government and private enterprises. While government websites and NWs in India have been breached, the private sector claims that it has not been similarly affected. It may also be that theft of intellectual property from private enterprises is not an issue here because R&D expenditure in India is only 0.7

5 "Securing our Cyber Frontiers", NASSCOM DSCI Report.

percent of GDP, with government expenditure accounting for 70 percent of that figure." As is the practice in developed countries the private players do not invest in securing their NWs in the correct proportion of their earnings and seek to hide these incidents because of the fear of loss of business. The report corroborates this view and says "Companies are also reluctant to disclose any attacks and exfiltration of data, both because they could be held liable by their clients and also because they may suffer a resultant loss of confidence of the public." Interestingly the report points out that the Official Secrets Act of 1923 has become outdated because of infiltration of government NWs and computers and observes that "cyber espionage has all but made the Official Secrets Act, 1923 redundant, with even the computers in the Prime Minister's Office being accessed, according to reports. The multiplicity of malevolent actors, ranging from state-sponsored to hactivists, makes attribution difficult; governments currently can only establish measures and protocols to ensure confidentiality, integrity and availability (CIA) of data." The report advocates legal support for Law enforcement agencies. The report states "Law enforcement and intelligence agencies have asked their governments for legal and operational backing in their efforts to secure sensitive NWs and to go on the offensive against cyber spies and cyber criminals who are often acting in tandem with each other, and probably with state backing." The report makes an generally accepted view that "Offence is not necessarily the best form of defence in the case of cyber security, as seen in the continued instances of servers of the various government departments being hacked and documents exfiltrated" which is debated by some experts.

A great deal of state-sponsored CNE is going on. The PLA stands accused of having broken into thousands of civilian and unclassified military systems, in the United States and elsewhere (e.g., Germany), to steal large quantities of information. The Chinese are also said to have dropped implants into such systems in ways that make it difficult to clean up individual machines without allowing them to become reinfected. Germany's chancellor, Andrea Merkel, felt confident enough in this attribution to complain to China's premier in person. China has steadfastly denied all responsibility.[6]

Cyber Security Challenges

Cyberspace is a man made domain and is ever expanding. It is characterized by its vast reach, easy access, speed and scope. National security, both external and internal, has traditionally been the responsibility of the state but cyberspace throws up a new challenge in national security not visualized in the other four domains of warfare. Warfare in the four domains of land, sea, air and space involved clash between the militaries that bore the brunt and the civilian population was by and large left unscathed. While in the earlier days this was an unwritten understanding between states and was therefore violated often depending upon the attitude of the victorious army, in the present times it is UN Regulations and the Geneva Conventions which now formally give protection to civilians and non-military targets. However, for cyberspace domain rules do not exist at present as nations are still to fully comprehend it primarily because no wars have been fought between cyber powers. The threats in the cyber domain extend beyond military targets to civilian infrastructure as well and hence draw the civil populace directly in the war fighting effort. The

---

6 In August 2007, on the eve of German Chancellor Angela Merkel's meeting with Chinese Premier Wen Jiabao in China, *Spiegel* magazine reported that Germany's domestic intelligence service, the Office for the Protection of the Constitution, had discovered a significant cyber-attack targeting computers in the German Chancellery and in the foreign, economic and research ministries in May 2007 ("Merkel's China Visit Marred by Hacking Allegations,"

Spiegel Online International, August 27, 2007). In this instance, the information was siphoned off the German government's machines using Trojan horse programs that sent German government data via the Internet to what is believed to be a PLA-supported locus of attack in Lanzhou, Canton province, and to Beijing. While the German government does not know exactly how much information was stolen, some estimates are in the terabytes, and

German security officials were able to thwart a 160-gigabyte data transfer. German security officials also said they estimate 40 percent of all German companies have been victims of nation-state–sponsored industrial espionage, with the majority of the activities originating in Russia and China. There is no word on whether these implants could have launched or facilitated a destructive cyber-attack or were instead simply meant to facilitate further.

Source- Cyber Deterrence and Cyber War by Martin C. LibiCki, RAND Corporation.

threats are consequently increasing at a bewildering pace.

Cyberspace is a vast, complex and rapidly changing battle space. The key to prevailing in a hostile cyber-space environment may lie in the ability to generate a comprehensive picture of that environment. In the kinetic realm, the fog of war is a term derived from Clausewitz referring to uncertain knowledge about the adversary, and the position and activities of the own forces in the midst of an operation. While situational awareness is a major challenge already in traditional warfare, the fog of cyber war may well be so thick that it could become the primary impediment to victory. Thus, developing the techniques and tools for cyber situational awareness would be paramount to achieving strategic, operational, or tactical advantage in this novel domain.

Cyberspace offers unique challenges in cyber security. These challenges exist at various levels- international, national-government, private sector, military and at the societal level. It is because of the wide array of targets that the cyber challenges that face us require challenging solutions.

At the international level no formal convention or regulation on cyber security exists. In the absence of globally accepted norms featuring cooperation across jurisdictions to track cyber criminals and their extradition makes it difficult for the law agencies to bring cyber criminals to justice.

There is still no clarity in the cyber security scenario among the nations in general and India in particular. There is still no sense of urgency though some nations who are constantly at the receiving end have begun to feel the heat. New threats are emerging every day which would present new complications and the impact could be beyond the present realm of thinking. Therefore the need of the hour is to enact a coherent cyber security policy which is reviewed constantly at the highest level periodically as new threats emerge. The policy should identify the national critical infrastructure, identify the vulnerabilities and suggest organizational measures to remove them. IDSA Task Report stresses upon this aspect when it states that "It is essential that more attention at the highest levels is paid to ensuring that cyber-related vulnerabilities that can impact on critical sectors are identified and removed. A coherent and comprehensive cyber security policy will have several major elements, including accurate conceptualisation of cyberspace threats; building of robust cyberspace through a variety of measures, including technical, legal, diplomatic, international cooperation; creation of adequate organisational structures; strengthening of PPPs; HR development; and implementation of best practices and guidelines." As an important proactive measure the policy could suggest is an organization which would be entrusted with the task of carrying out security audits of critical organizations and suggest remedial measures and monitor the follow up actions by affected parties in a time bound manner.

Protection of critical national infrastructure has emerged as a major challenge. The responsibility of securing the critical national infrastructure against the rising number of cyber-attacks has come within the ambit of national security. This responsibility, however, does not lie solely with the government; private sector too has a major role to play as part of the critical national infrastructure is owned and operated by the private sector. However, private sector's investment in security is driven more by business requirements and not by national security concerns. So how can government intervene? By giving incentives or by regulating the private sector? There is an ongoing debate on which direction the nations should take. Many believe that market forces cannot deliver the required investments and efforts for ensuring public safety and national security. Whereas some believe that too much of government intervention through regulations can undermine business innovation. [7]

The attacks on critical infrastructure of a nation are bound to happen and will only increase in future. The number of cyber security incidents involving potential attacks on critical infrastructure in US increased by more than 2,000 percent between 2009 and 2011, according to a new report from the Industrial Control Systems Cyber Emergency Response Team (ICS-CERT), reports Defence

7 Ibid.

Systems sister publication FCW. In 2009, ICS-CERT, which is part of the Homeland Security Department, received nine incident reports; that number jumped to 41 in 2010 and 198 in 2011. In 2009 and 2010, the energy sector was the target of the most incidents, accounting for a third of all reports in 2009 and for 44 percent in 2010. In 2011, water utilities saw 41 percent of the incidents reported to ICS-CERT, and attacks on multiple sectors made up 25 percent. A large number of incidents involved "sophisticated and targeted spear-phishing campaigns" that opened the door to theft and further network infiltration, according to the report.[8]

There is yet another area of global concern, namely the ICT global supply chain. Given the increased dependence on global ICT products, especially in operating critical sectors and growing realization of cyber risks, countries are doubting the integrity of these products, fearing that adversaries may introduce malicious codes / functions to do surreptitious surveillance, disrupt services, or at worst paralyze a nation. Alleviating such doubts and fears to continue benefitting from global ICT supply chain is one of the biggest challenges the world faces in cyber security today. Where some countries are trying to address this challenge by building global and national capabilities to address supply chain risks without undermining the international competitiveness and legitimate trade flow; others are focusing on developing indigenous products to reduce the dependency on foreign players.[9]

Two global trends within the information and communications technology environment, while providing greater efficiency and better services to users, will only increase vulnerabilities and the consequences of security failures. The first is *network convergence*: the merging of distinct voice and data technologies to a point where all communications – for example, voice, facsimile, video, instant messaging, computers, control of critical infrastructure, and the Internet – are transported over a common network structure, which will come to completion within the next five years. This

8 http://defencesystems.com/articles/2012/07/03/agg-cyberattacks-critical-infrastructure.aspx?s=ds_090712

9 Ibid.

convergence amplifies the opportunity for, and the consequences of, disruptive cyber-attacks and unforeseen secondary or tertiary effects on other parts of the critical infrastructure. The second is "channel consolidation": the concentration of data captured on individual users by service providers through emails or instant messaging, Internet search engines, Web 2.0 social networking means, and geographic location of mobile service subscribers, which increases the potential and consequences for exploitation of personal data by malicious actors.[10]

Another very important challenge requiring ongoing efforts is poor awareness and education about cyber security threats and the need to follow best practices, across different levels – ranging from school children to top government officials, and management in the corporate world. Adding to the problem is the non-serious and reactive approach towards security. Lack of knowledge and awareness among users increases the risk manifold. Because of poor awareness, we become vulnerable and easy victims of social engineering attacks, phishing sites, spurious email communications, etc. Many such cyber threats can be easily mitigated if individuals are aware and vigilant.[11]

The awareness and willingness along with the belief among government officials that cyber threat is real and lurking around may propel them to sit up and take cyber security in the right earnest. Hacking may still take place despite protective measures but the frequency will definitely reduce. Prompt reporting of such incidents will help law enforcements agencies to track the offender or at least take action to prevent further mischief. However, like the private sector, it appears the government officials are not inclined to give access to their compromised email accounts. A report in The Times of India substantiates this view.[12] This is hardly

10 DCAF HORIZON 2015 WORKING PAPER No. 7 "On Cyber Warfare" by Fred Schreier.

11 Ibid.

12 Can government officials claim right to privacy if their emails have been hacked and security agencies ask for full access to the contents of the accounts?

Efforts of Indian intelligence agencies to counter waves of cyber-attacks on government networks have run into an iron wall. Although access to the compromised email accounts of officials is critical for investigations, officials are less than keen. The officials

encouraging and may be detrimental to national security and also prove to be a setback in efforts to improve cyber defences because as the report observes "the move comes at a time when the government is strengthening its overall posture against cyber-attacks. A comprehensive policy is set to be approved by the Cabinet Committee on Security, detailing India's response to cyber-attacks targeted at government systems and other critical infrastructure. Part of the strategy is to create dedicated Computer Emergency Response Teams for various sectors, setting up of National Critical Information Infrastructure Protection Centre etc."

---

say that allowing the agencies to trawl contents of all their emails will breach their privacy: a position which is being supported by the National Informatics Centre (NIC), the custodian of all official electronic data.

Faced with regular attacks on government's critical infrastructure, agencies are discussing how much detail regarding the e-mails can be made available to investigators as officials are chary about private mails being scrutinized.

Sources said government found a clear pattern in cyber-attacks targeting government computers, networks and other infrastructure. Almost all these attacks gain entry into a computer or a network via emails of officials. Almost all of them are official emails provided to them by the NIC.

From phishing to acquire information such as usernames and passwords to planting Trojans that provide remote access to a user's computer and network, the attacks are consistent and widespread. Trojans can be used for downloading or uploading files from, or to, a system.

Sources in the military and intelligence agencies say NIC — the official holder of official emails and websites — has been fending off bids to access hacked official emails. In case of such foreign cyber-attacks, there are no police cases filed or any formal criminal investigation launched. Public email providers such as Google part with details of e-mails only when law enforcement agencies file formal cases and seek details.

The government agencies want access as soon as attacks happen so as to track down the attack as well as to initiate preventive measures. The logs of the e-mail would tell them where all these e-mails have been accessed from, and other details. A military source said, besides accessing the logs of affected e-mails they were also keen to get contents of emails that may have been hacked. "We would definitely like to know how much of information has been compromised," he said.

"What is there in the e-mail would tell us what has surely been lost," he added.

A senior official said the government is now set to draw up a policy guideline on accessing logs and contents of official emails of government officials. "We are primarily looking at the regular needs of intelligence agencies. They need quick access, but we have to ensure that there is no misuse," he said.

Source- The Times of India, Delhi, 13 May 2012.

Another type of challenge is the mushrooming of "objectionable sites." These sites pose a serious threat to the society and may hurt national pride and interests. The Indian Government has been regularly writing to ISPs to block such sites. According to Google Online content censorship in India has gone up by 49 percent. As part of its 'transparency report', Google said that it had received 101 content removal requests from Indian authorities between July and December in 2011, asking it to delete 255 items from its websites.[13] Of these, just five requests were made by courts. Recently Madras

13 According to the Google data, the company was asked to remove 130 items, including 77 videos on YouTube, because they were deemed defamatory. Another 25 items, including 24 videos, were considered hate speech. The interesting bit was that of these only 25 items — 23 on the blogs hosted by Google and two on other Google sites — were considered defamatory by a court.

"This is the fifth data set that we've released. And just like every other time before, we've been asked to take down political speech," Dorothy Chou, senior policy analyst wrote at the official Google blog. "It's alarming not only because free expression is at risk, but because some of these requests come from countries you might not suspect — Western democracies not typically associated with censorship."

National security and piracy, touted as primary reasons by government officials behind the push for control on the web, didn't lead to many content removal requests in India. Google was told to remove only two items because of copyright reasons and only 10 videos on You-Tube because they were considered a threat to national security. At the same time, the company was told to remove 22 items because of impersonation risk and seven items because the content was 'offensive' to religions. Also, requests were made to remove two videos from YouTube because they were too violent in nature and one item was deemed pornographic.

As far as removing the content was concerned, Google said it complied with 80 percent requests received from Indian courts. But for requests made by police or other government agencies, it complied in only 26 percent cases. "For the six months of data we're releasing today, we complied with an average of 65 percent of court orders, as opposed to 47 percent of more informal requests," wrote Chou.

While Google officials were not available to comment on Monday, in its earlier report the company had explained that it did not comply with all requests. "We received requests from (Indian) state and local law enforcement agencies to remove YouTube videos that displayed protests against social leaders or used offensive language in reference to religious leaders. We declined the majority of these requests and only locally restricted videos that appeared to violate local laws prohibiting speech that could incite enmity between communities," the report said.

Between July and December, Google also received 2,207 requests from Indian authorities seeking access to user data. In total, these requests targeted 3,427 accounts/people. Google said it complied with 66 percent requests.

Source - The Times of India, Delhi, 19 June 2012.

High Court Gave a ruling in which it directed that only the links of "objectionable sites" be blocked and not the site.[14]

---

14 The Madras high court has ruled that its April 25 order against internet piracy should not be used to block the entire website; only specific links should be blocked.

On an appeal filed by a group of ISPs, the court in an order on June 15 clarified that the content owners should give ISPs the specific web links through which the copyrighted material was being shared so that the ISPs could block them. Following the HC order, most of the websites blocked by ISPs, except Piratebay, have become accessible again.

In recent months, there has been a spurt in John Doe orders — orders against unnamed entities — in India. Film producers have gone to various courts and obtained such orders against those who might pirate their films. This has invariably happened a day or two before the film release. Armed with these orders, film producers have prevailed upon ISPs to block entire websites, leading to resentment among web users and a wave of protests by net activists.

The HC's June 15 order came after its April 25 John Doe order led to ISPs blocking several sites, including Vimeo. The move was severely resented and criticized by internet users in India, who blamed ISPs for the inconvenience caused to them. The blocking of sites also prompted Anonymous, a hacker collective, to raise the concern over what it perceived as web censorship. Anonymous attacked several government websites over the incident and even organized real-world protests in several cities.

The HC in its latest order said: "The interim injunction (dated April 25) is granted only in respect of a particular URL where the infringing movie is kept and not in respect of the entire website. Further, the applicant is directed to inform about the particulars of URL where the interim movie is kept within 48 hours."

Sunil Abraham, director of Centre for Internet and Society, a Bangalore based think tank that tracks internet policy, said the court clarification was much needed.

"There are two problems with John Doe orders. They lack specificity. It's against an anonymous infringer. These orders also allow petitioners to misuse them as they demand complete blocking of websites without taking recourse to identifying the pirates and the URLs through which copyright material is being shared," Abraham said. "The latest order addresses these issues. By asking ISPs to only block specific URLs it addresses major concerns about John Doe orders."

John Doe has of late become the favourite of film producers. Reliance Entertainment obtained several John Doe orders last year. Recently, producers of 'Gangs of Wasseypur' obtained such an order. After the film's director Anurag Kashyap received negative feedback from web users on Twitter, he said, "When my films were pirated, my investors and studio never blamed me for it but when the studio got a John Doe order for 'Gangs of Wasseypur', the internet blames me."

At the same time, he claimed he would try his best to make sure web users didn't suffer blanket bans on websites because of the order. "The order has been taken by investing parties to protect their investment but they have assured me that it will be used responsibly. I can argue with them about not taking down entire sites and just the URLs and they have assured they will do that," he tweeted. The Madras high court order is a welcome step in guarding the rights of internet users. The internet is all about free choice and free flow of information. Therefore, entire websites should not be blocked just because there might be some illegal content on them. Only specific

Google, which runs services like YouTube and Blogger apart from the widely used search engine, said the number marked an increase of 49 percent in such requests compared with January-June 2011 period. In terms of requests made by the government bodies excluding courts, India topped the list as it sent 96 requests to Google to remove content. However, in terms of number of items that governments wanted to remove, Brazil, US, UK, Germany and Spain were ahead of India.

Other major difficulties in addressing problems related to cyber security at an organizational level include: lack of high quality software development; treatment of security function as a cost centre; compliance driven approach to security; lack of multi-departmental coordinated road map; treatment of security as merely a technology issue and not a management issue; and difficulty in calculating Return on Investment (RoI) for security investment.[15]

Another issue which deserves the immediate attention of the authorities is E-activism. Today there are a host of websites dedicated solely to hoisting and advocating these petitions. Avijit Michael, country director, India, of Change-.org, says, "Websites like ours provide a number of tools to anyone who wants to see positive change. It starts with the petition tool to help one decide on the message and the target. It also allows a person to share the petition on social networks and, thus, mobilize more people. Finally, he can print the signatures and submit them to the target or mail them directly." When used well, along with media pressure on the target, an online petition, Michael says, serves to showcase how

---

URLs where pirated content is available should be blocked. An entire website may be blocked only when government and industry agree that it deals predominantly with pirated stuff. There should also be quick redress of copyright owners' grievances — illegal content should be blocked within, say, six hours, of verification. Websites on which a huge chunk of the content is pirated should be blocked for a specified period, say, three months, and given a chance to mend their ways. How huge is 'huge' — 5 percent, 10 percent or 15 percent? That may be decided by a committee comprising representatives of government and industry. The numbers mentioned here may sound arbitrary, but we have to start somewhere.

Source – The Times of India, Delhi, 22 June 2012.

15 Ibid.

many people support the issue. It has startled governments across the world — even in China, where internet is strongly controlled, with outspoken bloggers routinely being detained. [16]

In India, though, online advocacy is really yet to take off. It saw some success with the Pink Chaddi campaign against the Sri Ram Sene's campaign against Valentine's Day. But it was more controversy than content that it was noted for. The most visible would have to be the Anna Hazare's anti-graft movement where online petitions were used to drum up more numbers on the streets. Recently, West Bengal chief minister Mamata Banerjee took to the internet and Facebook to garner support for APJ Abdul Kalam as a presidential candidate. It failed, however, to create an online wave.

In a thriving democracy, dissent of opinion is a vital ingredient for its good health. However, it is dangerous when this E-activism gets exploited by groups inimical to our national interests. This again takes us to the issue of censuring the websites for any "objectionable contents." The tendency, however, to block links for parochial gains need to be curbed and hence necessary safeguards need to be incorporated in the law.

---

16 In April, an online petition on Change.org, a website promoting social change with internet petitions, received 2.2 million "signatures". The 'Prosecute the killer of our son, 17-year-old Trayvon Martin'-petition led to the arrest of George Zimmerman, a neighbourhood watch coordinator in Florida where the shooting took place.

Such internet activism has led to the emergence of free websites dedicated solely to hosting and advocating these petitions. There are dozens of them — Change-.org, Avaaz.org, to name a few But have such petitions worked? In many cases the answer would have to be a resounding 'Yes'. It was, however, the sheer power of online activism that led to the release of bloggers such as Ai Weiwei.

Massive campaigns were also launched during the Arab Spring to overthrow despots in the Middle East, and against the notorious Stop Online Piracy Act and the Protect IP Act — laws that threatened internet freedom. Other success stories included the release of two journalists, Laura Ling and Euna Lee, who were imprisoned in North Korea.

So, what will it take for internet petitioning to become a rage in India — something that becomes a movement in itself and is taken seriously by the government? For one, online activism here is severely limited by inadequate internet access. Also, the internet isn't as valued here as it is, say, in China or the US. But Michael is confident that as internet penetration grows, the number of online campaigns will increase. "Currently, on Change.org, we see at least 50 new campaigns every week," he says.

Source- The Times of India, Delhi, 14 June 2012.

Rumour mongering is another issue which the authorities need to take notice of as it can do incalculable harm. Using the social networking sites, like Twitter one can quickly spread rumours as was witnessed recently.

Bollywood's first superstar, Rajesh Khanna died and then rose from the dead on 21 Jun 2012, all in the span of less than 24 hours. As social networking sites oscillated between speculation and 'news' of Bollywood's 'Kaka' succumbing to his illness, following days of going without food, Akshay Kumar decided to sort fact from fiction. He brought out his dad-in-law on the balcony of his bungalow and later tweeted, "All those spreading rumours, a humble request, get your facts right before reporting. And for those genuinely concerned and inquiring about my father in law's health, he is doing fine now and on the road to recovery. Thank you for your good wishes." [17]

---

17 Rajesh Khanna happened to be one of over a dozen celebs who've been slain on the internet in death hoaxes this year. In January 2012, Lata Mangeshkar found herself dead online and had to take to her micro-blogging account to clarify she was hale and hearty. "All is well, by the grace of god," she tweeted, ending rumors of her ill health leading to death.

Another singer in the West, Cher was killed by rumor mongers online in January. Even Kim Karshashian fell for the prank and retweeted, "Did I just hear that Cher has passed away? Is this real? OMG!" Turned out Cher was just another victim of a celebrity death hoax.

An internet hoax about the death of Rowan 'Mr Bean' Atkinson went viral in late February. Earlier that month, in two separate instances, Hollywood actors Keanu Reeves and Eddie Murphy were made victims of snowboarding accidents and their death mourned by fans online till truth came to light.

In April, R&B singer Usher had to tweet a pic of his, a shirtless one, to dash rumors of his death, caused by a car crash. He also posted, "I must've died and went to heaven... Alive and cold kickin a**!!"

Rumors of actor Robin Williams' death doing the rounds of the internet in May were rather sordid. They claimed the actor had died by falling off a cliff in Austria!

In June alone, the internet has killed over four celebs, including Rajesh Khanna, who're actually far from dead. Tina Turner, Mariah Carey and American rapper Vanilla Ice have all died online this month and been resurrected by clarifications later.

Risen from the dead!

Here's a list of celebs in death hoaxes in 2012:

January: Lata Mangeshkar, Cher

February: Rowan Atkinson Keanu Reeves Eddie Murphy Chris Brown

April: Usher

The most disconcerting aspect of E-activism and rumor mongering is their exploitation by terror and separatists groups to whip up anti national feelings or, say, by Maoists to launch disinformation campaign against the state or the security forces. As regards the Armed Forces it has serious implications which will be discussed later.

Government Meets the Cyber Challenge

The Government of India has taken the initiative in meeting these challenges but a lot more needs to be done. Some of these are described in succeeding paragraphs.

Draft National Cyber Security Policy

The draft version of National Cyber Security Policy was released by the DIT on its website in March 2011 for public opinion. The draft policy aims to enable secure computing environment and adequate trust and confidence in electronic transactions. The draft policy tries to layout the cyber security ecosystem for the country. It covers the following:-

(a) Based on the key policy considerations and threat landscape, the draft policy identifies priority areas for action.

(b) Identifies PPP as a key component.

(c) Identifies key actions to reduce security threats and vulnerabilities.

(d) Establishment of a National Cyber Alert System for early watch and warning, information exchange, responding to national level cyber incidents and facilitating restoration.

(e) Defines role of sectoral CERTs and establishment of local incident response teams for each critical sector organization.

(f) Implementation of best practices in critical information and

---

May: Gabriel Garcia Marquez Robin Williams

June: Tina Turner Mariah Carrey Adam Sandler Vanilla Ice

Source – The Times of India, Delhi, 22 June 2012.

government infrastructure protection through creation, establishment and operation of Information Security Assurance Framework.

(g) Establishes framework for Crisis Management Plan for Countering Cyber-attacks and Cyber terrorism.

(h) Identifies priorities for action for legal framework and law enforcement capability development.

(j) Defines priorities for international cooperation for information sharing.

(k) Identifies indigenous Research & Development as an essential component of cyber security and enlists thrust areas for R&D.

(l) Identifies major actions and initiatives for user awareness, education, and training (capacity building).

(m) Defines responsible actions for network service providers, large corporates and small/medium & home users to secure information and systems.

(n) Identifies various stakeholders (ministries and government departments only) in cyber security and their responsibilities.

The final version of the National Cyber Security Policy, post public comments is yet to be announced by the government. The encouraging part is that the report has received overwhelming as response many comments (posted on the website), from companies to individuals, have been received.

CERT-In[18]

Government set up the Indian Computer Emergency Response Team (CERT-In) in 2003 as a nodal agency for responding to cyber security incidents. The charter of CERT-In states "The purpose of the CERT-In is to become the nation's most trusted referral agency of the Indian Community for responding to computer security incidents as

18 Source- www.cert-in.org.in/

and when they occur; it will also assist in implementing proactive measures to reduce the risks of computer security incidents."

CERT-In is a functional organisation of Department of Information Technology, Ministry of Communications and Information Technology, Government of India, with the objective of securing Indian cyber space. CERT-In provides Incident Prevention and Response services as well as Security Quality Management Services.

The Information Technology Act 2000 designated CERT-In to serve as the national agency to perform the following functions in the area of cyber security:-

(a) Collection, analysis and dissemination of information on cyber incidents.

(b) Forecast and alerts of cyber security incidents.

(c) Emergency measures for handling cyber security incidents.

(d) Coordination of cyber incident response activities.

(e) Issue guidelines, advisories, vulnerability notes and white papers relating to information security practices, procedures, prevention, response and reporting of cyber incidents.

(f) Such other functions relating to cyber security as may be prescribed.

The IT (Amendment) Act, 2008, recognizes CERT-In as a nodal agency for security incident management and provides it the authority it to call for information on security incidents from organizations. CERT-In, through a dedicated infrastructure, collects, analyzes, disseminates information on cyber security incidents. It monitors and investigates threats that affect computer systems and forecasts and generates alerts for cyber security incidents. CERT-In provides:-

(a) Proactive services in the nature of Advisories, Security Alerts, Vulnerability Notes, and Security Guidelines to help organisations secure their systems and networks.

(b) Reactive services when security incidents occur so as to minimize damage.

CERT-In in its Annual Report of the year 2011 gives out the Cyber abuse incidents as 13301. The details are at Appendix B. The trends of incidents reported to and handled by CERT-In and cyber-attack trends during the year 2011 are given at Appendix C. CERT-In has been tracking the defacements of Indian websites and suggesting suitable measures to harden the web servers to concerned organizations. In all 17306 numbers of defacements have been tracked. Most of the defacements were under .in domain, in which a total 9839 .in domain websites were defaced.

CERT-In collaborates internationally for the incident response, tracks incidents affecting both public and private sector and issues security guidelines and advisory on vulnerabilities. It provides technical assistance to organizations in resolving security incidents. It has helped establish sectoral CERTs in defence and banking sectors. To test preparedness of organizations operating critical information infrastructure, CERT-In conducts cyber security drills in partnership with the public and private sector. To help law enforcement agencies solve cybercrimes, CERT-In has developed standard operating procedures for cybercrime investigations. It organizes regular trainings and funds research and other projects in security to academic institutes and industry. It also engages with its counterparts in other countries for increased collaboration and information sharing. CERT-In has developed 12th five year plan on cyber security. [19]

Cyber Initiatives for Police

Ministry of Home Affairs (MHA) plans to launch a Cyber Crime Investigation Program (CCIP), which proposes to establish a Cyber Crime Police Station and a Cyber Crime Investigation and Forensic Training Facility in each State and Union Territory, and a central National Centre of Excellence for Cyber Forensics Services. The

19 Source- CERT-In

program will create a network of cyber police stations across the country, equipped with state-of-the-art technology and well trained police officers, which can collaborate to benefit from each other's experiences. The National Centre of Excellence will act as the guiding force, providing thought leadership to the Cyber Crime Police Stations and Cyber Crime Investigation and Forensic Training Facilities by conducting advanced research & development.

Under the Directorate of Forensic Science, under MHA, three Central Forensic Labs (CFSLs) have developed capabilities in cyber forensics. Also, there are 28 State Forensic Labs (SFSLs) that are acquiring capabilities in cyber forensics techniques and skills. Resource Centre for Cyber Forensics (RCCF) at Thiruvanthapuram, Kerala under Centre for Development of Advanced Computing (CDAC) has been established to develop cyber forensic tools and to provide technical support and necessary training to law enforcement agencies in the country.[20]

Security in e-Governance Projects

The National e-Governance Division (NeGD), under DIT, is the Program Management Office of NeGP. Among its various activities, including facilitating implementation of NeGP by various Ministries and State governments, the agency is also responsible for issuing cyber security and data security standards and guidelines for all the e-Governance projects under NeGP. For securing e-governance projects, Standardization Testing and Quality Certification Directorate (STQC) has developed e-Governance Security Assurance Framework (e-SAFE), which provides list of security controls based on the risk categorization of particular assets.[21]

Common Criteria Certification Scheme

This scheme has been set up by DIT to evaluate and certify IT Security Products and Protection Profiles against the requirements of Common Criteria Standards ver 3.1 R2, at Evaluation Assurance Levels EAL 1 through 4. Presently, the scheme provides national

20 " Securing our Cyber Frontiers" NASSCOM DSCI Report

21 Ibid.

certification. The scheme would also provide a framework for international certification through the National Mutual Recognition Arrangement with the other member countries of Common Criteria Recognition Arrangement (CCRA). Along with 24 other countries, India has already become a member of CCRA as a certificate consuming nation and soon will be recognized as a certificate producing nation. STQC is a certification body of the country with STQC IT, Kolkata centre as the Common Criteria Test Lab.[22]

NASSCOM and DSCI Initiatives

NASSCOM is an institution created by the corporate sector to guide their business through various initiatives. The initiatives taken by NASSCOM and DSCI show the seriousness of the private players in cyber security and deserve encouragement and active as well collaborative support of the government.

NASSCOM is the premier body and the chamber of commerce of the IT-BPO industries in India. NASSCOM is a global trade body with more than 1200 members which include both Indian and multinational companies that have a presence in India. NASSCOM's member and associate member companies are broadly in the business of software development, software services, software products, consulting services, BPO services, e-commerce & web services, engineering services offshoring and animation and gaming and constitute over 95 percent of the industry revenues in India and employs over 2.24 million professionals.

NASSCOM's Vision is to maintain India's leadership position in the global sourcing IT industry, to grow the market by enabling industry to tap into emerging opportunity areas and to strengthen the domestic market in India.

DSCI is a focal body on data protection in India, setup as an independent Self-Regulatory Organization (SRO) by NASSCOM, to promote data protection, develop security and privacy best practices & standards and encourage the Indian industries to implement the same.

---

22 Ibid.

DSCI is engaged with the Indian IT/BPO industry, their clients worldwide, Banking and Telecom sectors, industry associations, data protection authorities and other government agencies in different countries. It conducts industry wide surveys and publishes reports, organizes data protection awareness seminars, workshops, projects, interactions and other necessary initiatives for outreach and public advocacy. DSCI is focused on capacity building of Law Enforcement Agencies for combating cybercrimes in the country and towards this; it operates several Cyber labs across India to train police officers, prosecutors and judicial officers in cyber forensics.

NASSCOM Trusted Sourcing Initiative[23]

To promote India as a trusted outsourcing destination, NASSCOM initiated a 4E initiative for outsourcing industry for promotion and enforcement of security. It relies on Engagement with all stakeholders involved, Education of service providers, Enactment to create a policy environment, Enforcement of standards and constant checks. This initiative resulted in establishment of:-

(a) DSCI as a Self-Regulatory Organization with a vision to harness data protection as a lever for economic development of India through global integration of practices and standards conforming to various legal regimes. To achieve this vision, DSCI works closely with the Indian government, foreign governments, regulators, industry, clients, LEAs, think tanks and academic institutes in the areas of public advocacy, thought leadership, capacity building, cybercrime investigations and dispute resolution.

(b) Cyber Labs Program under which Cyber Labs were established in four major cities to build capacity of LEAs by training police officers in cybercrime investigations and cyber forensics.

(c) National Skills Registry (NSR) to build a robust and credible information repository on the knowledge professionals in the IT/BPO sector via background checks and verification.

23 Ibid.

Worldwide Cyber Security Summit

NASSCOM and DSCI have partnered with EastWest Institute (EWI) - a global think-and-do tank to host the 3rd Worldwide Cyber Security Summit in New Delhi on October 30-31, 2012. It will be India's first major international summit of cyber security experts from government, business, technology and civil society from around the world. The summit process will comprise forming three high-level working groups of Indian and international experts, each taking on a crucial cyber security issue. One group will develop ways to secure the global ICT supply chain.

Another will focus on agreements, standards, policy and regulations to secure the increasing share of our digital world powered by cloud computing. The third will focus on payload security. The first two working groups will be led by NASSCOM and DSCI.

DSCI Initiatives[24]

DSCI has developed strong linkages with the Indian government, industry and global think tanks and provided platforms to bring all the stakeholders in cyber security together for discussing cyber security issues and solutions. It has strengthened the government-industry interactions and has developed the operational capability to deliver cyber security projects in PPP mode. Following are some of the major initiatives undertaken by DSCI:-

(a) **DSCI Security Framework**. To overcome the checklist based and compliance based approach to security which fails to address the evolving threats, DSCI has developed DSCI Security Framework (DSF) which focuses on bringing dynamism in security. It is an improvement over existing security standards and frameworks as it enables an organization to focus on real threats in its environment, without worrying about compliance. It enables assessment of organization's maturity in implementing security in different areas with a view to continually improve the same. Such an assessment further helps organization draw a strategic plan based on evolution of different disciplines of

24 Ibid.

security, and their interdependencies, with continuous focus on protecting data. DSCI is promoting the implementation of DSF in the industry. DSCI has also developed DSCI Privacy Framework (DPF) which helps organizations design, implement and monitor privacy program.

(b) **LEA Capacity Building Programs**. Augmenting NASSCOM's efforts to build the capacity of LEAs in India, DSCI has expanded the Cyber Labs program. Presently, 4 out of 8 cyber labs have been funded jointly by DIT, respective state and DSCI. Through these labs over 9,000 police officers and other officials in the LEAs, including judiciary and public prosecutors for investigation and prosecution of cybercrimes, are being trained annually. The knowledge developed, over a period of time, has been systematized in the Cybercrime Investigation Manual and distributed to police stations across India. Based on its experience of running cyber labs, DSCI submitted a detailed project report to the MHA, which has been accepted by the ministry and the program will be extended to the entire country in the form of CCIP. This initiative will have active support of the industry through DSCI and NASSCOM. The DSCI core team on cyber forensics will liaise with the National Centre of Excellence (CoE), and contribute knowledge inputs to all their areas of work; it will mentor and guide the State agencies to operationalize the cybercrime police stations and training centres. DSCI will track cybercrimes, cyber forensic tools, emerging curricula, conferences and other developments to continuously develop the training material and update the content.

(c) **DSCI Excellence Awards**. To reward organizations and individuals who have shown high level of preparedness and have excelled in the area of information security, DSCI has institutionalized DSCI Excellence Awards. Among various categories, it also has India Cyber Cop Award category to recognize, reward and honour a police officer who has done the most outstanding investigation in solving a cybercrime to encourage the police officers who have put in extra efforts to learn cyber forensics to solve cybercrimes.

(d) **DSCI Chapters**. To create a network of security professionals in the country, DSCI has established 'DSCI Chapters' across major cities in India. Presently, over 1200 security professionals are connected together through these chapters. The chapters provide a platform to security professionals in India to collaborate and share best practices. It also provides a mechanism for DSCI to engage with the security experts in the country.

(e) **Cyber Security Awareness Program**. Under the DIT-NASSCOM funded Cyber Security Awareness Program (Nov'08 – Dec'10), DSCI conducted Cyber Security Awareness Campaigns across the country, published Security Surveys and Publication, conducted Training for over 700 government officials, developed Computer based Trainings, developed a national security portal, among other activities.

Critical Infrastructure Protection by PPP Model

National Security has traditionally been the sole responsibility of the governments across the four domains of warfare i.e. land, sea, air and space. With the recognition of cyberspace as the fifth domain of warfare, the entire landscape of traditional responsibility has undergone a change. As the world has moves into the information age, with increased dependence on information infrastructure for production and delivery of products and services, the responsibility of securing the critical information infrastructure (CII) against the rising number of cyber- attacks has come within the ambit of national security. This added responsibility, though it is its prerogative, however, does not lie solely with the government; private sector has a major role to play since more than 80 percent of the critical information infrastructure is owned and operated by the private sector.[25] However, private sector's investment, the world over, in security is driven by business interests and not by national security concerns. DIT, Government of India, has identified the national critical information infrastructure in Indian context as Defence, Finance, Energy, Transportation and Telecommunications.

The analysis of some of these sectors shows that a significant

25 Ibid.

part of the CII is owned and operated, to a varying degree, by the private sector in India:-[26]

(a) **Telecom Sector**. It is mostly governed by private players, except MTNL and BSNL. The global undersea cable communication infrastructure (GUCCI) is largely owned by private players.

(b) **Banking Sector.** More than 30 percent of the transactions are done online, and the value of these transactions is over 80 percent of total transaction value, has a large number of foreign and private banks

(c) **Stock Exchanges.** The major stock exchanges BSE and NSE are private players, wherein most of the transactions are done through the electronic medium.

(d) **Airline.** It is dominated by private players, with Air India being the only government enterprise.

(e) **Energy and Utilities**. Though this sector is largely dominated by government players, the distribution in major cities is largely controlled by private partners.

Presently an animated debate is raging the world over on the issue- how should government intervene? By incentivizing or regulating the private sector? Though strong and effective PPPs are obviously essential, such questions need to be debated and discussed in detail before a viable solution which while keeping the national security interests paramount, address and protect the business interests of the private sector to their complete satisfaction. It is important that the PPP model evolved generates the firm belief of well-being in the private sector.

NASSCOM-DSCI Report analyses the US model which advocates market driven approach. It provides interesting inputs for India to evolve its own model.

US policy focus since Clinton Administration (1998) has been on voluntary PPP and information sharing, with market driven approach

26 IDSA Task Force Repot

to address the problem of critical infrastructure protection. The policy has emphasized on assessing available alternatives to direct regulation including providing economic incentives to encourage the desired behaviour and to regulate only in case of market failure. However, this US policy approach has been criticized primarily for following three main reasons:-[27]

(a) Underestimating antitrust, liability and competition related issued in information sharing by private organizations.

(b) Undermining issues in sharing of classified information by the government with the private sector.

(c) Wrongly assuming that organizations will take action if they are made aware of the threats.

The existing policy approach, advocates believe, fails to understand that the market forces cannot deliver the required investments and efforts for ensuring public safety and national security – voluntary efforts will always be inadequate.

To this extent, the cyber security legislation proposal released by the US government last year focuses on improving cyber security for the citizens, critical infrastructure, and the Federal government's own networks and computers. For critical information infrastructure protection the proposal aims at establishing a regulatory framework to enhance cyber security of critical infrastructure which includes: owners and operators of critical infrastructure to develop cyber security plans; third party audit of the cyber security plans and reporting to Security & Exchange Commission of the US. Also, to improve voluntary information sharing, it provides industry, state and local governments the required immunity to share cyber security related information with the Department of Homeland Security.

The report offers balanced arguments on the approach India should take-Regulate or incentive the private sector? It cautions that "though regulations are necessary they should not add to cost without necessarily improving security of critical information

27 NASSCOM-DSCI Report

infrastructure." It further warns that "too much of government intervention through regulations can also undermine business innovation" thereby making it in competitive. The Report suggests "the better approach would be to incentive the private sector to invest in security beyond what is required by business requirements through appropriate instruments such as the government funding, tax reliefs, awards and recognition, liability protection, cyber insurance, etc."[28] The Report advocates that "only when such market driven approach fails, should the government think of bringing light weight legislation for critical information infrastructure protection that is developed in partnership with the industry." This argument may not be acceptable to those in- charge of national security as the cost of failure may be too heavy or unacceptable.

The IDSA Report "INDIA'S Cyber Security Challenge" understandably offers a view that is less liberal on national security which cannot be compromised under any circumstances." The Report argues "the government cannot leave it to the private sector alone for securing its own CII. This is because if any cyber-attack takes place on CII owned by a private company, the consequences of such an attack may have an adverse impact on the entire nation and not restricted to the company owning the CII. For example, if there is a cyber- attack on one of our national stock exchanges, it could possibly bring down the entire trade operations, impacting the economy and creating panic among investors. Therefore, there is an urgent need of appropriate collaboration and partnership between the government and the private sector for securing CII. The private sector needs to be greatly involved in government's cyber security initiatives through various mechanisms, including PPP."

Sharing Information. The private sector has always been hesitant to share information with the government bodies on its

28 IDSA Report also reinforces this view 'the government must also create incentives for industry to invest in security of CII beyond what is necessitated by companies' business plans. Examples of such incentives could be tax deductions and rebates on security investments, lower cost loans for SMEs that implement best security practices, reduced liability for improved security, recognition, etc

vulnerabilities less it gets adverse publicity which would harm its business interests and drive away its customers. A viable solution could be to create a separate body, like CERT-In, which could have their representatives also which though would be tasked to share information would also be responsible for coordination of security measures in close association with CERT-In. It would be necessary to create such bodies for separately for each CII. The IDSA Report points out some difficulties in this approach "difficulties they have encountered include private entities' inability to share information because of liability, anti-trust and business competition risks. From the government side, difficulties of sharing classified information with the private sector have been reported. It seems that many of the information-sharing activities will require even legal changes to make this programme work." This is a tall order in terms time and effort but cannot be ignored.

The Government of India is moving in this direction. A report[29] suggests that while "CERT-IN (Computer Emergency Response Team India) would be responsible for protection of most of the cyber space, NTRO would be tasked to protect the critical infrastructure such as important government networks. NTRO would be tasked to create the National Critical Information Infrastructure Protection Centre (NCIPC), which would be a command and-control center for monitoring the critical infrastructure. It would be a round-the clock center, providing real time response to cyber security breaches.

The proposal before NSC also envisages creation of sectoral CERTs in order to respond quickly to protect power distribution networks, Air Traffic Controls, traffic networks and other areas that heavily dependent on networked systems, and thus are susceptible to attacks."

Given the increasing linkage between cyber security and national security and the involvement of multiple stakeholders, it is very crucial that the cyber security in India is positioned at the highest level within the government. This will give cyber security the much needed impetus and will help address inter-agency

29 The Times of India, Delhi, 11 June 2012.

concerns and improve coordination.

ICT Supply Chain Risks

ICT supply chain, in its reach and characteristics, reflects a high level of globalisation. In fact, that has been one reason for the success and continuous growth of the Internet. There is a growing trust deficit in the global ICT supply chain. Countries fear that their adversaries could plant attack vectors in the imported ICT products and services which could be used against them. Many countries, including India, are responding to this threat by emphasizing on development of indigenous ICT products and services especially for critical sectors and government departments, even though the Internet technology and services are the result of global innovation, which is spawning new products, services and companies – which is required for continued growth of economies. The Indian draft National Telecommunication Policy reflects India's approach to the ICT supply chain problem - *"To provide preferential market access for domestically manufactured products with special emphasis on Indian products for which IPRs reside in India to adequately address the strategic and security needs of the country consistent with international commitments."* The US policy, on the other hand, emphasises on building global and national capabilities to address supply chain risks without undermining the international competitiveness and legitimate trade flow:-

(a) Understand threats, vulnerabilities, and consequences associated with acquisition decisions.

(b) Develop and employ tools to technically and operationally mitigate risk across the life cycle of products.

(c) Develop new acquisition policies and practices that reflect the complex global market place.

(d) Develop partnership with industry to develop and adopt supply chain and risk management standards and best practices.

India should be able to mitigate security risks arising from procurement of ICT products especially from foreign vendors and yet take full benefits from the global supply chain that includes access to world class products, services and expertise at competitive prices. Giving preference to domestic vendors for national security reasons may not be the right policy direction, primarily for two reasons – Firstly, deploying domestically developed products may not necessarily reduce the supply chain risks, since these need to be tested globally in real life environment. Secondly if other countries take such an approach to this problem, it will adversely impact India's outsourcing industry, which will be set to lose out to domestic companies in such countries. Therefore, to effectively address such risks without affecting business competitiveness and country's image as a promoter of global trade and market, India should build its capacity to mitigate ICT supply chain risks.[30]

The IDSA report also talks of concerns in the ICT supply chain. It says" From the Indian perspective, there is need to pay attention to two types of concerns:-

(a) Concerns With Respect to Global Products. There is concern with respect to vulnerabilities in products offered by global technology providers, which are deployed in critical sectors.

(b) Services Delivered From Offshore. Concerns with respect to services being offered from the country to the rest of the world, like application code development offered by Indian companies."

The Report further says "DIT may undertake a focused program for security assurance in the ICT supply chain". The first requires setting up of testing labs; the second requires a joint effort of DIT, in partnership with NASSCOM and DSCI, to assure secure delivery of services from India.

The Report recommends that "the Government should incorporate IT Supply Chain Security as an important element of e-security plan to address security issues."

30 NASSCOM-DSCI Report

Indigenous Cyber Security & R&D

India needs to develop its own cyber security systems in-house and invest in R&D which would be immune to foreign intervention or mischief. This would require creating capabilities in the field of cyber security which provide the nation with adequate proactive, deterrent and reactive tools. Private sector can provide stellar support by investing in cyber security R&D by attracting the best talent available in the country and bringing out products which are comparable to the best in the world.

Capacity Building: Cyber Specialists

India has a dearth of cyber security manpower required to defend corporate and government ICT infrastructure and this shortage is expected to grow in future as the digitization of processes increases, resulting in increased number of cyber-attacks and crimes. To prepare for the future, a competent cyber security workforce needs to be created. The Government should focus on creating awareness in the society, target the school children who are net addicts and are not necessarily cyber security conscious and are easy targets by introducing cyber security in school curriculum and finally creating a workforce of security professionals in the country, keeping in view the requirements of the future. This would require introducing security-related courses in formal education in engineering courses, and postgraduate courses. Simultaneously, advanced security courses should be designed for the working professionals to update their skills. There is a continuous need for providing training and education to all professionals working in the critical sectors – from general awareness to specialized training and advanced training, depending on the work profile of the professionals followed by advanced training to the key personnel.

NASSCOM Report suggests to " start with a Competency Framework that assesses the security skills requirements, identifies existing gaps and challenges, defines competency areas across different security roles (leaders, auditors, managers, administrators, developers, etc.) and devises strategies and programs for building the capacity such as security certifications, cyber security courses and specialization in schools, graduate and post graduate programs, career path in government, etc. should be created and implemented."

The NASSCOM Report offers some suggestions on the roles the Government and the Industry could play in evolving the PPP model for cyber security. Apart from what has been mentioned in preceding paragraphs, it suggests that the Government and Industry, both should provide incentives such as recruitment in government, internships and scholarships to students pursuing specialization in cyber security. Implicit in this is the idea that creates awareness about cyber security early during the formative years and impressionable age so that it becomes a habit and comes naturally to them. This will help the nation in becoming "cyber secure "in the years to come. While the Report suggests that the Government should provide indigenous certification that is recognized and accepted globally, it calls upon the Industry to consider cyber security as a rewarding career option.

Conclusion

The cyber challenges we face as a nation are multidimensional raging from those which pose a threat to national security, CII, private industry and finally to the very core of the society fabric as it affects the daily routine of the population cutting across gender and age groups. Radical problems require radical solutions. Cyber security is an issue of extreme importance which, in future, will increase in intensity and range and therefore need to be addressed with utmost urgency and seriousness at all levels.

CHAPTER 11

IMPLICATIONS FOR INDIAN ARMED FORCES

Introduction

India has been a victim of cyber-attacks as any other country. The scope, enormity and methodology of attacks have been different in accordance with the aim of the attacker. Most of these attacks have been said to have originated either from China or Pakistan. The targets included government institutions to military establishments. Recently the high profile target was the Common Wealth Games web site.

A recent incident highlights the enormity and the seriousness of cyber-attacks. Texas college researchers hacked into and hijacked a drone of the US Homeland Security before the eyes of the officials operating it. Using a technique called 'spoofing' where a signal from hackers imitates the one sent to the drone's on-board GPS, the researchers managed to take control of a small but powerful drone in mid-air. During the experiment conducted at the University of Texas stadium, the small red drone soared into the sky following a clear set of commands entered into its computer. Shortly after, the aircraft veered to the side, making it obvious that it was no longer following its original orders. Then, the drone hurtled toward the ground as if given a self-destruct command and was saved in the last moment. And the hijacking was just for a $1,000 wager.[1]

1 But the incident has unnerved Homeland security officials, as the spoofing has made it possible for anyone with a $1,000 and a plan to turn a harmless UAV into a missile and crash it into a building. The hijackers team led by Professor Todd Humphreys at Austin Radio-navigation Laboratory said his team was able to build the most sophisticated spoofing system yet that tricked the drone into following a new set of commands. "Spoofing a GPS receiver on a UAV is just another way of hijacking a plane," Humphreys said. The stadium display was not the first time government officials witnessed spoofing in action. Last Tuesday, officials from the Federal Aviation Administration and Department of Homeland Security watched as Humphreys' team repeatedly hijacked a drone from a remote hilltop in New Mexico. Source- The Times of India, Delhi, 02 July 2012.

The Armed Forces have taken steps to factor in the threats posed by cyber-attacks in the overall national security environment. However, cyber security transcends the traditional levers of national security and calls for active involvement of Government, Industry and the military. One may also argue that Society also has a stake in cyber security if one follows the arguments advanced in the preceding chapters. To get these diverse institutions with conflicting interests and responsibilities on board would the task of the Government of the day and which by all means is not going to be easy. This aspect has also been analysed in the preceding Chapter. The discussion will now be restricted and analysed from the military angle.

Defence Procurement in India

The trajectory of India's national development is based on the core values of democracy, secularism and peaceful coexistence. A stable and peaceful regional and global environment is necessary to achieve the aim of growth and prosperity for our citizens, according to the Ministry of Defence of India.

India has a land frontier of 15,200 km, a coastline of 7,516.6 km and an exclusive economic zone of 2.2 million sq km, as well as island territories, vital offshore installations and airspace to defend. The Indian forces, therefore, have to be kept prepared and well equipped to repel any external threat.

India's defence spending has grown manifold since the country announced its first defence budget in 1950, to USD 30 billion in 2009-10, according to the Economic Survey 2010-11. Of this, approximately 40 percent relates to capital expenditure which is currently driven by equipment modernisation programmes in each of the three services — the army, the air force and the navy. India is also amongst the world's top countries in terms of defence expenditure, including imports of defence hardware. In fact, India currently procures approximately 70 percent of its equipment needs from abroad, but the government's aim is to reverse this balance and manufacture 70 percent or more of its defence equipment needs in India. This provides an immense opportunity for both domestic and foreign players in the defence sector.

As a percentage of GDP, India has been able to maintain defence expenditure within a range of 2 percent to 3 percent, in line with other major developed nations, signifying a fairly steady focus on defence within the economy to date. The government, as the sole purchaser of defence equipment, spends heavily with defence expenditure accounting for close to 15 percent percent of Central government expenditure.

Today the Armed Forces have embarked on the path of modernization. Weapon Systems and communications have almost revolutionized the way the wars will be fought in time to come. However, the armed Forces have to shake off the shackles of inefficient and unresponsive system. Ongoing efforts at modernization of the armed forces, however, unless accompanied by significant political reforms, may fail to change India's military-strategic position, particularly with respect to Pakistan. Despite importing large numbers of conventional weaponry over the last three decades, if India wishes to effectively confront critical security challenges it must address a civil-military imbalance that hampers coordination and an illegitimate procurement process that threatens to further entrench government corruption.[2]

The Indian armed forces are undergoing rapid modernization,[3] with investments in such areas as a missile defence system and a nuclear triad.[4] India's arsenal includes nuclear weapons with a triad of delivery mechanisms. In recent years, India has been the world's leading arms importer, accounting for more than 9 percent of global imports. Russia, Israel, and to some extent, France, are the primary military suppliers of Indian armed forces. The country's capital expenditure for defence equipment may reach US$112 billion between 2010 and 2016. Since 1962, the IAF has maintained close military relations with Russia, including cooperative development on programs such as the Fifth Generation Fighter Aircraft (FGFA) and the Multirole Transport Aircraft (MTA).

2 Cohen, Stephen P. and Sunil Dasgupta, "The Drag on India's Military Growth", The Brookings Institution, September 2010

3 http://www.iht.com/articles/2007/09/19/news/missile.php?page=2

4 http://en.wikipedia.org/wiki/Indian_Armed_Forces

The Indian defence budget was US$48.6 billion during FY-2012, at about 2.5 percent of GDP, with additional spending on infrastructure in border areas and for paramilitary organizations.

Analysis of the Central Intelligence Agency indicates that India is projected to possess the fourth most capable concentration of power by 2015. According to a report published by the US Congress, India is the world's leading arms purchaser.

Policy and Promotion[5]

Ministry of Defence (MoD) is in charge of all defence-related activities spanning the army, navy and air force. Before proceeding further, it would be appropriate to examine he government policies for the defence sector. The major policies and promotions for the defence sector can be summed up as follows:-

(a) **26 percent FDI Permissible.** Presently, the FDI limit in the Indian defence sector is 26 percent. The sector was opened for private sector participation in May 2001, with 100 percent private sector ownership permissible and FDI of up to 26 percent. The aim in limiting foreign investment to 26 percent is to develop defence technologies within the country, and if the FDI is hiked, the foreign firms only will supply defence products to India and local firms will still be dependent on overseas suppliers. [6]

(b) **Higher FDI limits in Pipeline**. The Department of Industrial Policy and Promotion (DIPP) has suggested the FDI limit to be raised to 74 percent and the proposal is under consideration by the government. When accepted, this will raise foreign investment and enable the transfer of foreign technologies to India.

(c) **Increasing Capacity**. The focus of India's defence planning is on increasing capacity to meet the needs of the armed forces and to establish a reliable mechanism for inter-

5 http://www.investindia.gov.in/?q=defence-sector

6 http://www.defence.pk/forums/indian-defence/92274-interview-raj-kumar- singh-secretary- defence-production-india.html#ixzz1zAsB8Vxq

service, inter-departmental and multi-level coordination. In the near future, the role of the private and foreign sector is likely to rise to meet the ministry's goals.

(d) **Long-term Integrated Perspective Plan**. India's defence sector needs modernisation as obsolete equipment currently accounts for 50 percent of equipment, whereas the MoD's required profile would have this at 30 percent. The proportion of state-of-the-art equipment also needs to grow from its current level of 15 percent to 30 percent. Hence, during the last decade, the Indian defence industry has been in the process of undertaking one of the largest procurement cycles in the world. The current cycle, which includes acquisitions drafted under the long-term integrated perspective plan (LTIPP), is expected to include procurements worth USD 100 billion by 2022.

(e) **Big Procurement Drive**. As part of the LTIPP program, the Indian armed forces have announced some significant forthcoming procurement. The largest announced procurement is the USD 10.5 billion MMRCA procurement for 126 combat aircraft, which will be the largest aircraft procurement deal worldwide since the 1990s. There are several other billion dollar-plus deals that are making India's current procurement cycle one of the most attractive markets for defence companies worldwide. In the survey of CII Defence Division members conducted by KPMG, approximately 62 percent of the companies believe that the Indian market is an attractive proposition for foreign defence companies owing to India's large procurement plans.

(f) **Dedicated Defence SEZs**. India's first SEZ for aerospace in Belgaum, Karnataka, was inaugurated in November 2009. The government is considering the establishment of dedicated SEZs on similar lines catering specifically to the defence sector along the lines of IT, automobile and other specialized SEZs that already exist in the country. This would provide defence manufacturers and service providers (especially foreign companies) a suitable tax friendly environment and also aid in promoting exports of products and services.

Major Players[7]

India maintains an extensive defence industrial base with 40 ordnance factories and eight defence PSUs that are engaged in the manufacture of state-of-the-art weapons and systems for the armed forces. The eight defence PSUs are: Bharat Earth Movers Limited, manufacturing specialized heavy vehicles for defence and re-engineering solutions in automotive and aeronautics; Bharat Dynamics Limited, an engineering company; Bharat Electronics Limited, another engineering company; Garden Reach Shipbuilders & Engineers Limited, a transportation equipment manufacturing company; Goa Shipyard Limited, a transportation equipment manufacturing company; Hindustan Aeronautics Limited, a transportation equipment manufacturing company; Mazagon Dock Limited, a transportation equipment manufacturing company; and, Mishra Dhatu Nigam, a steel manufacturing company.

(a) In terms of value of production, defence PSUs account for more than 65 percent of the total industrial output of all defence public sector entities in India. During 2007-08, the value of production by defence PSUs totalled nearly USD 4 billion.

(b) The private sector has been playing a significant role in the defence industry as sub-contractors and ancillary industry, and suppliers of raw materials, semi-finished products, parts and components to defence PSUs, ordnance factories, base workshops of the army, base repair depots of the air force, and the dockyards of the navy, etc.

(c) Foreign companies account for the majority of procurement from the private sector in India, with approximately 70 percent of Indian defence procurement coming from overseas sources.

7 Ibid.

(d) Currently, the defence market for private sector firms in India, which includes outsourcing from DPSUs and ordnance factories, is estimated to be worth USD 700 million. This spend is expected to increase steadily with the growing participation of private players in the Indian defence industry.

(e) Major Indian industrial houses such as the Tata Group, Ashok Leyland, Mahindra Group, the Kirloskar Brothers, Larsen and Toubro, and Wipro have diversified into the defence sector, forming joint ventures with foreign companies for both strategic and produce-specific projects. For instance, Wipro has got the Foreign Investment Promotion Board's (FIPB) approval to manufacture, design and develop software for the Indian defence industry. Wipro has signed an agreement with Swedish defence firm Saab. Under the agreement, Wipro will manufacture, deliver and market Saab's entire suite of land electronic defence systems in India. The land electronic defence system will provide active protection to light and medium combat vehicles, as well as to main battle tanks against engagement by weapons such as rocket propelled grenades, anti-tank missiles, mortars and artillery shells.

(f) Some of the prominent potential deals in the air force sector are: a USD 10,000 million deal for 127 multi-mission role combat aircraft with bidders such as Lockheed Martin, Boeing, Dassault, UAC, EADS and Saab Gripen; a USD 1,000 million deal for six transport aircraft; a USD 700 million deal for 12 heavy lift helicopters with potential bidders being Boeing, Sikorsky, Bell, Westland, Eurocopter and Mil-MI Design Bureau, etc.

(g) Similarly, some potential deals in the army sector are: a USD 3,000 million deal for 197 light observations/utility helicopters with bidders such as Elbit, Thales, Marconi, Motorola, Ericsson, Raytheon and Honeywell; a USD 1,100 million deal for Future Infantry Soldier as a System (F-INSAS) with bidders such as Elbit, Thales, Marconi, Motorola,

Ericsson, Raytheon and Honeywell; and a USD 2,170 million deal for howitzers, etc.

(h) For the Navy, some of the potential deals in the pipeline are: a USD 3,500 million deal for seven Scorpene Submarines; a USD 7,600 million deal for 12 stealth frigates; and a USD 1,000 million deal for 16 multi-role helicopters (MRH). Bidders for all these deals are expected to be companies engaged in electronics, weapons control, fire control, navigation systems, turbine engine manufacturing, generators, standoff weapon systems, etc.

(j) Some of the foreign collaborations for internal security include a tie-up of Raytheon with the Indian Space Research Organisation (ISRO) for the installation of GPS systems at 100 airports across India at a project cost of USD 22 million; and tie-up of Lockheed Martin with Wipro Technologies for opening up a network centric operations centre in India providing Net-enabled capabilities and solutions for potential civil and military applications.

The above discussion was considered vital to highlight the role played by various actors in dense procurement and hence their accountability to the nation for any act of omission or commission in the discharge of their duties.

Cyber Challenges for the Military

The Indian Armed Forces are no longer sourcing their requirements only from PSUs. In their bid to modernize and get the best they are now moving to the private sector and are also buying equipment commercially of the shelf (COTS). This willy- nilly makes the Forces dependent on the private sector who primarily is acting as front end of foreign manufacturers.

The foreign manufacturers, at the behest of their governments may introduce a virus which may lie dormant and undetected for months. Another difficulty is getting the private sector, which is driven by monetary profits, to invest in cyber security measures. This vulnerability can easily be exploited by the adversary while launching the cyber-attack.

The most important challenge before the military in the cyber era is the dependence on foreign manufactures for arms and equipment. This issue has been dealt with in detail in the preceding chapter. Any weapon system or equipment the country imports will have a "cyber-element" incorporated in it. This implies handing over the remote control to the host country which can press it whenever its interests demand. The damage could be from destruction of the System, malfunctioning at a critical time, loss of command and control to stealing sensitive information or espionage. Will it lead us to "stone- age" warfare; we are probably staring at it in not too distant a future.

Let us examine this aspect in a little more detail and from military point of view.

The current trends towards digitization, automation, and interoperability need not be mutually exclusive of security. However, the cyber security challenge can only be addressed effectively by fully under-standing the wide range of the real "threat vectors" existing, which fall into four broad categories: supply chain and vendor access, remote access, proximity access, and insider access to ICT systems.[8]

With respect to the supply chain, it is widely accepted that the global economy has given nations the ability to compete and purchase services in an expanding market that has driven down prices and promoted rapid invention and innovation. But the global supply chain also has substantially increased our vulnerabilities to adversarial manipulation of hardware and software. Computers or the architecture they ride on can be poisoned with dormant capabilities that can be awakened by adversaries. Even if our ICT systems come out of the factory in pristine condition, they can be manipulated by the delivery service, the wholesaler, the retailer, the installer, the repairman, or through the downloadable firmware update or patch. Supply chain and vendor operations are very difficult to monitor. Even without a global supply chain, these same

8 DCAF HORIZON 2015 WORKING PAPER No. 7 "On Cyber Warfare" by Fred Schreier.

exploits could be introduced domestically by organized crime, disgruntled employees, or foreign intelligence services.

Remote access by network intrusion or hacking is another avenue of attack. We see most of this threat vector either because it is the greatest problem or because it is the most easily tracked. Systems administrators typically are overwhelmed by the quantity of warnings issued by automated intrusion detection, prevention, and firewall systems, and by the additional need to study the logs associated with other technology services and applications. In fact, our visibility into remote access security is so great that an organization must prioritize its review and response efforts. Hacking and remote access provided by malicious email attachments and drive-by downloads might or might not be the worst of problems, but they are the most visible. From a strategic point of view, it is important to ensure that the volume of the perceived remote threat and the resources directed against it are not considered to the exclusion of other equally pernicious threat vectors.

Proximity access refers to the abilities adversaries have when they are physically close to our ICT systems but not directly inside them. The interception of wireless signals is a good example of this vector. Through common techniques such as passive electronic monitoring of information being transmitted, joining a wireless connection and obtaining the ability to access other computers connected to the same wireless network – so-called peer-to-peer connections – or the attacker posing as a legitimate wireless network in order to lure unsuspecting users, wireless connected devices and access points can turn into a significant cyber security liability. Wireless keyboards can present similar opportunities for eavesdropper, broadcasting keystrokes through the air, even user IDs and passwords.

Finally, insider access must be addressed. Current employees, contractors, and trusted business partners have unique opportunities to do harm because they have been provided authorized access to our physical and digital spaces. Once authorized, they can operate from within without being challenged by the hard outer shell of gates and guards, intrusion prevention devices, and firewalls.

Operating from the inside also provides a distinct perspective on an organization's security weaknesses, including technical gaps, lapses in policy enforcement, knowledge of where the crown jewels are located, and even vacation schedules of security staff, just to name a few. Although a cyber-attack is more likely to come from an outsider, research indicates that when an insider does strike, the damage can be substantially greater.

These threat vectors can only be efficiently resolved by seeking the best options for lowering the factors that are used in the formula for risk assessment: Risk = Threat x Vulnerability x Consequence. Lowering any of the three variable factors will lower the risk. And driving any of the factors to zero will eliminate the risk altogether. Policymakers, strategists, and those who operate on the front lines of cyber security should carry out their direct and indirect roles in ways that help to lower the threat, vulnerability, and adverse consequences associated with supply chain and vendor access, remote access, proximity access, and insider access. Anything less leaves the advantage with the adversaries.

Indian Armed Forces today are more dependent on civil infrastructure than ever before. Prior to independence the dependence was rather low. The cantonments were located well away from the hustle bustle of cities and the soldier was by and large insulated from the civil society. All his requirements were met within the periphery of his citadel. The dependence was mainly restricted to power, railways and fuel and required direct dealing. Other requirements like weapon systems; communications etc. were met through public sector. The requirements were few and aspirations were low.

The Forces are dependent for power on the National Grid and for mobilization to a large extent on Railways which use automated systems for their functioning. They are thus susceptible to cyber-attacks. In Dec 2008 Eastern Railways web site was hacked and could only be traced to Toronto in Canada. It had messages pasted by Pakistani hackers "Whackerz- Pakistan (24 Dec-2008 Financial Express). The website of CBI, country's premier investigating agency, was also hacked. According to Times of India (16 Aug

2010), Indian enterprises lost Rs 58 lakh due to cyber-attacks. This was set to increase if companies do not take appropriate protective measures.

Network for Spectrum[9]

Indian Armed Forces are dependent upon BSNL for their long distance communications. This dependence is set to reduce once the OFC under the Project "Network for Spectrum" is completed. India is investing ₹ 9,970.16 crore (US$2 billion) to build a dedicated and secure optical fiber cable (OFC) network for exclusive use of the Army, Navy and Air Force. This will be one of the world's largest closed user group (CUG) network.

India is poised to have an exclusive pan-India Optical Fibre Cable (OFC) for its Defence Forces which will help them to vacate the radio waves they currently occupy. The proposal for the pan-India OFC is currently being processed and it will be to the tune of $ 1.3 billion.

The need for such an exclusive OFC is strategic since all the three armed forces require a robust communications network. A dedicated and highly secure state-of-the-art OFC network for the Army, Navy and Air Force will enable improved voice and data services and boost homeland security as well.

The $1.3 billion OFC proposal envisages a network to be laid out over 60,000 km to provide connectivity for 129 army, 162 air force and 33 navy stations. In a reply to the Parliament, Defence Minister AK Antony has indicated that this allocation is in addition to the roughly $ 2 billion approved for the Defence forces' communication network in 2009. Antony added that the alternative network will be implemented to facilitate vacation of spectrum by the Defence services.

The Union Cabinet had approved the roughly $ 2 billion plan to build an alternate optic fibre cable (OFC) network for the Defence services in December 2009. However, the state-owned BSNL, to

9 http://www.defencenow.com/news/675/pan-india-optical-fibre-cable-net work - for-defence-forces-at-an-additional-cost-of-$13-billion.html

whom the project was awarded, overshot its budget for building the alternate communication networks in 2010 by a huge 50 percent. BSNL had sought an additional funding of over $ 1.19 billion from the Centre for the same.

Human Resource Factor

The soldier for the Armed Forces will continue to come primarily from the rural sector. Implementation of new education policy has opened up the doors of elite schools to under privileged children in India. Also, the efforts of the Government to provide education to children in the hinterland have yielded positive results. This forced the three services to revise the minimum educational qualification required for recruitment. Today the soldier has a mentionable educational background which includes computer education. The soldier, particularly from the progressive states, is aware of internet, usage of mobile telephones and it would not be a surprise if he is addicted to social networking sites like Facebook.

This addiction to social networking sites comes with a baggage. Social networking sites feed anxiety and can make you feel insecure, a new study in UK has found. A survey of hundreds of social network site users found that more than half of them admitted that the sites have changed their behaviour, and half of them said their lives had been altered for the worse.[10] This will pose a new set of problems

---

10 Most commonly, those who suffered a negative impact from social media said their confidence fell after comparing their own achievements to those of friends online. Two-thirds said they found it hard to relax completely or to sleep after spending time on the sites, while one quarter of them said they had been left facing difficulties in their relationships or workplace after becoming confrontational online, the Daily Telegraph reported.

The research, conducted by Salford Business School at the University of Salford in UK, also demonstrated the addictive powers of internet, with 55 percent of people saying they felt "worried or uncomfortable" when they could not access their Facebook or email accounts. More than 60 percent of people said they felt compelled to turn off electronic gadgets in order to have a break, with one in three of those surveyed saying they switched the devices off several times each day.

"If you are predisposed to anxiety it seems that the pressures from technology act as a tipping point, making people feel more insecure and more overwhelmed," said Nicky Lidbetter of charity Anxiety UK, which commissioned the poll.

She said the charity was surprised by the high proportion of people who found that the only way to ensure a break from the demands of their devices was to switch

for psychologists when recruiting people for the military.

The breaking up of the joint family system and propagation of small family norms though has made the soldier more aware of his responsibilities and has curbed his happy and carefree attitude; he still remains resistant to change his habits and attributes which he imbibed while growing up in rustic environs of his village. The village life instills in him a strange sense of security with respect to his environment and he remains immune to the threat which is not visible. This trait manifests itself when he is exposed to cyber security. Any amount of sermonizing in the air will not convince him. What is needed is the practical manifestation of the threat, not once but at regular intervals. Top down approach if implemented would require the officers to practice cyber security drills very meticulously and in clear visibility of the men they command. This would go a long way in creating cyber awareness.

Youngsters joining the Services are definitely adept in computers and are regular on social networking sites. It is quite common to see officers in 10 to 15 years or below regularly visiting these sites. Add to this the lady, who is also computer savvy, also updating her status on these sites. In fact, any social event, personal or official, will invariably get posted along with photographs, where possible. Jurisprudence demands that some photographs be avoided. Even the movement of the officer on exercise or temporary finds a mention. It even extends to other officers in some cases. It was, therefore, not surprising to find four commander level officers of the Indian Navy facing a full-fledged inquiry for using online networks to share sensitive information such as location of ships, frequency and location of patrolling, nature of ammunition on board etc.[11]

---

them off, as they were not capable of simply ignoring their mobile phones, BlackBerry devices and computers.

Dr Linda Blair, a clinical psychologist said many people suffered increased anxiety because they failed to take charge of the demands being placed on them.

Source - The Times of India, Delhi, 09 July 2012

11 http://www.rediff.com/news/report/indian-army-draws-loc-on-internet-use-for-officers/20120127.htm

While the world of internet and social networking sites is being increasingly embraced by citizens, companies, or even the governments across the globe, the Indian Armed Forces are bracing against cyber-attacks, cyber honey traps after several incidents of possible hacking and honey trapping came to light.

A new policy on use of social networking sites and internet is now being implemented. It is said that cyber-attacks have the ability to cripple a nation's ability to defend itself. In view of this, the Indian Army is actively bracing itself to deal with even the faintest cyber-attack -- direct or indirect.

Very recently it has been found that Facebook and Orkut profiles of several officers were hacked and infused with Trojans.[12] After several such incidents were reported, the officials have been instructed to use internet and social networking sites strictly and only for personal use. A police letter to this effect has been drawn out by the director general of military intelligence with detailed instructions on use of internet.

The letter states, "As a policy, use of internet through email and social networks is permitted only for private use, and under no circumstances will the personnel disclose their official identity on the internet in any form whatsoever."[13] Service personnel have been refrained from uploading any information pertaining to their ranks, units or formations, appointment, place of duty or place of movement, contact numbers, pictures in uniform or with backgrounds depicting any defence establishment.

Officers have also been asked to not comment on matters related

---

12 A preliminary investigation has also revealed that the hackers, suspected to be from Pakistan or China, would 'make friends' with other members on the friend list of the officer whose profile has been originally hacked. After a chatting with the 'friend' of the officers, via Facebook chat, the hacker (who is pretending to be the officer) suggests that he has found an interesting online application which helps in preparing power point presentations very easily which in turn help in studying and official presentation before the commanders. The hacker then sends a link. On clicking the link, system of the target officer hangs and the entire data gets wiped out or infused with a virus.

Source- http://www.rediff.com/news/report/indian-army-draws-loc-on-internet-use-for-officers/20120127.htm

13 Ibid.

to the policies or activities of the Indian Defence Services, Ministry of Defence and the government. One of the other restrictions is forwarding of chain mails pertaining to the armed forces to avoid addresses being given away by way of bulk mails. Any groups such as NDA 53, SODE 97, DSSC 65, formed by any course, batch, or unit have been asked to be deleted with immediate effect. Use of email IDs which give out any direct or indirect hint of affiliation with the forces have also been banned.

Internet usage and social networking is becoming an intrinsic element of personal lifestyles and is emerging as a major tool for exchange of information.

The impact of internet, in particular and information revolution in general has been extensively discussed in the earlier chapter. While in the past, a number of guidelines have been issued on the use of internet and social networking sites, they have not been implemented in the desired manner, leading to a large number of cases of breaches in security of information.

It is increasingly clear that it is not only the man in uniform but also his family which needs to be cyber security savvy. Otherwise information relating to national security might find its way, unwittingly onto the social networking sites.

Advantages and Risks: Networked Forces [14]

Today, "Bombs are guided by GPS satellites; drones are piloted remotely from across the world; fighter planes and warships are now huge data-processing centers; even the ordinary foot-soldier is being wired up." With this wiring up, the Internet has enabled the most recent military innovation: *networked forces*. A networked force enables the expansion, acceleration, and qualitative improvement of command and control, and helps to improve situational awareness that can reduce uncertainty. It may change the way how wars are fought. A networked force is more effective than a non-networked one of comparable size. Networked air defence is much more combat effective than an aggregation of individual

14 DCAF HORIZON 2015 WORKING PAPER No. 7 "On Cyber Warfare" by Fred Schreier.

air-defence units. Ships, aircraft, and fighting vehicles connected by data links hold the promise to fight more effectively than non-networked units who rely solely on radio/voice communications. This increase in effectiveness makes military networks clearly a valuable and legitimate target for attack.

Advanced, post-industrial societies and economies are critically dependent on interlinked computer information and communication systems. Sophistication has itself become a form of vulnerability for enemies to exploit. Disruption of civilian infrastructures is an attractive option for countries and non-state actors that want to engage in asymmetric warfare, and lack the capacity to compete on the traditional battlefield.

The use of network technologies and exploitation of cyberspace for intelligence collection, surveillance, reconnaissance, targeting, and attack has become a normal part of military activity. Cyber warfare aims at disruption of crucial network services and data, damage to critical infrastructure, and creation of uncertainty and doubt among opposing commanders and political leaders. Cyber-attacks can be directed at targets over very long strike distances using relatively inexpensive tools. However, cyber-attacks seem generally not very likely to be decisive in the sense that the engagement of strategic weapons or a main force conventional attack can be. No one will likely win a victory or war using only cyber-attacks. But cyber-attacks do offer advantages. Cyber-attacks will certainly be part of future military conflict since it is known with a sad certainty that war has a healthy future. What is not known is with confidence are the forms that warfare will take.

The amount of advantage provided by cyber- attack will depend in part on the scope and length of a conflict. Cyber- attacks may well be more valuable in short conflicts. In a conflict limited in time and scope, the disruption created by cyber- attacks in services and logistics may provide an initial advantage. But the longer the conflict lasts, the probability increases that the utility of this advantage will decline as an opponent adjusts. In contrast, attacks against command and control, such as those that disrupt data and undermine confidence in the own information, could have a sustained cumulative effect, and increasingly hamper an opponent's ability to resist. Cyber-attacks thus introduce a new dimension in the ability to create uncertainty in the mind of opposing commanders. Uncertainty does not only create a large part of what Clausewitz called the 'fog and friction of war': it slows decision making, amplifies caution and timidity, and increases the chance of errors. Misleading an opposing commander has always been part of warfare. But cyber-attacks provide a new and more intimate capacity to undertake this, and potentially offer a significant advantage for deception, and thus for undermining confidence.

A similar kind of uncertainty and indecision can be produced by manipulation of data in a cyber-attack. Beyond scrambling data to deny an opponent access to it, a more difficult and damaging attack consists of manipulating data in order to make it misleading or incorrect. A cyber exploit that surreptitiously manipulated data in ways unfavourable to the opposing commander provides new promises for cyber conflict. In addition, it also provides possibilities to sabotage targeting and weapon systems, to take over control of missiles, Unmanned Aerial Vehicles (UAV) – this has already been demonstrated as mentioned earlier, robots, and radars, or to mislead or disrupt the controls even of jet fighters. Data manipulation could also create havoc with operational planning. And it is not hard to imagine cyber-attacks that effectively interfere with logistics plans and chains: by giving false locations of depots, by rerouting supplies or making it appear that there are shortages or surpluses when the opposite is the case.

Weapon systems are ever more dependent on software, computer hardware, and battle space networking. While the security of these weapon systems advances in step with the development and implementation of cyber technology, they can be increasingly affected by cyber-attacks. Aircraft are a good example. In the past, 100 percent of an aircraft's performance and capabilities were defined by hardware – the physical makeup of the aircraft. In more recent advanced aircraft, 75 percent or more of its performance and capability is dependent on software. Without software, some aircraft would not be controllable. Through software, aircraft performance is gaining some independence from physical configuration, and therefore software dependence and hardware independence are growing. But even fifth generation multirole fighters are not closed systems; external information systems can update and integrate information for combat operations during the flight. Through these external connections, not just the information systems, but the basic software and hardware systems of these fighters can be attacked. Vulnerabilities increase in proportion of the number of code lines deployed.

The doctrine of network-centric warfare, a cornerstone in the ongoing transformation efforts of a number of Western armed forces and the Indian Armed Forces as well, seeks to translate an information advantage, enabled in part by IT, into a competitive advantage through the robust networking of well-informed geographically dispersed forces. It draws its guidance from the concept of team warfare, and the integration and synchronization of all appropriate capabilities across the various services, which is part of the principle of joint warfare. This networking, combined with changes in technology, organization, processes, and people, may allow new forms of organizational behaviour. Specifically, the theory of network-centric warfare contains the following four tenets:-

(a) A robustly networked force improves information sharing.

(b) Information sharing and collaboration enhance the quality of information and shared situational awareness.

(c) Shared situational awareness enables self-synchronization.

(d) The above in turn, dramatically increase mission effectiveness.

There is no doubt that the effectiveness of network-centric warfare has greatly improved. US forces engaged in Operation Desert Storm, involving more than 500,000 troops, were supported with 100 Mbit/s of bandwidth. The forces in Operation Iraqi Freedom, with some 350,000 warfighters, had more than 3'000 Mbit/s of satellite bandwidth, which is 30 times more bandwidth for a force 45 percent smaller. US troops essentially used the same weapon platforms used in Operation Desert Storm but with significantly increased effectiveness. Good C4ISTAR (command, control, communications, computers, intelligence, surveillance, target acquisition, and reconnaissance systems) systems are at the heart of successful military operations.

However, in view of the many architectural and design challenges, it is not yet clear whether the vision of network-centric warfare is soon realizable. Since network-centric warfare focuses so much on distributed information, the armed forces must be wary of the effects of false, misleading, or misinterpreted information entering the system, be it through enemy deception or simple error. Just as the usefulness of correct information can be amplified, so can the repercussions of incorrect data entering the system achieve much greater non-positive outcomes. In addition to this, there are potential issues arising from the very nature of any complex, rapidly-developed artificial systems arising from complexity theory, which implies the possibility of failure modes such as congestion collapse or cascading failure.

Cyber Security

India as a nation fares poorly when it comes to cyber security. A Symantec study, in 2009, states that Indian enterprises lost Rs 58 lakh due to cyber-attacks. This was set to increase further if companies do not take appropriate measures to protect themselves from various threats that lead to not just financial setbacks but also loss of crucial data, it further added. Social engineering was already one of the primary attack vectors being used and Symantec estimated that the number of attempted attacks using social engineering techniques was sure to increase in 2010.

According to rankings released by Symantec in their study" 2009 Global Internet Security Threat Report", Brazil has supplanted Germany as the globe's No. 3 origination source of malicious net traffic, while India has zoomed to No. 5, The United States and China maintained the first and second spots respectively in the rankings as the top nations of origin for various types of cyber-attacks in 2009 compared to 2008. It stated that India is No. 2 in delivering malicious code, and No. 3 in spewing spam. India fared poorly in cyber defence in the recently released report in 2012, published by Brussels based Security and Defence Agenda (SDA)-a think tank. It indicates that we as a nation are not learning fast enough to make tangible progress in this field.

The above reports are indeed disturbing and give an indication of our indifferent approach to the serious issue of cyber security. If India has to take its rightful place in world arena, we need to be more proactive and institute measures and provide safety mechanisms to prevent any breaches. Though CERT-In is doing its best, incidents do happen. In its Annual Report for the year 2011, CERT-In has disclosed the wide range of its activities. See Appendix D.

It is evident that the civil society will be the biggest sufferer in the event of cyber-attacks. Hence it is imperative that it gears up to the challenge. However, it is easier said than done. India would require a vast pool of qualified personnel and large resources to implement some degree of cyber security. Is that pool available? This is question which is difficult to answer given the disinclination of the private players to boost up their cyber defences. The bottom line is that till we do not move society as a whole and nation as a whole we will continue to remain vulnerable.

It is imperative that information flow must continue uninterrupted and the nation should put in place best practices, resources and people to ensure there are no outages. However, when every other system is interconnected the susceptibility of the network increases. Therefore "Information Assurance" becomes a critical factor and one needs to identify the criteria for its protection.

The increased interconnection of information systems and data inherent in these trends pose threats to Information Assurance, which comprises of five essential criteria for the protection of information and the own systems against unauthorized access: availability, integrity, confidentiality, authentication, and non-repudiation.[15]

15 DCAF HORIZON 2015 WORKING PAPER No. 7 "On Cyber Warfare" by Fred Schreier.

(a) Availability applies to the information itself, its supporting technology and the people who operate and serve the infrastructure.

(b) Integrity refers to the trustworthiness of information and system or process reliability.

(c) Confidentiality is about denying access to the information and sensitive aspects of supporting technology, to those persons without authorization.

(d) Authentication refers to assuring that those who do access the information or supporting systems have the requisite authorization.

(f) Non-repudiation is linked to authentication and, effectively, is the digital signature.

The principle that applies to functionally-interdependent systems, whereby the failure of one component can impact on the functionality of one or more other components, also applies to Information Assurance. Thus, if any of the above criteria are compromised for any reason, at least some elements of information and/or functionality and efficiency of related information infrastructures is also likely to be compromised. The more serious the compromise, particularly in key areas or system choke-points or nodes, the more significant the impact will be on functioning and efficiency. Identifying existing vulnerabilities, or creating vulnerabilities that will enable Information Assurance to be compromised, is an important part of the "targeting process". The effective implementation of Information Assurance involves a wide range of security processes and procedures, as well as physical measures. One important measure is redundancy and diversity, which is intended to counteract the effects of any failure within, or compromise of, a system, or at least to minimize those effects. However, the high-end functioning and efficiency of many of the processes, systems, services, and capabilities we rely on and take for granted is dependent on current-generation hardware and software. For high-tech systems, in particular, the rapid changes in technology resulting in increasingly more powerful hardware and software, means that planned redundancy and diversity to provide effective backup and continuity, must also largely keep pace technologically with primary-use hardware and software. Hence, *redundancy and diversity must be recognized as part of the Information Assurance equation*, and must therefore be factored into targeting considerations.[16]

One fundamental problem is the lack of design and analysis methods which are scientifically proven to master the enormous complexity of future interconnected digital systems, especially regarding safety, reliability, functionality, and security – privacy, authenticity, and data security. Developing solutions for this fundamental problem will be one of the most important challenges for the computer science and web science research communities.

Estonia offers the closest example, in modern times, of what can befall a nation if adequate measures are not taken to ensure Information Assurance. The lessons from the cyber-attack on Estonia must be understood properly and suitable remedial measures must be instituted. Critical National Infrastructure must deploy foolproof cyber security systems. US have invested heavily in providing stringent protective measures to its nuclear plants. The underlying idea is clear. National interests have to be protected at all costs.

Cyber Security and Armed Forces

The anonymity, global reach, scattered nature, and the inter connectivity of information networks continue to reduce the probability of detection and discovery of the origin of an attack, thus making attribution a permanent problem. Attackers can use ever more means of deception, most of them offering plausible deniability. Smart hackers can route attacks through countries with which the victim's government has poor diplomatic relations or no law enforcement cooperation. Even successful investigations often lead only to another hacked computer. Thus, states and governments still face the prospect of losing a cyber-conflict without ever knowing the identity of their adversary.

16 Ibid.

Hence, responses limited to the level of the nation-state are inadequate: coordinated international activity, with all the associated problems of reaching agreement and then acting in concert, is what is required. The enemy can only be known through close international cooperation. Thus, his vulnerability can be learnt of and exploited through such cooperation.

A very significant aspect of change is mostly out of control for the forces deployed are the changing nature of vulnerabilities and threats. There are many thousands of known vulnerabilities in IT systems, and new ones are discovered every day. The cyber security company Sophos analyzed 95,000 malware pieces in its labs every day in 2010, nearly doubling the number of malware they tracked in 2009. This accounts for one unique file every 0.9 seconds, 24 hours per day, each day of the year. The threat experts of the company see 30,000 new malicious URLs each day – 70 percent of which are legitimate websites that were hacked. This is a clear sign that the malware threat continues to grow at an alarming rate.[17]

Nation states opponents are constantly developing new methods and mechanisms to exploit these vulnerabilities. The problem is that it is cheap to develop a cyber-weapon, while defending against it costs a lot. Some of the most complex, commercially available defence software now has between 5 and 10 million lines of code. In contrast, the average malware has stayed more or less constant over the last decade at 170 lines of code. Thus, what was considered impregnable yesterday may show subtle weaknesses today, and may likely be compromised tomorrow. Thus, cyber defences must be in a constant state of flux to accommodate both changing ICT systems and changing threats. But because the traditional manual techniques are failing to provide the security needed, automated systems are required that continuously monitor security postures, and provide risk-based situational awareness to decision makers. Hence, to protect their vital assets, the armed forces must meet the threats proactively with a system-wide defensive approach employing superior technology.

Two aspects are relevant for computer security, which must not

17 DCAF HORIZON 2015 WORKING PAPER No. 7 "On Cyber Warfare" by Fred Schreier.

be lost sight of and remembered. First, that security depends on a combination of technology and policy; and second, that no system is totally secure. It is safer to assume that there will be breaches, and work out how to minimize the damage. That means storing, and moving around, as little data as possible; anonymizing records and linking to personal details stored in a separate database; using encryption to protect data in transit, and using Intranet solutions where possible.[18]

Security architectures are built on the premise that successful attacks will occur. The rapidly changing and inherently open nature of cyberspace makes this inevitable. The ultimate protection against attacks is to air-gap critical systems from sources that cannot be trusted. But this comes with high costs in timeliness, flexibility, and functionality. To retain functionality while still offering robust security, cyber defences are built in layers. Even if an attack penetrates the first layer, deeper layers of defences are designed to contain the attack before it can reach critical systems. Much like physical defences, layered defences can provide incident response teams the time to shut down an attack before it causes unacceptable damage.

With effective contingency plans, processes, tools, and competencies in place for the event of an intrusion or disruption, incident response teams can react swiftly to contain and eradicate the threat. With the help of timely incident reports, they can assess any system damage or data loss and move quickly to resume operations. And with recovery procedures and workarounds already thought out, incident response teams can quickly move forward after an attack to recover lost data or configuration information. They then can restore systems and tests to help ensure that all components are again in compliance, and thus reestablish mission assurance and confidence. A continuing review of security audit files provides the opportunity to learn from the incident, so the lessons can be applied to help to improve existing security provisions and prevent recurrence.[19]

18 DCAF HORIZON 2015 WORKING PAPER No. 7 "On Cyber Warfare" by Fred Schreier.

19 Ibid.

Cyber-attacks may rise to the level of a national security threat when adversaries have invested enough time and effort into creative and well-timed strikes on a critical national infrastructure target such as the electrical grid. National security planners should consider that electricity has no substitute, and that all other infrastructures, including computer networks, depend on it. Because the cyber-attack threat to critical infrastructures is strategic in scope, the national response must be equal to the task: public awareness, investment in education, scientific research, the development of cyber law, and international cooperation. Because cyber security is evolving from a technical discipline to a strategic concept, and because cyber-attacks can affect national security at the strategic level, national leaders must look beyond the tactical arena. The quest for strategic cyber security involves marshaling all of the resources of a nation-state. In this quest for strategic cyber security, it is advisable to put emphasis on a security system architecture that employs multiple tiers of defences, that can be segmented under attack, and that has a healthy component of resiliency to allow speedy recovery.

The main improvements that could be made would be to strengthen mechanisms for global cooperation and capacity building. "The United Nation's Internet Governance Forum already brings together stakeholders from the public and private sector as well as civil society groups from around the world, and has actively considered security issues. If the UN decides to continue the existence of the forum, it would be an ideal venue for further global debate."[20]

The Indian Armed Forces, with the three components of army, Navy and Air Force, have put their own defence mechanisms for cyber security. These are primarily on the premise that defence systems are "isolated". However, as was pointed out earlier that it just takes a USB flash drive containing a malicious program to bring down the entire network. Hence isolation of networks is a fallacy and must be viewed as such. Policies must also be put in place to ensure a standard for private companies' computer and network

20 Ibid.

security. Some of the measures suggested are:-

(a) Policies may be enacted so that the military knows which techniques they are and are not allowed to perform, when engaging in cyber warfare.

(b) The Indian military mindset has to evolve to include high tech well-trained computer security experts and create properly dedicated cyber-attack and defensive units and these experts should be part of these units.

(c) Create defensive plans against known attack methods.

(d) Increase funding for computer security research.

(e) Increase public awareness of the potential threat and give tips for effective computer security practices.

An interesting article on different ways to plan against cyber-attacks is at Appendix F. It makes an interesting reading and makes some very valid points. The start point to defending against cyber-attacks is to understand own network and focus on the basics. This can be achieved by taking following measures:-

(a) Focus on the basics.

  (i) Understand your network.

  (ii) Monitor it to provide real time situational awareness.

  (iii) Enforce configuration and patch policies that are prioritized based on vulnerabilities and risk.

(b) Phishing e- mails will possibly get through as people click on the attachments- Make it tough for the attacker to move around by ensuring systems are properly configured and patched.

(c) Strict human security procedures.

(d) Convergence of trained people and well defined processes employing latest in technology to defend networks

Cyber-attacks, when launched, would use communications as the medium. Indian Armed Forces are dependent upon BSNL for their communication backbone and thus becomes as vulnerable as BSNL itself. Any attack on BSNL infrastructure would cripple the defence backbone and in the event of cyber war it would have serious repercussions. The fielding of DCN further increases this vulnerability. Hence it is important for the Armed Forces to work out the paradigm of cyber security for their backbone network.

US, France, China, Russia and Israel have created cyber commands to face the threat of cyber war. US CYBERCOM is headed by a four star general and comes under its strategic command. Its mandate is to coordinate cyber warfare efforts across the full spectrum of military conflicts as it seeks to protect over 15000 networks. It has components of Army, Navy and Air Force. It therefore synergies the cyber warfare efforts under one coordinated domain. Perhaps India could take a leaf out of US experience. The only difficulty would be to get the three services on the same platform. The advantages of unified and coordinated effort to protect the information systems do justify the necessity of this approach.

Today more personnel are computer savvy in the three services than a few years before. Indian Army gets a fresh intake of 60,000 personnel every year. Training these personnel in cyber security at their respective training institution is a must if cyber security culture is to take roots in the army.[21] Officers are computer literate and some of the PBORs also barring a few who definitely are in a minority today. How many of them are aware of the looming cyber threat is difficult to answer. Hence education of the officer class to cyber threats needs to be addressed on urgent basis.

Army grants computer loans to its personnel to buy the computer. Earlier it was only availed by the officers but it has changed now. In fact with increased purchasing power and computers being taught in schools it is not uncommon to find a computer in the home of PBOR. This again brings us to the issue of

21 This was stated by ADG MO while speaking in the session "Indian Cyber Security- Way Forward" at IDSA.

flash drives. Move of the flash drive between office and home could be frequent as in some stations internet connection is available/ feasible in the office only. Hence isolation of the networks may not be the solution. Stuxnet is a case in point.

Militaries Scramble for New Skills

The growing worries about the threat of cyber warfare are moving the militaries towards recruiting the computer specialists they believe may be central to the conflicts of the 21st century. However to attract specialists will be a major problem and tougher will be to find people to command them. While there will be many keys to the success of the Armed Forces in defending the cyber domain, the most important factor in all this will be their ability to recruit, train and retain the talent in this arena which is both unconventional and unfamiliar to many of our military leaders.

The Armed Forces may adopt an approach that identifies, assesses and mitigates the cyber threats; however it would be vitally important to invest in attracting the right type of personnel for the "cyber cadre" as they would be critical to operating and gaining the advantage in cyberspace. Technology will play a dominant role, there is no doubt, but it is the cyber warrior who will hold the center stage. Making people priority will enable the Armed Forces to react to all changes and advancing technology and to actively meet the threats and opportunities that these technical advantages present.

Militaries, that had barely considered the internet only a few years ago, are building new centres and training hundreds or even thousands of uniformed personnel. Herein lies the problem. Only a few people are of top notch quality, whom one would want to employ on high profile operation like the Stuxnet. Commanders say that they are trying to change the rules on issues like hair length to fitness. However the militaries will struggle to attract or retain these specialists due to stiff competition from private sector. It is all about having a small but sustainable number of very good people with imagination and will as well as technical know-how. Many experts feel that offensive cyber warfare capability- particularly anything potentially lethal such as the ability to paralyze networks – should be kept in the hands of the directly accountable military, not the shadowy spy agencies.[22]

The Indian Armed Forces, through a variety of recruitment programs, offer many professional development opportunities and have managed to recruit and retain an all-volunteer world class force. The armed forces offer number of courses, both in military institutions and civil, and a clear, well defined path for career enhancement. While some of these programs and courses may be suitable for recruiting, training and retaining cyber warriors (possibly), a whole new perspective is needed to attract both the quality and caliber of talent necessary to defend the nation's networks against ever increasing cyber threats. When viewed with the challenge of competing with the private sector recruitment for top notch talent the armed forces will need to do some serious thinking.

Cyber practitioners thrive on the ability to foster innovative and unconventional thinking in a highly collaborative environment. This would be in conflict with the highly regulated environment that promotes a regimented career path, which ultimately emphasizes and promotes general leadership over technical expertise in a specific domain. Some of the highly skilled and talented individuals in cyber domain may not have leadership aspirations or the flair for it, yet they might be very effective as technicians rather than leaders. Since the armed forces rely on rank based assignments, the cyber security talent will most likely resist assignments outside their area of expertise. Hence, the armed forces to meet this challenge may have to consider providing a viable career path for recruiting and retaining these cyber warriors.

How will the armed forces find the solution to the above problem is difficult to answer? Some suggestions are offered below:-

(a) **Develop a viable career path for individuals with specialized cyber skill sets, and advertise this aspect in recruiting advertisements giving wide publicity.** The Armed Forces

22 Thomson Reuters 2011

should not limit their options when identifying the attributes of a cyber-warrior and his or her typical career path. Officer, PBOR and even civilian career paths may be considered as options. Some services may find it beneficial to devise a NCO or JCO career path for cyber warriors (Similar to that in MES) that are willing to invest the time it takes to develop and hone specialized, technical expertise in the cyber domain. Additionally, leadership positions should not necessarily be a required outcome in career progression unless specifically desired. While the military needs cyber warriors in its officer ranks, providing an officer path alone will not yield the large number of resources that are needed. For those cyber warriors who do desire leadership positions, the option of promoting these technical liaisons into leadership roles may be offered. The military needs technical liaisons to explain the mission impact of identified cyber threats and vulnerabilities to military leaders and decision makers.

(b) **Find methods for embracing diversity of thought and collaboration in the controlled environment of military life.** The environment in which cyber warriors will thrive is a highly collaborative one that encourages free thinking and innovation. Working side by side in a think-tank-like environment can provide motivation for like minds to collaborate and excel. This will reduce formal training costs because often the best training in this domain can occur by physically or virtually co-locating several passionate people to facilitate their knowledge sharing.

(c) **Do not force cyber warriors into alternate career paths**. Due to the specialized nature of the skill sets required by the cyber warriors, this discipline tends to draw people extremely passionate about the subject, individuals who will be largely disinterested in assignments outside the cyber domain and will serve the military best behind a computer rather than on the battlefield. The Armed Forces should re-examine their rotation policies/practices and rank-based assignments when allocating resources within the cyber domain.

(d) **Find ways to reward technical expertise and increase retention**. This is a challenging task because private industry typically offers higher packages for the very skill sets the military is seeking. There are many methods for providing incentives, including more traditional tools already in use, such as monetary incentives and specialized training; however the best way to reward the cyber warrior is with the opportunity to learn something new. *The opportunity of working in an environment that allows for exercising the latest and most innovative technologies will be the military's best retention tool.* The introduction of simulated environments to promote skill building, collaboration, and innovation could in many cases be its own reward for the cyber warrior.

(e) **Raising Cyber TA Battalions.** Raising of TA battalions for cyber warfare may be considered as this would give limited liability to the cyber specialists to serve the military. It could be a motivation for some as it provides them with an opportunity to serve in the military as well as allow them to pursue their regular career. However, with the serious shortage of cyber security professionals it is difficult to fathom how this could be achieved. One aspect, however, is clear. The raising of cyber TA battalions would require a totally different approach and the military needs to look at with a fresh mind if this is to succeed. Their role, organization and equipping policy will be at stark variance with a conventional TA battalion. The terms of embodiment may also need a relook if cyber specialists are to be motivated to join. Moreover, the private sector where they would otherwise be working will have to be encouraged to spare them. This may not be a tall order as most IT companies maintain bench strength of about 20 percent of the workforce.[23] The current slowdown in IT industry offers

23 A bench, up to a point, is a necessary evil. Even though these employees don't earn anything for the company, there will inevitably be a bench formed by employees who would have just completed a project and would not have another to immediately work on. A bench is also needed—as a strategy-—to quickly get a project going when the company receives an order (a client will not accept a situation where his work cannot

the Indian Armed Forces a unique opportunity wherein the workforce sitting idle and waiting eagerly for projects as well as the companies may be quick to respond to the proposal.[24]

Training would be the most important factor to create a competent pool of cyber specialists. Some countries have already taken the first step. As part of an effort to strengthen cyber defence and cyber warfare skills among young army officers graduating from France's Saint-Cyr Coëtquida, the institution's new chairmen of cyber defence has identified three key objectives and four teaching themes to catapult skills beyond their present level, reports Aviation eek's.[25]

---

be immediately implemented). It's like a manufacturing company that keeps investing to ensure there's always some excess factory capacity that can be used when an order suddenly flows in.

24 In normal times, IT companies have about 20 percent of their employee base on the bench. But as of the quarter ended March, the employee utilization rate (which is the opposite of the bench proportion) had fallen to about 67 percent for many, including Infosys, Wipro and MindTree — which means some 33 percent of their employees were on the bench. Considering that Infosys has 1.5 lakh employees, nearly 50,000 today are not earning any revenue for the company. For TCS and iGate, the utilization rate has dropped by about 4 percentage points over the last one year.

"There are companies with a bench size of up to 40 percent today," says an HR professional at a tier-1 IT firm who did not want to be named. Nirupama VG, MD of HR consultancy Ad Astra, says the bench size has gone up for many companies by 10 to 15 percentage points.

C Mahalingam, HR head at software product engineering services company Symphony Services, says the churn duration (the time an employee spends between completing one project and getting into another) used to be 45 to 60 days, but with opportunities dwindling, the duration is getting longer. "This opens up a huge resource management challenge and is the biggest concern for HR managers today," he says. Companies are reacting to the bench problem in multiple ways. Infosys Technologies has said it will delay the joining dates of the freshers it hired this year, some of them to as late as mid-2013. iGate has said it will delay the joining by one to two quarters. Many others are said to be taking similar measures. Most are reducing the extent of hiring they are doing this year. "Companies also handle benches by increasing the training period and using them for internal projects," says Navin Kumar, CEO of IT skills development firm.

Source – The Times of India, Delhi, 10 July 2012.

25 Daniel Ventre, who began working in his new position on July 2, has established these three objectives:-

Introduce students to the subject and provide on-the-job instruction to higher ranking officers throughout the French armed forces.

The first four teaching themes, which are subject to change, focus on territory (where do cyber-attacks come from and where are they aimed and why), human factor (who are cyber warriors?), national strategies, and threat measurement from both quantitative and qualitative standpoints, the story said.

The U.S. military is also accelerating its cyber warfare training programs in an aggressive expansion of its preparations for conflict on an emerging battlefield. The renewed emphasis on building up cyber warfare capabilities comes even as other defence programs have been trimmed. Along with unmanned aircraft and special operations, cyber warfare is among the newer, more high-tech and often more secretive capabilities favoured by the Pentagon's current leadership.

In June, the U.S. Air Force's elite Weapons School—the Air Force version of the Navy's famed "Top Gun" program—graduated its first class of six airmen trained to fight in cyberspace. The new course, at Nellis Air Force Base in Nevada, trains airmen working at computer terminals how to hunt down electronic intruders, defend networks and launch cyber-attacks.[26]

"While cyber may not look or smells exactly like a fighter aircraft or a bomber aircraft, the relevancy in any potential conflict in 2012 is the same," said Air Force Col. Robert Garland, commandant of the Weapons School. "We have to be able to succeed against an enemy that wants to attack us in any way."

The training effort comes amid a push by the Obama administration to rapidly deploy offensive and defensive techniques across the government, including at the Central Intelligence Agency, other intelligence agencies and the Department of Homeland Security. Cyber warfare techniques have been deployed in an

---

Establish a high-ranking research program with public and private partners, both military and civilian, French and foreign and with other international research centres.

Set up a center of cyber defence expertise at the Saint-Cyr Coëtquidan schools.

Source- By Defence Systems Staff Jul 05, 2012

26 http://online.wsj.com/article/SB10001424052702303684004577508850690121634.html?mod=googlenews_wsj

apparent U.S. and Israeli campaign to undermine Iran's nuclear program, elements of which were reported last month by the New York Times. The U.S. also contemplated using cyber weapons to incapacitate Libyan air defences in 2011, before the start of U.S. airstrikes.

The military's cyber buildup began in 2008, leading to creation of a formal "U.S. Cyber Command." The command marshals computer-warfare capabilities from across the military and integrates them with expertise at the National Security Agency. Some of the defences could someday be extended to the private sector.

Overall the Air Force spends about $4 billion a year on its cyber programs, though the training initiatives are a fraction of that cost. Other military services also are taking steps to strengthen cyber warfare capabilities and training. The Navy is revamping courses for 24,000 people trained each year at the Center for Information Dominance each year. "It is that full span, from peace time to war and everything in between," said Capt. Susan Cerovsky, commander of the Center for Information Dominance.

James Cartwright, a retired Marine general and former vice chairman of the U.S. Joint Chiefs of Staff, argues the new emphasis on cyber training is critical. But he said the military should do a better job publicizing that it is working to hone all of its cyber capabilities—both defensive and offensive. "For cyber deterrence to work, you have to believe a few things: One, that we have the intent; two, that we have the capability; and three, that we practice—and people know that we practice," Gen. Cartwright said.

The full range of U.S. cyber weapons is a closely guarded secret. U.S. officials have said the military is developing weapons aimed at cutting off power to precise, limited locations. "Our curriculum is based on attack, exploit and defence of the cyber domain," said Lt. Col. Bob Reeves, who oversees the cyber course as commander of the 328th Weapons Squadron.

The U.S. also has acknowledged it has cyber weapons that could help suppress enemy air and sea defences. Israel used cyber techniques to hide its aircraft in a 2007 attack on a Syrian nuclear facility, according to current and former officials.

Such methods are taught at Weapons School, officials acknowledge. The course focuses on combining cyber power with more traditional combat, said Lt. Col. Reeves. That includes "affecting an adversary's computer system in a way that allows us to fly in an airstrike more effectively, with less resistance," he said.

Lt. Col. Steven Lindquist, one of the inaugural students, said the course asks officers to study how an attacker could launch a cyber-attack against an Air Force command center or an individual airplane, and to construct defences. An Air Force "aggressor" team at Nellis then tests the defences. "The Air Force aggressor acts as a hacker coming against us and we see how our defensive plan measured up," said Lt. Col. Lindquist.

The Air Force Weapons School provides advanced training for a handful of elite officers each year in traditional skills, like teaching aerial combat, reconnaissance and bombing, and also for the growing ranks of drone pilots. ***Adding the cyber-warfare course to the most elite school, officials say, is important to changing the mind-set of the military, where many still regard radios, telephones and computers as communications tools—not targets and weapons.***

"We know this is a contested domain," said Lt Col Timothy Franz, Staff Director for the Air Force Office of Cyberspace Operations. "There are people out there trying to get into your telephones and networks for military purposes, and we recognize that having similar capabilities is imperative for the future fight."

The current threat environment therefore demands a highly capable force of cyber- warriors to defend our military networks and critical infrastructure. The Indian Armed Forces must shift their human capital paradigm to achieve recruiting and retention success in the cyber domain. This would necessitate a major change in mind set and then among others from policy, recruitment, training, postings and promotions to allocation of resources with simplified procurement policies. The essence is best summed up in the words of BH Liddell Hart :-

> *"The only thing harder than getting a new idea into the military mind is getting an old one out."*

Even in the era of shrinking military budgets, funding for cyber security is going up. The Pentagon's 2012 budget allocated $2.5 million to improve cyber capabilities. In Dec last year US Army announced its first "cyber brigade" was operational, whilst the US Navy and Air Force have their own cyber "fleets" and "wings". Not only are they tasked with protecting key US military systems and networks, but they are also working to build offensive skills that US commanders hope will give them an edge in any future conflict. " For better or worse, it is American military that is leading societal thought in how to think about things cyber," former CIA director and Air Force Gen Michael Hayden told a security conference in Munich.

The above discussion leads us to the conclusion that firstly Indian Armed Forces must plan to have cyber specialists. They have to be permanent and led by cyber specialists' officers. Secondly, cyber domain requires a joint mind set. Hence the biggest challenge the military must overcome, is itself. Only then can the information be shared 100 percent without which cyber war cannot be fought in a coordinated manner. Lastly and the most important deduction is that the Armed Forces must plan for the contingency when their networks and PBXs' are rendered ineffective by a sustained and massive cyber-attack. Perhaps the time has come for the militaries to look at **Stone Age warfare** a new look.

It would indeed be an interesting and enlightening experience if the Armed Forces in any of their major exercises render their systems as "cyber-attacked." The aftermath could be a scene of total confusion and chaos. Hence the Indian Armed Forces must plan, train and incorporate in their operational plans the contingencies when all or selective cyber systems are attacked. US Armed Forces have already started training for such contingencies.

Conclusion

The Indian Armed Forces cannot fight the cyber war in isolation. The private, government and the military will have work in a coordinated manner to prevent and defeat the threat. Any weakness in this is likely to be exploited by the adversary and will result in chaos and confusion thereby lowering the morale of not only of the nation but also that of the military as it will not remain insulated from the repercussions of these attack. Hence a nodal agency needs to formulate the common ground policy and suggest measures for all key institutions and government institutions.

CHAPTER 12

RECOMMENDATIONS

I do not know with what weapons World War III will be fought with, the fourth will be fought with sticks and stones

– Albert Einstein

Cyberspace of a nation, unlike the other four domains which have physical dimensions, is part of the global cyberspace; it cannot be isolated to define its boundaries since cyberspace is borderless. With its increasing reach to people and its extensive usage by the by the business community and the governments alike, cyberspace is expanding at a fast pace. Therefore, there is a need to put in place a system which is dynamic, flexible and ever evolving to address new challenges and threats.

Since cyberspace affects every individual, organisation, government, military and system therefore, it is but natural that in order to secure our cyberspace all stake holders must share the responsibility.

It would be pertinent to mention here that two studies have been carried out recently- Securing our Cyber Frontiers by DSCI and INDIA's Cyber Security Challenge by IDSA. Both studies have examined the subject in an adept manner and have given suitable recommendations. These recommendations are given in Appendix E.

Government

(a) Declare Cyberspace as the fifth domain of warfare.

(b) Prepare a National cyber Security Policy which should lay down the ground rules for protection of own cyberspace clearly defining the responsibilities of various stake holders in cyber security.

(c) Threats in cyberspace are enormous which are increasing in scale and complexity every single day. Hence it requires a serious intellectual effort to first comprehend the problem, identify the areas of threat, suggest measures to mitigate the threat. The Government should therefore set up a competent Cyber Security Task Force.

(d) There is a requirement of dealing with cyber threats at the highest levels in the echelons of the Government. Some experts have suggested that in view of the speed, reach, and scale of the threat and most importantly to resolve coordination issues between various government agencies and ensure swift and timely response, a National Structure for Cyber Security should be created directly under PMO. The IDSA Study Team[1] with its wide experience in Government and Industry has suggested that "NSA through NIB should be put in charge of formulating and overseeing the implementation of the country's cyber security policy within the ambit of a larger national security policy. This body should be serviced by the NSCS for policy measures and DIT and other departments (e.g. Telecom, space, etc.) for operational measures." To what extent will the Government accept the recommendation is a matter of detail. What is more important here is that while releasing the Report Mr Shiv Shankar Menon, the NSA, said that the Report has come at a time when the Government is in the Final stages of preparing a "whole of government Cyber Security Architecture."

(e) International cooperation is very crucial to handling threats in cyber space. CERT India has MoU with the respective CERTs of US, Japan and South Korea. This needs to be expanded further with other friendly countries.

---

1 The Study Team was headed by Shri Nitin Desai- Diplomat and former member NSAB. Some of the members included the present DG CERT and the former DG CERT who is now the CEO of DSCI, a retired Lt General and the Director of IDSA.

(f) Educate the Government staff, Centre and States, at all levels from top to bottom, on the repercussions of cyber-attacks and train them on cyber security. The Head of the Department must ensure best cyber security practices are followed in his Department. Accountability at all levels, if ensured, will mitigate the threats to a large extent. People will only implement a measure if they are convinced and have belief in it – this can be achieved through training.

(g) There is acute shortfall of competent cyber security specialists in the country. The Government should open Institutions or run courses in existing institutions on cyber security. The aim should be to meet the shortfall by 2015 by when internet usage is expected to grow 9 times from what it was in 2011.

(h) Four percent of Indian population is on Facebook. Most of it is young school children. It is therefore felt that introducing cyber security as a compulsory subject in schools from class VI onwards would create cyber security awareness.

(j) Set up Labs which can check the laid down cyber security specifications. Whenever any equipment is procured by any agency, government or private, it must be made mandatory to be sent to these labs for not only checking the cyber security aspect but also the Manufacture and User specifications.

(k) Identify the National Critical Infrastructures, put in place adequate cyber security measures, maintain an updated database on them and carry out regular cyber security audit. PPP in this field should be encouraged.

(l) Stress on indigenous R&D in cyber security. This may require involvement of both, the public and private sector. It is time that trust is reposed in the private sector if India is to surge ahead as it is already a major power in IT.

(m) Develop Cyber Forensic capability to deal with cyber-crime and cyber- terrorism.

(n) Enact laws to provide the LEAs the necessary support to deal with cyber security issues.

Armed Forces

(a) Enunciate Cyber Warfare doctrine. Cyber boundary must be clearly defined.[2]

(b) Establish a Cyber Command. It is recommended that it should be a triservice body responsible for all aspects less operational aspects, which would fall in the domain of operational commanders, of cyber warfare. Both the Study Reports, IDSA and DSCI, recommend establishment of Cyber Command for building offensive and defensive capabilities.

(c) Establish a Centre for Cyber Security at any of the training institutions like CME, MCTE or MCME. Basic and advanced courses may be run at these institutions. In addition, vacancies on cyber security courses at civil institutions in India and abroad must be sought regularly to keep abreast in this field. advances, study and analyse their application in operations and disseminate them to the environment. The changes in the field of cyber warfare are going to be at a very rapid pace and hence the necessity to keep abreast at all times is vitally important. This can be achieved by creating an organization which continuously monitors these advances, study and analyse their application in operations and disseminate them to the environment. It should maintain close linkages with industry and acdemicia. In the long run a tri-service institution "College for Cyber Warfare Studies" could be established at Bangalore.

(d) Create a pool of trained manpower in cyber security and position them at key locations/formations. There is a urgent need of creating a separate Cyber Cadre which could be trained in cyber operations. It would be imperative to

---

2 The cyber/ kinetic boundary is the decision point when a commander must decide whether and how to move from a purely cyber war to one involving conventional forces, or kinetic weapons. Crossing the boundary is an escalatory step that may lead to the war spiraling out of control.

change the existing mindset of the military to protect their career interests as discussed in the previous chapter. These are briefly described below:-

(i) Develop a viable career path for individuals with specialized cyber skill sets, and advertise this aspect in recruiting advertisements giving wide publicity.

(ii) Find methods for embracing diversity of thought and collaboration in the controlled environment of military life.

(iii) Do not force cyber warriors into alternate career paths.

(iv) Find ways to reward technical expertise and increase retention.

(e) Raise Cyber TA battalions at the scale of one per Command.[3] The role, organization and equipping policy of these units will be different from a conventional unit. More importantly the qualifications required for joining would need a careful analysis as they would be required not only to fill the cyber voids but also supplement the regulars in cyber operations. Their terms of engagement, working regimen, promotion and pay aspects etc would have to be innovative and attractive enough to get best talent. However, the tendency to retain them for long stretches needs to be avoided as it may be counterproductive as they may lose their sheen.

(f) Wargame cyber operations. Invoking "cyber blackout" during formation exercises is the key to preparing troops for cyber warfare.

(g) It is time for the armed forces to give a relook at "Stone age warfare". The contingency when all cyber systems fail, for whatever duration, plans and drills need to be in place and all personnel trained for such an eventuality- it is a tall order.

---

3 Strength of Cyber TA Battalion will be much less compared to a normal TA Battalion as its role and hence its organisation and equipping policy will be different.

(h) Cyber warfare should be included in the basic military training of all ranks like other operations of war.

Individual

(a) All ranks need to be educated in cyber warfare. This could be through courses of instruction, talks and other avenues like sainik samellans, roll call etc.

(b) Awareness among all ranks of the dangers and risks posed by cyber attacks is a must.

(c) All advisories issued by Army Cyber Security Establishment must be read and understood by all ranks. Presently these are read by very few, understood by select few and implemented by special few. In a unit they rarely go beyond the confines of the regimental headquarters. It is imperative that these advisories are read and understood by all ranks. This can be given the right kind of impetus if it is treated as a command function.

(d) All ranks should be made aware of good cyber forensics.

(e) Spread awareness on the flip side of social networking sites among all ranks and their families. Ladies and particularly teenage children need to be sensitized about not disclosing anything on these sites which even remotely suggests military linkages.

(f) Lastly, it may impressed upon that a PC/ Laptop and the smartphones, which are now available with various apps, can be accessed by a hacker anytime from anywhere.

Appendix A

TOOLS OF CYBER WARFARE

Nuke Ping Flood. This is a flooding attack on the public Internet; it relies on misconfigured network devices, allowing packets to the computer hosts on the network. The attack sends an overwhelming number of ping packets choking the network and ultimately closing it down.

Reflected Attack. A reflected attack takes place when an unsuspecting user is enticed to follow a malicious link to a vulnerable server that introduces (reflects) the malicious code back to the user's browser: malicious code or scripts are injected via any method that produces a response as part of a valid HTTP request. Some common examples of responses are error messages, search engine results, or submitted web forms.

DOS. A denial of service (DOS) attack is an assault on a network that floods it with so many additional requests that regular traffic is either slowed or completely interrupted. It is characterized by an explicit attempt to prevent legitimate users of a service from using that service. One of the advantages of this type of attack is that it can be executed with limited resources against a larger and more sophisticated computer or network. For example, an attacker with an old PC and a slow modern may be able to disable much faster and more sophisticated machines or networks.

DDOS. A distributed denial-of-service (DDOS) attack is one in which a huge number of compromised systems attack a single target, thereby causing denial of service for users of the targeted system. The flood of incoming messages to the target system essentially forces it to shut down, thereby denying service to legitimate users. When conducting a DDOS attack, an aggressor utilizes thousands of infected computers--known as zombies or bots--to concurrently attack a single system. DDOS attacks are difficult to stop because the data flooding the system originates from multiple computers and multiple locations.

PDOS. A permanent denial of service attack is an attack that damages a system so badly that it requires replacement or reinstallation of hardware. It is a pure hardware attack which can be much faster and requires fewer resources than DDOS.

Common Weapons/ Techniques. Cyber weapons are usually basic programs that have the objective to defend or attack a target. Most of them are freely available on the Internet but others which are sophisticated are not freely available. Some of the common tools of attack are given in succeeding paragraphs.

Hacking is the most common tool to cause maximum damage with little funding and is most difficult to detect and defend. Further it provides the attacker a high degree of deniability and does not have limitations of distance or place. Let us examine some of the basic tools of hacking.

Security Exploit. It is the most commonly method used for cyber reconnaissance and attack. It is a prepared application that takes advantage of a known weakness. It is a piece of software, data, or commands that utilize a bug, glitch, or vulnerability to cause an unanticipated behaviour to occur on computer software, hardware, or electronic devices. This can allow the attacker to take control of the computer, permitting its use for other tactics, such as DDoS. An exploit may be used to gain low-level entrance to a computer, after which a hacker can search for further exploits to attain high-level access such as system administrator (root). This tactic is known as privilege escalation.

Vulnerability Scanners. Vulnerability scanners may be used to identify exploits. Port Scanner can be used to find weaknesses of computers on a network. They check to see which ports on a specified computer are 'open', available to access, and sometimes will detect what program or service is listening on that port. Once an open port has been found, large quantity of data can be sent to cause a buffer overflow. This can cause exposure of data, memory loss, and/or a crash within the compromised system.

Spoofing. A spoofing attack occurs when a person or program fools another into thinking it is someone or something else. One example is the man-in-the-middle attack, in which person X gets person A to believe they are person B, and they get person B to believe they are person A, thus gaining access to information sent in both directions. This is accomplished by monitoring packets sent from A to B, guessing their sequence and number, knocking them out with a SYN attack, and injecting packets from X. Firewalls may defend against these attacks, if they have been configured to only accept IP addresses from the intended correspondent.

Phishing. Phishing imitates a webpage such as a bank's website. When the user enters their data, such as passwords and usernames, the fake website catalogues their information. It is often used in conjunction with URL spoofing, using an exploit to display a false URL, and DNS cache poisoning to direct the user away from their intended site and then back again when the data has been collected. As a precaution some websites require a user to arrive at their login page from a specified referrer page, but these referrer pages may also be spoofed.

Trojan. Trojans are notorious for installing backdoor programs. It appears to perform a desirable function, while secretly performing malicious functions. Trojans can be used to gain remote access, destroy data, download data, serve as a proxy, falsify records, or shut down the target computer at will. The Pentagon, defence-related think tanks, and defence-related contractors were the target of a combined spoofing and Trojan attack in 2008. Trojans were hidden in email attachments designed to look as if they were sent from a reliable source. The Trojan was designed to bury itself into the system, covertly gather data, and send it to an internet address in China. Due to the ability of hackers to route their activity through foreign computers, security experts were unable to determine if China was the final destination.

Virus. A virus attaches itself to a program or file so it can spread from one computer to another. The virus spreads across disks and networks by making copies of itself. In addition to self-replicating code, a virus normally contains a payload. Cyber attackers can program the payload to have malicious side effects such as data corruption or destruction. Almost all viruses are attached to an executable file, which means the virus may exist on a computer but it cannot infect that computer unless the user runs or opens the malicious program.

Worm. A worm operates similarly to a virus in that it spreads from computer to computer. However, unlike a virus, a worm has the capability to travel without any help from a person. It does this by taking advantage of file or information transport features on a system, which allows it to travel unaided. The biggest danger with a worm is its capability to replicate itself on a system. Thus, rather than a computer sending out a single worm, it could send out hundreds or thousands of copies of itself. Due to the copying nature of a worm and its capability to travel across networks, the end result in most cases is that the worm consumes too much system memory or network bandwidth, causing web servers, network servers, and individual computers to stop responding.

Logic Bomb. A logic bomb is malicious code designed to execute if specific events occur or at a predetermined time. Once triggered, it can take down the computer, delete data, or activate a DOS attack by generating bogus transactions.

Digital Manipulation. Digital image manipulation is the alteration of an image using computer program tools and software to produce a contrived image, which often reflects new meaning. This technique involves already existing imagery, such as photographs or videos. Doctoring photographs has been around as long as photography itself and now digital photographic manipulation is so sophisticated that it is sometimes impossible to discern whether people or objects in a photograph were actually there when the photo was taken.

Appendix B

ABUSE STATISTICS

In the year 2011, CERT-In handled more than 13000 incidents. The types of incidents handled were mostly of Phishing, Malicious Code, Website compromise & propagation of malware and Network Scanning & Probing.

The year-wise summary of various types of incidents handled is given below:-

Security Incidents	2004	2005	2006	2007	2008	2009	2010	2011
Phishing	3	101	339	392	604	374	508	674
Network Scanning / Probing	11	40	177	223	265	303	277	1748
Virus / Malicious Code	5	95	19	358	408	596	2817	2765
Spam	-	-	-	-	305	285	181	2480
Website Compromise & Malware Propagation	-	-	-	-	835	6548	6344	4394
Others	4	18	17	264	148	160	188	1240
Total	23	254	552	1237	2565	8266	10315	13301

Appendix C

INCIDENTS TRENDS

The trends of incidents reported to and handled by CERT-In and cyber-attack trends during the year 2011 are as follows:-

(a) Web site intrusions and drive-by-download attacks through compromised websites. Around 4394 malicious URLs were tracked in ".in" space. Most of the attacks were facilitated through attack tool kits such as Techno XPACK, Phoenix Exploit Kit, Neo spolit, Eleonre and Blackhole.

(b) Prominent client side vulnerabilities exploited in the drive by download attacks were in Adobe PDF, Flash, Java Runtime Environment, Internet Explorer and Mozilla Firefox.

(c) Malware trends indicate that malware affecting mobile platforms such as Android and Symbian were on the rise.

(d) Banking Trojans and key logger families were widely propagating. Prominent Trojans observed were ZeuS, Carberp, SpyEye, Torpig, Pushdo etc.

(e) Rougue antivirus programs such as MacDefender, Winwebsec etc. were delivered to users through SEO poisoning.

(f) Malicious Spam and identity theft schemes were leveraging Social networking sites and features therein

(g) Targeted attacks were on the rise involving exploitation vulnerabilities in Adobe PDF and MS Office.

Appendix D

ACTIVITIES CERT-In:2011

The summary of activities carried out by CERT-In during the year 2011 is given in the following table:-

Activities	Year 2011
Security Incidents handled	13301
Security Alerts issued	48
Advisories Published	81
Vulnerability Notes Published	188
Security Guidelines Published	4
White papers/Case Studies Published	3
Trainings Organized	26
Indian Website Defacements tracked	17306
Open Proxy Servers tracked	3294
Bot Infected Systems tracked	6277936

Appendix E

RECOMMENDATIONS OF STUDY GROUPS

NASSCOM - DSCI REPORT

Major recommendations are listed below:-

1. Create a **National Structure for Cyber Security** which clearly defines roles and responsibilities for every stakeholder, establishes coordination & information sharing mechanisms, focuses on building Public Private Partnership models and creates environment for enhancing trust between the industry and government.

A fully empowered head for Cyber Security should be appointed, positioned at the highest level within the government.

2. Design and Implement a **Competency Framework** for building a competent and adequate Cyber Security Workforce. The Competency Framework should assess the security skills requirements, identify existing gaps & challenges, define competency areas across different security roles and devise strategies and programs for building the required capacity.

3. Create and maintain an **Inventory of Critical Information Infrastructure** in the country to provide the required visibility over the critical information infrastructure and help prioritize deployment and monitoring of the protection measures.

4. Establish a **Centre of Excellence for Best Practices** in Cyber Security to institutionalize the development, sharing, collation, distribution and implementation of best practices in the country.

5. Establish a **National Threat Intelligence Centre** which should integrate all the existing information sources such as sectoral CERTs, intelligence bodies, security alerts issued by security vendors,

threats seen by critical sectors and industry to enable cross-domain awareness and a comprehensive view of cyber threats at a national level.

6. Build **Capacity of the Law Enforcement Agencies** in Cyber Crime Investigations and Cyber Forensics by establishing training facilities in every state and union territory.

7. Build **Lawful Interception Capabilities** for balancing national security and economic growth by establishing a national centre for performing research in encryption and cryptanalysis.

8. Establish a **Centre of Excellence for Cyber Security Research** to develop solutions that will protect country's information infrastructure in the future by defining and executing a research roadmap developed based on country's research needs.

9. Set up **Testing Labs for accreditation of ICT products** to mitigate security risks arising from procurement of ICT products especially from foreign vendors and yet take full benefits from the global supply chain that includes access to world class products, services and expertise at competitive prices.

10. Establish a **Cyber Command** within the defence forces to defend the Indian Cyberspace. The Cyber Command should be equipped with defensive and offensive cyber weapons, and manpower trained in cyber warfare.

The study concludes:-

> "The government should implement the above recommendations in parallel through effective public-private partnerships. The industry should actively support the government in the implementation of these recommendations.
>
> Government and industry cannot overcome the cyber security challenge in isolation; the imperative is to work together in a trusted and collaborative environment, leveraging each other's strengths to strengthen the cyber security posture of the country and take lead in global cyber security efforts."

The study forcefully argues for PPP in cyber security and gives out tangible arguments' which merit serious consideration. Ms Vijay Latha Reddy, Deputy NSA, has also spoken highly of the study report and stated that findings of the report would be considered during formulation of the policy.[4]

The Report states that DSCI can leverage the above credentials to deliver the following services (not limited to) to enhance cyber security in the country and specifically with respect to the implementation of the CSAG recommendations:-

(a) **Advisory and Consultation** – DSCI can provide strategy, policy and program related inputs to the government after consulting the industry on specific subjects.

(b) **Define Partnership Models** – For implementing specific cyber security initiative or program in PPP mode, DSCI can consult both the government and the industry and recommend best possible partnership model that is capable of meeting the strategic goals of such a project / initiative. As a section 25 not-for-profit company, it can develop approach for executing projects with government funding, through industry that is acceptable by the government.

(c) **Program Management and Execution** – For a particular PPP project, DSCI can provide the program management services – defining governance mechanisms, monitoring performance and completion, managing budgets & resources, communication, etc. DSCI can also be appointed as the agency for end to end project execution – requirement definition & consensus, deployment of in-house resources or sourcing, procurement of infrastructure (IT & non-IT), development of content, distribution, etc.

(d) **Knowledge Partner**- DSCI can act as a knowledge partner in PPP projects to provide the required expertise during conceptualization and implementation.

4 This was stated while chairing the session "Indian Cyber Security- Way Forward" held during the release of IDSA Report by NSA.

(e) **Create Platforms** – DSCI can create platforms for bringing together the government and industry for discussions on specific issues and concerns.

(f) **Establish Centres of Excellence** – DSCI can build and operate Centres of Excellence (CoE) on different subjects that are of mutual interest to the government and the industry. Such CoEs can be established for creation, sharing, compilation and dissemination of Best Practices in security, Research in cyber security, Technology trends, among others.

(g) **Training** – DSCI can conduct ongoing trainings for identified set of audiences in government and / or industry by arranging relevant experts in security and establishing the required training environment, which can be repeatedly used for conducting training sessions.

(h) **Outreach** – To increase education and awareness level within the country, DSCI can conduct cyber security campaigns across the country bringing together government, industry, LEAs, academia, school children, home users, etc.

(j) **Information Sharing Environment** – Being a third party, DSCI can act as an 'Information Clearing House' for enabling information exchange within industry and between industry and government.

One of the most valuable suggestion of the Report is regarding point of contact and finding the right people for the right task. It also proposes to become the knowledge base for future PPP projects. The report states " DSCI will act as 'Single Point of Contact' for both the government and industry in PPP, helping government and industry save efforts to identify right people, institutions, expertise, channels, etc. The knowledge and learning of running PPP projects will get consolidated at DSCI and can be leveraged to design and run PPP projects in future. Also, a common infrastructure (IT & non-IT) can be created through DSCI, which may be reused for PPP projects, resulting in cost and resource optimization. Very importantly, DSCI, as an interfacing agency, can solve the 'who will do what' problem which is very common in a multi-stakeholder environment and more so when government and industry both cannot afford to allocate resources on full time basis for executing projects."

IDSA Report

General Recommendations

(a) In view of the rapidly growing threats to national security in cyberspace there is urgent need for the government to adopt a cyber-security policy. The government should immediately adopt such a policy so that urgent actions in a coordinated fashion can be taken to defend India's economy and society against cyber-attacks.

(b) Cyber security policy will necessarily be an evolving document in view of the changing nature of cyber vulnerabilities, risks and threats. The government will need to review the document periodically.

(c) Cyber security should be regarded as an integral component of national security. Urgent attention should be given to the issues of cyber- crime, cyber-terrorism, cyber warfare and CII protection.

To Government

(a) The **NSA**, through NIB, should be put in charge of formulating and overseeing the implementation of the country's cyber security policy within the ambit of a larger national security policy. This body should be serviced by the NSCS for policy measures and DIT and other departments (e.g. Telecom, space, etc.) for operational measures.

(b) A Cyber Coordination Centre should be established at the operational level, staffed by personnel from the relevant operational agencies. This centre would serve as a clearing-house, assessing information arriving in real time and assigning responsibilities to the agencies concerned, as and when required.

(c) MHA should be the nodal agency for handling cyber-terrorism. To handle cyber-terrorism and cyber-crime, a slew of measures will be needed, ranging from monitoring and surveillance, investigation, prosecution, etc. Cyber-terrorism should be regarded as a part of the nation's overall counterterrorism capabilities. The National Counter Terrorism Centre being set up should have a strong cyber component. NIB, with MHA as the nodal agency, should be tasked with the responsibility of formulating and implementing a policy to deal with cyber-terrorism. The issues of ethical hacking and immunity for defence and intelligence officers should be considered.

(d) MHA should also be the nodal agency for dealing with cyber- crime. In dealing with cyber- crime, some of the measures needed will overlap with those required to deal with cyber-terrorism but extra effort will be required to ensure greater awareness, strengthening of the legal framework, law enforcement, prosecution, etc. Particular focus should be placed on awareness and enforcement. MHA, in collaboration with DIT and the Law Ministry should make a necessary roadmap in this regard.

(e) Headquarters IDS should be the nodal agency for preparing the country for cyber warfare in all its dimensions. The necessary structures should be created in a time-bound manner. Since cyberspace is integral there should be an appropriate interface between defence and civilian departments. NIB should smooth out the difficulties.

(f) NSCS should be given the nodal agency for coordinating the efforts to protect critical infrastructure of the country. This will require identification of the critical infrastructure and formulation and implementation of strategies to ensure protection of each component from cyber- attacks.

(g) DIT should be tasked with creating the necessary cyberspace situational awareness, strengthening PPP, promoting international cooperation, and other residual measures. DIT will necessarily have other nodal agencies. The interface between DIT and other agencies should be smoothed out by the NIB.

(h) Cyber security education, R&D and training will be an integral part of the national cyber security strategy. The government should set up a well-equipped National Cyber Security R&D Centre to do cutting edge cyber security R&D. This Centre should be a PPP endeavour. Cyber security research should also be encouraged in public and private universities and institutions. DIT could come up with a roadmap for cyber security research in the country. The country's strengths in ICT should be leveraged. DRDO should conduct specialised research for the armed forces and NTRO should do so for the country's intelligence agencies.

(j) DIT's CERT should be the nodal agency, much like the Met Department for weather forecasting, to create and share cyberspace situational awareness in the country. DIT should make public awareness of risks, threats and vulnerabilities in cyberspace and how these should be managed.

(k) Disaster management and recovery must be an integral part of any national cyber security strategy. The DIT should be the nodal agency for such efforts. It should coordinate its efforts with NDMA and also other government departments as well as private bodies.

Specific Recommendations

(These recommendations deal with specific technical and legal measures to strengthen cyber security. They are being flagged in view of their criticality. They can be part of the action plans and roadmaps to be developed by NIB, NSCS, DIT, MOD, MHA, etc.)

(a) There is need to place special emphasis on building adequate technical capabilities in cryptology, digital signatures, testing for malware in embedded systems, operating systems, fabrication of specialised chips for defence and intelligence functions, search engines, artificial intelligence, routers, new materials, SCADA systems, etc. Cyber security should be mandatory in computer science curriculum and even separate programmes on cyber security should be contemplated.

(b) Emphasis should be placed on developing and implementing standards and best practices in government functioning as well as in the private sector. Cyber security audits should be made compulsory for networked organisations. The standards should be enforced through a combination of regulation and incentives to industry.

(c) The government should launch a National Mission in Cyber Forensics to facilitate prosecution of cyber criminals and cyber-terrorists.

(d) International cooperation is crucial to handle cyber- crime, cyber-terrorism and in managing risks in cyberspace. It is necessary to participate in multilateral discussions on rules of behaviour in cyberspace. The government should also consider joining the European Convention on Cyber- crime. A 24x7 nodal point for international cooperation with cyber authorities of other countries should be set up. The Indian agencies should also participate in regional fora on cyber security. Engagement of Indian cyber authorities with internationally renowned cyber professional bodies should be encouraged.

(e) The impact of the emergence of new social networking media, and convergence of technologies on society including business, economy, national security should be studied with the help of relevant experts, including political scientists, sociologists, anthropologists, psychologists, and law enforcement experts. It should be ensured that the issues of privacy and human rights are not lost sight of and a proper balance between national security imperatives and human rights and privacy is maintained.

Cyber Warfare

(a) Need to lay down red lines, define objectives and enunciate a doctrine.

(b) Flesh out a policy of proactive cyber defence with emphasis on actions taken in anticipation to prevent an attack against computers and NWs.

(c) Raise a Cyber Command and build up offensive capabilities.

(d) Create a pool of trained people such as Cyber TA Battalions who can provide "surge capacity" to bolster the country's resources during critical periods or in the event of hostilities.

(e) Study the impact of social NWs with respect to national security and perception management, especially during crisis.

Critical Infrastructure

(a) Government should initiate a special drive of implementing practices in the critical infrastructure sectors and provide necessary budgetary support for such implementation.

(b) Develop security expertise for protection of CII by providing hands-on training to professionals, especially from the government sector.

(c) Government should establish a preparedness of critical sectors such as security index, which captures preparedness of the sector and assigns value to it. Operationalise the mechanism for routinely monitoring preparedness.

(d) Government should incorporate IT Supply Chain Security as an important element of e-security plan to address security issues.

(e) Government should promote R&D in private industry through active government support for industry-led research projects in the areas of security. Establish enabling mechanisms to facilitate this.

(f) Government should focus on creating a workforce of security professionals in the country keeping in view the requirements of the future.

(g) PPP model should be explored for taking security to the regions and industry sectors.

(h) Strengthening telecom security – one of the key pillars of cyber security, especially through development of standards and establishment of testing labs for telecom infrastructure (equipment, hardware).

(j) Capacity building in the area of cyber-crime and cyber forensics in terms of infrastructure, expertise and availability of HR and cooperation between industry, LEAs and judiciary.

Legal

(a) Need for trained and qualified experts to deal with the highly specialised field of cyber security.

(b) Awareness with regard to the threat to ICT infrastructure needs to be created and the necessary legal provisions to ensure cyber safety must be developed.

(c) Substantive laws dealing with illegal access, illegal interception, data interference, misuse of devices, computer-related forgery, child pornography, etc. must be implemented.

(d) Procedural laws need to be in place to achieve cooperation and coordination of international organisations and governments to investigate and prosecute cyber criminals.

(e) The police must work closely with both governmental and non-governmental agencies, Interpol and the public at large to develop a comprehensive strategy to address the problems.

(f) Lobbying at an international level for the harmonisation of existing national legislation to ensure that such laws provide a fair measure of deterrence to cyber criminals and cyber-terrorists, thereby making cyberspace a safer place for national and international transactions.

(g) Government must put in place necessary amendments in existing laws or enact a new legislation like a Data Protection/ Privacy Act so as to safeguard against the misuse of personal information by various government agencies and protect individual privacy.

Miscellaneous

(a) Examine the impact of cloud computing and wireless technologies and formulate appropriate policies.

(b) Make it a mandatory requirement for all government organisations and private enterprises to have a designated Chief Information Security Officer (CISO) who would be responsible for cyber security.

(c) Establishment of a cyber-range to test cyber readiness.

(d) More powers to sectoral CERTs.

(e) Establish an online mechanism for cyber- crime-related complaints to be recorded.

Appendix F

WAYS TO PLAN AGAINST CYBER WARFARE

By Calum Macleod, *in* Security *JULY 06, 2012 ShareNew*

It may not be particularly sensitive or sophisticated and is generally associated with life and death battle on the front line – yet the old British Army adage "Proper Planning and Preparation Prevents Piss Poor Performance", (or the "seven Ps") could not be more appropriate when battling the growing threat of cyber warfare. As organisations brace themselves for attacks, planning and preparation are everything.

In reality, no matter how good or well we think we are, those who are now targeting our organisations are better trained, have unlimited resources, and are extremely capable! Cyber Warfare is a very real threat, and as in any war, weapons do not distinguish between legitimate and innocent targets.

Collateral damage is never avoidable, and management will be held accountable for harm to the organisation regardless of its source. Recently, a number of security specialists demanded an international treaty to halt online weapons. In reality though this sounds a little like a weapons manufacturer asking for a ban on weapons!

The Target of Choice

Flame, Stuxnet, Duqu, and Mediyes are the high-tech weapons, and are likely only the tip of the iceberg when it comes to what is lurking beneath. The target, however, in many cases is the same: SSL certificates. Each of these pieces of malware have been signed by a digital certificate owned, or appearing to be owned, by reputable companies, and issued by trusted authorities such as VeriSign, and Microsoft – or again appearing to be.

In spite of all the cries that SSL is not safe, and that there are problems with the trust model, the fact of the matter is that SSL is probably the best we have right now to protect ourselves. No one claims it is perfect, but I have yet to see a better and more secure alternative.

Passwords are certainly not the way to go – they're being hacked left, right and centre. Some will argue that OTP token-based solutions do the job, but it's not so long ago that RSA were replacing millions of them because they were hacked! The biggest problem with SSL certificates is that most organisations have applied no Proper Planning and Preparation for the use of certificates, and as a result are vulnerable to attack.

Contrary to popular opinion, Microsoft did not invent Excel to be a certificate management or policy enforcement system, although given the extensive use of Excel among PKI departments; they could probably rebadge it and charge a fee! But then in most companies this is the level of sophistication that exists. So here are some guidelines that might be helpful, even if you're convinced that Excel does it all!

Review your Private Key Management Processes

The market for stolen SSL certificates is purportedly worth $5 billion, and since most organisations do not have system-generated inventory, it's probably unlikely that you would notice one or two going missing. Also since you have no inventory, would you even know if a private key your admins had access to, tied to a certificate issued by any one of 650 plus CAs, from anyone of 54 countries, went walkabout?

In the same way that you probably stop your admins having access to root passwords, the same steps should be taken to control their access to private keys. For example, how many organisations, as a matter of policy, replace private keys that have been directly accessed by administrators when those administrators are reassigned or leave the organisation? How often are keystore passwords changed, or do you even have keystore passwords, and is there any separation of duties related to key access. These are just some of the basic steps you should be taking.

Introduce SSL and SSH Policies and Review them Annually

In many organisations, a Certificate Practice Statement (CPS) does not even exist, and where it does certificate policies and the certificate practice statement are generally out of date. For example a CPS should cover topics including minimum key lengths, approved cryptographic algorithms, approved trusted root certificates, administrative access to private keys, etc.. There are many other points, but the important thing is that the CPS remains current. Last year's CPS may already be out of date given developments in the industry.

Ensure that Keys and Certs are Compliant with Policy

When you consider how much time is spent on enforcing password policies, you would think that keys and certificates would also benefit from the same TLC. When organisations are still using key lengths less than 2048 and MD5 hashing algorithms, it should not come as a surprise that they are vulnerable. Can you have really even have a policy without the ability to enforce it? Certainly Excel aids nothing there. Deploying wildcard certificates across multiple systems with a long validity periods is not good practice. You might as well use the same admin password on all your systems! If you have policies, then enforce them!

Have a System-generated Inventory of Keys and Certificates

Relying on manual entry in a spreadsheet does not qualify as an inventory! The general status of most IT departments is that they only have a view of a fraction of the total number of keys and certificates that are deployed. In most organisations, the management of keys has been so diluted across various groups that most organisations don't even know how many Certificate Authorities they use.

IT departments should perform network and on-board scans periodically and ensure that details such as the locations for certificates and private keys, owners or contacts are identified, and all relevant attributes of the certificates are collected. It is curious why organisations talk about having the on-going problem of finding the person responsible when a certificate expires. You would think that when this occurred once, action would be taken to stop this re-occurring – or is this just too obvious!

Prepare for a Certificate Authority (CA) Compromise

Just because Microsoft, VeriSign, and a host of others have been compromised doesn't mean you will be. But then would you even know, because it's not just the 650 plus CAs that you have to think about, but the over 1400 root certificates trusted by your systems. And these are only the external ones.

Apart from ensuring that you have active contractual relationships with more than one vendor, and don't end up in a Diginotar scenario where you have to shut down your internet business, you also need to be able to be ready to rapidly replace all certificates issued from each CA currently in use, assuming you know what they are. And of course this assumes you know where they keys and certificates are, which brings us back to having a system-generated inventory of keys and certificates. There's no point is simply getting new certificates if you don't know who needs them!

Safeguards to Prevent Migration of Non-production Keys and Certificates to Production

In a recent check on a single production server at a global, Fortune-ranked organisation: instead of the 5 certificates they expected to find, there were in excess of 190! When systems move from development, to test, to production, very often the keys go with them. Not only are the keys being exposed to multiple administrators, but test environments and developers have much less regard for security than, say your average hacker. It is important that test CAs and test certificates should not be trusted on production systems, and certificates, and private keys used in tests do not move into production

Do a Sanity Check

Like any IT security measure, its ultimate purpose is to ensure that your business runs safely and smoothly. No one can predict when or where the next breach will occur. Enterprises must prepare to act immediately and implement these steps to ensure control throughout the lifecycle of keys and certificates. If they don't then the simple result is that they are placing your business at risk. And don't think you won't be compromised, because you will.

Effective key and certificate management controls can make or break a business – so take the initiative and prepare your organisation for war by strengthening your defences and closing the doors on your attacker.

Source - http://www.businesscomputingworld.co.uk/7-ways-to-plan-against-cyber-warfare/

BIBLOGRAPHY

1. Cyber Power and National Security edited by Franklin D Kramer, Stuart H Starr and Larry Wentz

2. Cyber Warfare and Cyber Terrorism by L J Janczewski and Andrew M Colarik

3. Estonia – http://en.wikipedia.org/wiki/Estonia

4. Cyber Attacks on Estonia short synopsis by Merike Kaeoless

5. Cyber warfare, the truth in a real case by Muhammad Saleem and Jawad Hassan

6. Lessons from cyber-attacks on Estonia – GCN interview on 13 June 2008 with Lauri Almann

7. Principles of War for the Information Age by Robert R Leonhard

8. Technological change and the future of Warfare by Michael O'Hanlon

9. Cyber warfare operations: development and use under internationallaw–http://www.thefreelibrary.com+warfare+ operations

10. Imaging India by Nandan Nilekani, Penguin Books, India.

11. ICTs and Indian Social Change, edited by Ashwani Saith, M Vijayabaskar and V Gayathri, SAGE Publications India Pvt Ltd.

12. "Art of War" by Jomini

13. "The Principles of War", by Carl Von Clausewitz.

14. Beaufre, Andre, Introduction to Strategy (London, 1965).

15. Fuller, John F. C., Foundations of the Science of War (London,

1925).

16. Sun Tzu "Art of War".

17. DCAF HORIZON 2015 WORKING PAPER No. 7 "On Cyber Warfare" by Fred Schreier

18. Times of India, Delhi, 12 June 12.

19. Times of India, Delhi, 13 June 12.

20. Times of India, Delhi, 29 March 12.

21. Times of India, Delhi, 10 May 12.

22. Securing our Cyber Frontiers - NASSCOM-DSCI Cyber Security Advisory Group Report.

23. Cyber Deterrence and Cyber War by Martin C. LibiCki, RAND Corporation.

24. Times of India, Delhi, 13 May 12.

25. Times of India, Delhi, 13 June 12.

26. Times of India, Delhi, 14 June 12.

27. Times of India, Delhi, 22 June 12.

28. IDSA Report "INDIA'S Cyber Security Challenge".

29. Times of India, Delhi, 11 June 12.

30. Times of India, Delhi, 02 July 12.

31. Cohen, Stephen P. and Sunil Dasgupta, "The Drag on India's Military Growth", The Brookings Institution, September 2010.

32. Times of India, Delhi, 09 July 12.

www.ingramcontent.com/pod-product-compliance
Lightning Source LLC
Chambersburg PA
CBHW031359270326
41929CB00010BA/1243

* 9 7 8 9 3 8 4 4 6 4 1 1 0 *